Between
EAST
and
WEST

Between EAST and WEST

Writings from *Kultura*

ROBERT KOSTRZEWA

EDITOR

HILL AND WANG · NEW YORK
A division of Farrar, Straus and Giroux

Library of Congress Cataloging-in-Publication Data
Between East and West : writings from Kultura / Robert Kostrzewa, editor.—
1st ed.
Translations from the Polish.
1. Poland—Intellectual life—1945–   I. Kostrzewa, Robert.   II. Kultura
(Paris, France)
DK4437.B48   1990   943.805—dc20   89-38196

All the selections in this book originally appeared in *Kultura*. The introduction, by Konstanty A. Jelenski, was first published, in slightly different form,
in *Le Débat* (February 1981) under the title "*Kultura*, la Pologne en exil."
Copyright © 1981 by Editions Gallimard.
Grateful acknowledgment is made to the following publications for permis-
sion to reprint previously published material, in English translation, some
of which appears in this book in a slightly different form: *Cross Currents*,
"About Our Europe" (originally titled "Central European Attitudes") and
"Dostoevsky and Western Intellectuals," both by Czeslaw Milosz (No. 5,
1986); *Survey*, "Two Fatherlands; Two Patriotisms," by Jan Jozef Lipski
(Autumn 1982), and "The Hair Styles of Mieczyslaw Rakowski," by Leopold
Tyrmand (Summer 1982); Foreign Policy Research Institute and *Orbis*,
"The Suppression of Solidarity" (originally titled "The Crushing of Solidar-
ity"), by Ryszard Kuklinski (Winter 1988).

To Jerzy Giedroyc

CONTENTS

III · What We Write

Robert Kostrzewa

PREFACE

THE MAGAZINE GRAVEYARD is a densely populated place. Yet hundreds of journals are launched all over the world each year. Few of them are worth reading and even fewer will survive to celebrate their tenth-anniversary issue. But there are a handful of journals which not only attract successive generations of readers but also make a difference in the way people think and look at the world. This anthology is an attempt to introduce to American readers one such publication.

It is often the case with book projects that they begin with a passing remark. The story of this anthology is no different. In the autumn of 1986 I spoke with a German sociologist and political writer, Ralf Dahrendorf, about *Kultura*, a Polish émigré monthly review published in Paris by the Institut Littéraire. During the conversation, I showed him a small book of *Kultura's* articles published in German translation. He suggested that I should prepare a similar volume for the English-speaking reader. More than two years later, when I was about to complete my work on this book, I realized how dangerous passing remarks could be if they are taken seriously.

But the two years spent on this anthology were hardly wasted. The fortieth anniversary of the Institut Littéraire, celebrated in 1986, called for a tribute to this distinguished cultural institution which, for almost half a century, with modest means and thanks to the total devotion of its small staff, has so profoundly influenced several generations of Poles. A large part of my own political education took place on the pages of *Kultura* and the books published by the Institut Littéraire. When I was about seventeen, I first saw several old issues of *Kultura* at the Warsaw home of one of my high-school friends. They were on the top shelf of an overloaded bookcase, hardly visible in the darkest corner of the room. It was in the midseventies, when Polish *samizdat* was still in its infancy. For many Poles, *Kultura* was the most authoritative voice not only on Polish affairs but also on general historical, social, and literary issues. One read *Kultura*, smuggled into the country by Poles returning from visits to the West, with that kind of intellectual curiosity and mounting excitement which one feels encountering something forbidden and dangerous.

Later I was lucky to get hold of a number of books published by the Institut Littéraire. I read, for the first time, Solzhenitsyn's *The Gulag Archipelago* and Koestler's *Darkness at Noon*, Gombrowicz's novels and diaries, and Milosz's poems and essays. Even Albert Camus's *The Rebel* could not be officially published in Poland at that time, and I remember the pride and feeling of superiority over my classmates when in literature class, to our teacher's astonishment, I was able to ask questions about *The Rebel*. How much I then understood of what I read was not the issue. What mattered was the discovery that out there, somewhere in the mythical West, there was another world, another way of thinking and looking at things. At that time, accurate information and informed opinion about Poland as well as about the international scene could only be obtained from such Polish-language foreign radio broadcasts as Radio Free Europe, Voice of America, and the BBC, or from the pages of *Kultura*. *Kultura* was simply the most important intellectual forum where Poles, both in exile in the West and in captivity in the East, could meet and exchange ideas freely, albeit in the case of the latter the use of pseudonyms was a common practice which protected them from the punishing hand of the totalitarian state. Over the years, *Kultura*, by challenging official Poland's publishing monopoly, helped to preserve Polish culture. The magazine's constant presence and vitality has testified—if only in a symbolic fashion—to the Poles' unfading spirit of resistance, abroad and at home, to a Soviet-styled totalitarianism. Those in

Poland who decided to join the clandestine opposition were often students of *Kultura*'s political thought. The postwar generations of Poles, including the Solidarity generation, began their political education by reading the pages of the Paris-based review.

In the late 1970s, many other independent publications were launched—often with conceptual and material support from *Kultura*—both in Poland and in the West. *Kultura* was no longer one of a handful of uncensored journals available to Polish readers. With the emergence of Solidarity in 1980, other émigré periodicals as well as dozens of independent journals mushroomed in Poland. *Kultura*, however, did not have to compete. Thanks to its remarkable strength, the review has retained the prestigious position it earned in more than forty years of publication.

The staff of *Kultura*, at both the journal and the publishing house, has never exceeded eight people (editorial board, administration, support staff, and distribution combined). This is not only an achievement beyond the imagination of the bureaucratized publishers of Eastern Europe and the Soviet Union, but it is a world-class phenomenon. The explanation lies in the people running *Kultura* since its inception. They have been a group of close friends, utterly devoted to their work, who have practically given up their personal lives for *Kultura*. Even more impressive is that the editorial board of the monthly review, the publishing house, and the historical quarterly *Zeszyty Historyczne (Historical Notebooks)*, which Institut Littéraire started to publish in 1962, rest virtually in the hands of one man, the now eighty-three-year-old Jerzy Giedroyc. Mr. Giedroyc has a rare combination of moral integrity, enormous editorial skill, a benevolently dictatorial managerial style, and an ability to bring together so many talented contributors to create not merely a publication but a distinguished cultural institution and a lively intellectual milieu. For many years, *Kultura* was both a tribune for well-known, respected writers and columnists and a refuge for controversial authors, who, if not for *Kultura*, would have perished in the whirls of émigré existence.

Kultura and the Institut Littéraire first gained worldwide recognition by publishing several Polish and Russian manuscripts rescued from the hands of censors and the secret police. These included works by such Russian authors as Siniavsky, Daniel, Amalrik, and Solzhenitsyn. Under the imprint of *Biblioteka Kultury (Kultura Library)*, books were first published by Czeslaw Milosz, later a Nobel Prize winner, Witold Gombrowicz, Leszek Kolakowski, and Adam

Michnik. Among some 450 titles published by *Kultura* over the years are books by George Orwell, Aldous Huxley, Boris Pasternak, Ignazio Silone, Graham Greene, Raymond Aron, and Simone Weil.

Between East and West is the third collection of writings from *Kultura* to appear in English translation. The previous volumes—two companion anthologies, *Kultura Essays* and *Explorations in Freedom: Prose, Narrative and Poetry from Kultura*—were published by the Free Press in 1970 under the editorship of the late Leopold Tyrmand. The present collection is a selection of writings from the past two decades of the magazine. The years covered in this anthology were marked by many serious losses in *Kultura*'s "inner circle." Several regular contributors—for example, the magazine's main political commentator Juliusz Mieroszewski, the renowned novelist Witold Gombrowicz, essayists Pawel Hostowiec (Jerzy Stempowski) and Konstanty Jelenski, poets Jozef Wittlin and Kazimierz Wierzynski, as well as one of *Kultura*'s pillars, its manager and public-relations man, Zygmunt Hertz—died. They all belonged to a generation of Polish intellectuals who stayed in the West after World War II when it became clear that the catastrophe of the Nazi destruction was going to be followed by another national calamity—the Soviet occupation. They were driven to exile by bitter necessity and the desire to oppose defeat in the hope of ultimate victory. They were committed to what they considered their historical mission—the preservation of Polish culture. They regarded *Kultura* as the most effective vehicle for the accomplishment of such a mission. Their work resulted in the magazine's Golden Era of the 1950s and 1960s.

In recent years, *Kultura*'s Old Guard was gradually replaced by younger writers and journalists. Some of them are émigrés of the late 1960s and the early 1980s; others live in Poland and send their contributions through whatever channels are available to them. With the birth of Solidarity in 1980 the émigré community began to play a much greater role in Polish politics. Contacts between Poles living in the West and those at home became more frequent and mutually productive. Copies of *Kultura* and the books published by the Institut Littéraire were not only smuggled into the country but also reprinted by underground publishers. Since 1988 the magazine has also had its "Polish" edition published simultaneously by one of the independent presses in Warsaw. Today one can buy *Kultura*, as well as other uncensored publications, at numerous independent distribution centers throughout Poland.

In the era of *glasnost* the nature as well as the content of public discourse in Eastern Europe and the Soviet Union has changed dramatically. What one can openly say or write today was simply impossible a year ago. Some people may wonder whether there is still a need for *Kultura*, or does it belong to the ancient past of the Cold War? One can answer this concern with another set of questions. Is there really freedom of speech and expression in Poland or Hungary today, or is this freedom still partial and limited? Are the political reforms being implemented in the Soviet Union and Eastern Europe so substantial and far-reaching as to guarantee that the practice of free and open discussion will last, or could the current "thaw" be followed by a future "freeze"? Perhaps in time *Kultura* won't be needed, but writing its obituary today is as premature as writing an obituary for the Soviet Union itself.

In presenting this anthology to English-speaking readers, I hope to accomplish two goals: to introduce *Kultura* and its intellectual milieu to a broader audience, and to present—if only in an incomplete and fragmented fashion—several important issues and concerns which the Poles have been trying to cope with in recent years. All the essays in this book were written before the events of spring and summer 1989, which brought Solidarity into the government. I believe, however, that the passions and problems explored in these articles and short stories remain pertinent and shed much light on where Poles have been, where they are today, and where they are headed.

The momentous changes that are currently unfolding in Poland and in other countries of Eastern Europe may greatly weaken the Soviet Union's hold on several nations and recast the overall balance of power, not only on the European continent, but in the world at large. As the Soviet grip on its European satellites is relaxed, the rigid division of Europe may give way to a much more fluid and fragmented arrangement. For the West, the fast-changing and confusing reality of Eastern Europe could become the major political challenge of the remainder of the century. It is therefore extremely important that people in the West familiarize themselves with at least some of the seemingly intractable problems that have tormented the East Europeans for the past fifty years.

There are many people without whose help, contribution, and encouragement this anthology would never have been conceived, or completed. I am greatly indebted to all of them.

I should like to express my appreciation to the Central & East European Publishing Project at Oxford, England, for financing the translations for this volume. I am especially indebted to Ralf Dahrendorf, Chairman of the International Committee of the Oxford Project, and Elizabeth Winter, its Executive Director, for their resourcefulness, encouragement, and invaluable advice.

I am grateful to the Barbara Piasecka Johnson Foundation for its generous financial support, which made it possible for me to be relieved from other obligations while working on this book.

I also extend my thanks to the competent translators of this volume, some of whom wish to remain anonymous. I want especially to thank Maya Latynski, Jadwiga Kosicka, Michael Kott, Jerzy B. Warman, and Linda Coverdale.

I am indebted to Steve Wasserman, publisher of Hill and Wang, for his faith in the importance of this project, immense patience, and valuable editorial recommendations, which contributed greatly to turning this anthology into what I hope is a readable book.

Special thanks go to my good friends Gregory Gorzynski, Joanna Kranc, Pawel Mayewski, and Jacek Niecko, for support and advice at the most crucial moments.

The greatest credit, however, has to be given to Jerzy Giedroyc, the editor of *Kultura*, who—with the help of his brother Henryk Giedroyc and Zofia Hertz, his most faithful collaborators over the past forty years—was able, against all odds, to create and provide continuous leadership to a journal of such high intellectual quality and importance as to forever imprint its name in the history of publishing.

Between
EAST
and
WEST

Konstanty A. Jelenski

INTRODUCTION

THE YEAR WAS 1956 or 1957, a few months after the "Polish October" and Gomulka's return to power. I and a few friends from Poland were discussing the limited influence an individual might hope to have on the course of events in Poland despite the recent upheavals there. Curious about the concrete workings of the system, I proposed a game: everyone would write down the names of fifteen Poles in the order of their relative individual importance, potential or real. Two names headed the lists, of course: those of the first secretary of the Party and the primate cardinal of Poland (sometimes *ex aequo*). Next came two or three members of the Politburo, followed in extended order by the chief of political police; the editor of *Po Prostu*, the leading opposition weekly at that time; a certain general suspected of nostalgic nationalist yearnings; Jan Nowak, head of the Polish section of Radio Free Europe (the American station in Munich); the liberal poet Antoni Slonimski, then president of the Polish Writers' Union; and a few other independent intellectuals whose prestige had weathered the storms of Stalinism. Among the last names mentioned, but appearing on every list without exception, was that of Jerzy Giedroyc, the editor in chief of *Kultura*, a monthly review founded

3

by émigrés in 1947 and published in the Parisian suburb of Maisons-Laffitte, with a circulation of a few thousand readers. Although I had been a frequent contributor to *Kultura* from the first and was well aware of both its high literary standards and the attractive aura that surrounded it as a forbidden fruit in the intellectual circles of Warsaw, I still found that unanimity of choice both disproportionate and incomprehensible.

A quarter of a century later, in 1979, Nowa (an independent publishing house with ties to KOR, the Workers' Defense Committee), which publishes and distributes in Poland works rejected by government censors (and which, functioning outside all economic channels, paradoxically constitutes the only authentically communist enclave in the country), issued an anthology of writings from *Kultura* as one of its first publications. Here is the preface Adam Michnik wrote for that book:

Kultura has been appearing for thirty-two years now and richly deserves a monograph, for it already has its own history and legend. *Kultura* accompanies the Polish intelligentsia through good times and bad, as do the books it publishes under its own imprint with their distinctive covers. The vital importance of this review and publishing firm—which are constantly hounded by customs and security forces—can be seen in the catalogue of books and authors whose presence in Polish intellectual life springs directly from the work accomplished by a very small editorial staff. The list is a long and distinguished one: Gombrowicz, Milosz, Kolakowski, Stempowski (Hostowiec), Herling-Grudzinski, Vincenz, Czapski, Jelenski, Hirszowiczowa, Wierzynski, Bienkowski, Hlasko. It is thanks to *Kultura* that we have the full text of Witos's memoirs, the writings of Stawar, as well as the documents and reminiscences published by *Kultura* in the quarterly *Zeszyty Historyczne* (*Historical Notebooks*). We may also add a large number of translations: Koestler and Orwell, Aron and Camus, Simone Weil and Djilas, Boris Pasternak's *Doctor Zhivago*.

It was in *Kultura* that the works of the Russian dissidents were published for the first time, including texts by Solzhenitsyn, Sakharov, Amalrik, and Siniavsky. The review reports regularly on the situation in Lithuania, the Ukraine, and Byelorussia. *Kultura* has long supported the idea of an entente with these nations and was the first to declare that the claims put forward by some Poles regarding the once Polish cities of Wilno and Lwow should be abandoned.

This policy does not represent capitulation in the face of undeniable and arbitrary subjugation, but a realistic approach, in keeping with the hopes of independence and democracy fueled by recent events in Poland. The same reasoning lies behind *Kultura*'s opposition to the perpetuation of the "state in exile." From the very beginning, the review has taken the position that it is absolutely necessary to maintain contact with the homeland, with those here on the banks of the Vistula River who strive to broaden the sphere of democratic liberties. At the same time, however, one also reads in its pages that "Poland is not bounded by the land where the Vistula flows," because those who have emigrated also belong to the Polish community.

In exile, *Kultura* was accused of crypto-communism, while in Poland the press denounced its ties to the intelligence agencies of the United States, Germany, etc. When the review scathingly criticized the Polish government's anti-Semitic campaign in 1968, they were even accused of Zionism.

In short, it is largely through *Kultura* that the Polish intelligentsia has been exposed to a certain continuity of political thought and a nonconforming model of national culture, an independent standard against which to judge our values and attitudes.

This preface is not a panegyric. *Kultura* often disturbs us and provokes disagreement. Many of the opinions and judgments expressed in its pages stem from a misunderstanding of how things really are in Poland. When we compare present-day emigration with the "Great Emigration" of the last century, however, we are forced to admit that although the nineteenth-century Polish émigrés had their "bards," they had nothing like *Kultura*. I have seen with my own eyes the modest means and frankly ascetic life of these alleged "agents of every national secret service," and I can personally attest to the generous spirit in which they endure the isolation and sacrifices involved in the pursuit of their goals.

The editorial opinions of *Kultura* were written by Juliusz Mieroszewski until his death in 1976, after which his pen was taken up by Gustaw Herling-Grudzinski. These editorials always followed the line laid down by the editor in chief, Jerzy Giedroyc, whose closest colleagues—from the very beginning—have been Zofia and Zygmunt Hertz.

This selection of pieces is not only a fascinating literary document, it also bears witness to the Polish democratic opposition's gratitude toward these few people, without whose efforts our intellectual life would be greatly impoverished.

If I've quoted this preface in its entirety within the main text of my introduction instead of placing it in a marginal note, it's because this preface says everything succinctly, in a publication representative of the Polish left-wing opposition, and it was written, moreover, by a young man born after the war, whose family belongs to the old elite of the Communist Party.

It remains for me to elucidate the truly mysterious process whereby a review and some books banned in Poland—which must therefore enter and circulate through the country in secret, in a necessarily small number of copies, written by people whose names could not even be mentioned in the media before the birth of Solidarity—have managed to create a legend that shines throughout all Eastern Europe, including the U.S.S.R. This is of course due in part to the high quality of the work published by *Kultura* and even more to the particular nature of the Polish intelligentsia (we'll come back to this idea), but the principal merit belongs to one man, Jerzy Giedroyc, who was almost unknown to his compatriots when he set out on this adventure.

The editor of *Kultura* comes from an old princely family of Lithuanian stock, some of whose descendants were Russified, others "Polonized." He belongs to a branch that met with financial ruin in the nineteenth century and thereupon gave up a title that was considered inappropriate at the time if one had been reduced to earning a living as a doctor or an engineer. Born before the First World War, he spent his childhood and adolescence in Russia, moving to Poland only a few years after the Revolution of 1917. I believe that his exceptional destiny was determined by an initial paradox: Giedroyc is a born political animal, but he was born without most of the qualities that make a politician. He is timid, rather touchy, a loner, incapable of giving a speech, someone who finds it very difficult to communicate with others (which explains his voluminous correspondence), a man who speaks no foreign language except Russian (even his French has remained rudimentary after forty years in France). What luck for Polish culture these impediments turned out to be! If he'd become a minister in the government in exile in London, *Kultura* would never have seen the light of day. Now, what does a young man fascinated by politics do if the political world is closed to him? He founds a review, of course. That's what Giedroyc did in 1929 by publishing *Polityka*, a rallying point for young supporters of Jozef Pilsudski, independent intellectuals from both ends of the political spectrum, whether leftists or conservatives. I might point out here that the names of the two principal weeklies in communist Poland after the

Second World War, *Polityka* and *Kultura*, were taken—strangely enough—from the two reviews founded by Giedroyc, so that anyone in Poland referring to the original *Kultura* (the "real" one) must call it "the Paris *Kultura*." As for the first *Polityka*, it already contained the seed of one of the governing ideas that would influence *Kultura* in exile. The aging Marshal Pilsudski's dream of a federation with Poland's neighbors to the east (Lithuania, the Ukraine, and Byelorussia) was a familiar one for Giedroyc and his friends, but they were also aware that any sort of nostalgia for the old Jagellonian empire smacked of colonialism, for that "union of equals" under the rule of a Lithuanian dynasty had in fact "Polonized" the elite of the other partners, finally creating a situation similar to the one in Ireland (if not Algeria). In 1937, a contributor to Giedroyc's review wrote: "The Jagellonian idea brings along in its wake certain illusions that we must quickly dispense with for our own good. We must admit that neither the Lithuanians, nor the Ukrainians, nor the Byelorussians have the slightest desire to become Polish—and we must respect their wishes." Clearly, *Kultura*'s support since its inception for the abandonment of territorial claims to Wilno and Lwow—a position roundly denounced by the great majority of Polish émigrés as a "betrayal"— is rooted in something other than simple political opportunism.

If I'm correct in thinking that Giedroyc became the founder and editor of a review as a result of his unsuitability for the more direct give-and-take of politics, then he certainly picked the proper arena for his talents. I don't think he has ever written an article in his life (his personal contributions, signed "The Editor," are limited to those rare occasions when a clear statement of his views on some major topic is appropriate, and they are both short and to the point). He has an exceptional flair for detecting the slightest sign of talent or originality, as well as the stubborn patience required to win over and inspire those whom he wants to contribute to the review, and, above all, he is a master of surprise, a genius of the dramatic stroke who never loses sight of his long-term objectives. He has also been very lucky, especially in the early years of the review, but he has proved quite adept at turning favorable circumstances to the best advantage, practically without ever leaving his tiny office cluttered with books and files, where he sits in front of his typewriter busily weaving his network of contacts. It's said that he has no friends, that he uses people seduced by his obvious charm, that he despises his countrymen. It's true that he has a huge ego and is not easily impressed (as far as

I know, he has only two heroes: Pilsudski and de Gaulle). These alleged character flaws have played a positive role, however, in his destiny as an émigré. His passion for independence led him to distance himself immediately from all entrenched authority and to refuse any kind of financial aid that might have caused problems for him later on.

In 1947, there was still a veritable Polish state in exile in London, with its own "legitimate" government (the Presidential Constitution of 1935 had given the head of state the right to name his successor in case of war, thus making the office self-perpetuating), officially recognized embassies in foreign countries (I often traveled in Europe until the early 1950s with a Polish passport renewed by the government in London through their embassy at the Vatican), a parliament, countless institutions, a writers' union, and various publications. The wave of political emigrants consisted largely of veterans who had left their country to continue fighting against the Germans on every Western front (two army corps, one parachute brigade, a navy, and an air force). For a long time, they would remain convinced that they had "carried their country with them on the soles of their shoes," thus belying the old Polish proverb. This conviction surfaces even in our language. We never say "Poland," but "the Homeland." We say "the Warsaw government" because the Polish government, the Republic, is in London. This strong sense of legitimacy gave a certain cohesion and definite power to Polish émigrés right after the war, and it was sometimes an invaluable trump card. The first director of the Polish section of Radio Free Europe, which was established by the Americans in Munich at the height of the Cold War, was Jan Nowak, who had belonged to a democratic left-wing opposition students' movement before the war, during which he became a hero of the Resistance, operating as a secret courier between London and the Home Army. Jan Nowak was "appointed" to this post by his legitimate government, so that, although he was a salaried employee working for the Americans, he considered himself "seconded" to them, which reinforced his feelings of independence vis-à-vis his immediate "superiors" and surely helped him to convince them, for example, that Gomulka should be supported unstintingly in October of 1956 in order to spare Poland the fate that befell Hungary.

Giedroyc saw the problem in different terms. It might be useful to note that an émigré journal is usually founded by people who have left their country to fight from abroad against a regime they refuse to accept and under which they have personally suffered. Neither Giedroyc nor any of his original colleagues has ever lived for a single day under the communist regime. After the Yalta Conference, however, Giedroyc foresaw that a long period of exile awaited those Poles who found themselves outside the country because of the fortunes of war, and he conceived the idea of founding a publishing house with the help of a few friends, among them Jozef Czapski, Zofia and Zygmunt Hertz, and Gustaw Herling-Grudzinski. At the time, they were all soldiers in the second Polish army corps, commanded in Italy by General Anders. A loan from the "Soldiers' Fund," which was established by the Polish military authorities to facilitate entry into civilian life abroad, financed the purchase of a small printing press in Rome, and the Institut Littéraire made its debut in 1946. The following year, thanks to the sale of the press, Giedroyc and his companions at the Institut moved to Paris, where they rented a small house in Maisons-Laffitte and brought out the first edition of *Kultura*. It was typical of Giedroyc that he scrupulously, as soon as possible, repaid the loan he had received, so that he might feel free to criticize the policies of the Polish politico-military establishment in exile without being accused of "ingratitude." The financial organization of the enterprise has always been (and still is) something like a kibbutz or a phalanstery. Board and lodging are provided, and the editor and his four colleagues receive the same salary (twenty years before the French newspaper *Libération* instituted this same arrangement), which is pegged at the level of the guaranteed minimum wage. This income is assured by subscription fees, which quickly climbed to ten thousand (the price of a year's subscription in 1987 was 440 francs, or about $70, with subscribers in some twenty countries who receive their copies through the kind offices of about fifty distributors). All profits go toward the publication of books, which the Institut could begin undertaking only in 1953, after the repayment of all its outstanding debts. In an article devoted to Zygmunt Hertz, who died in October 1979, Czeslaw Milosz evokes *Kultura*'s birthplace: "A rented house on avenue Corneille, ugly and uncomfortable, and the bitterly cold winter (the potbellied stoves stuffed with coal to no avail), the Parisian suburbs, and that neighborhood with its kilometers of avenues all lined with chestnut trees, so reminiscent of nineteenth-century Tver or Sarajevo . . . Those who pick up a bound volume of back issues of *Kultura* or a copy of a book published by the Institut Littéraire, and those who will do so one day, should stop and think for a moment of the saucepans, the meals prepared by the same three or four people on the editorial staff, the page proofs, the administrative drudgery, the housework, the dishwashing, the shopping (luckily, French markets are excellent), and they should multiply these kinds of domestic chores by days, months, and years. Not forgetting all that wrapping paper and stout string, then having to bundle the packages off to the post office and mail them out." All this is true, but there is no need to invoke a "generous" acceptance of "sacrifices" on the part of the staff, as does the young Polish writer whose preface I quoted above (an interpretation that would be shared by any young Frenchman or American of his generation). The founders of *Kultura* had just spent five or six years in the army, and several of them had been imprisoned in the Siberian Gulag before their enlistment. Whatever tastes for comfort and luxury they'd had were long gone. However, there is another reason why the adventure of *Kultura* would probably be impossible to repeat nowadays. We belonged to a generation and a country that took for granted the material sacrifices involved in founding a small, prestigious literary review, for serious literature rarely provided a decent living to anyone. Only the bell jar of emigration, moreover, has permitted *Kultura* to last as long as it has while preserving the same high standards, without being either destroyed by competition from other periodicals or subsidized by advertising or a major publisher (and especially not by any state).

I should like to take this occasion to correct for the first time, but once and for all, a thesis put forward by the Polish authorities in various articles and a police pamphlet devoted to *Kultura*, as well as in the course of several trials of political dissidents whom they accused of being agents "run"—through *Kultura*—by the CIA. I have been a frequent contributor to the review, and I have worked since 1952 as a secretary for the Congress for Cultural Freedom (and on the editorial board of the review *Preuves*), which turned out to be secretly financed by the CIA through several small "respectable" American foundations. This was an open-and-shut case, according to the official Polish view of the matter, which cast me as a high-class international secret agent "at the center of the Washington–Bonn–Tel Aviv Triangle." In a scenario right out of a cheap spy novel, I supposedly received Giedroyc in a luxurious office, where I regularly handed over to him thick wads of dollars and passed on the instructions of my shadowy cohorts. This is neither the time nor the place to describe the Congress and its role during the 1950s and 1960s. In this particular case, the fanciful police version pales before the irony of what really happened. Giedroyc and Czapski were among the founding members of the Congress for Cultural Freedom at the time of the big meeting in West Berlin in 1950 (Czapski had known Nicolas Nabokov, the secretary general of the Congress, since the 1920s), and it was thanks to these two friends of mine at *Kultura* that I became a member of the Congress—not without some difficulty, moreover, since it took the full authority of Raymond Aron to get me in. I must admit that we had hoped this group of distinguished anti-fascist and anti-Stalinist intellectuals, who so closely resembled *Kultura*'s "self-image," would be of some assistance to the review. Such was not the case, however, and when *Kultura* was evicted from its lodgings, my best efforts obtained a donation of only two or three thousand old francs from the Congress. Giedroyc launched a public fund-raising drive in the review, whose readers responded miraculously by donating the fifteen million francs necessary to buy a different house in Maisons-Laffitte. (This gift, like all donations, was duly reported in the review.) My other attempts to obtain anything whatsoever from the Congress for *Kultura* all ended in failure. Years later, when the news of the secret CIA funding broke, the executive secretary of the Congress, Michael Josselson, assumed full responsibility for the scandal. Like most of the friends and members of the Congress, once the initial shock had worn off I found I had lost none of the affection and esteem I felt toward this man, who had managed to assure complete freedom for all the reviews and other undertakings of the Congress. (Hannah Arendt told me one day that Josselson's most difficult project must have been safeguarding that freedom from the CIA.) During one of our numerous subsequent conversations on this topic, he told me: "Now you understand why I never wanted to help *Kultura*. For an émigré review, it could have turned out to be a dangerous liability." As for giving "instructions" to Giedroyc, whose liberal and democratic convictions are beyond reproach, he has always behaved as a perfect autocrat as far as the review is concerned. I know what I'm talking about, because for a time I was a member, with three other friends, of a *Kultura* "collective" that was co-opted by Giedroyc, probably in an effort to present the readership with what he felt was a suitable image of the workings of the review. None of the members of the collective ever knew what was going to be on the next table of contents, which always remained

one of the best-kept secrets in our little world where everything
became known sooner or later, if only to a few people. I'm convinced
that Giedroyc is still pained by the fact that at least one of his three
closest colleagues—who share his life—found out this secret in the
end when the review went to press. So it's not surprising that this
first and only collective quickly dissolved, without this ever being
discussed among us or mentioned in the review. We had no inkling
at the time of *Kultura*'s prodigiously successful future, but we already
knew that the exclusive passion of this man—completely devoid of
personal ambition but determined to affect the destiny of his country,
of all Eastern Europe (I might go so far as to think: of the whole
world)—was a greater moving force than any collective effort. The
Poles understand this very well, particularly the ones who now flock
to Maisons-Laffitte almost as though they were on a pilgrimage to a
kind of Colombey-les-Deux-Eglises in exile. And there's a touch of
admiration in the affectionate irony of the young Polish writer who
refers, in one of the new "independent" reviews, to "the sovereign
principality of Maisons-Laffitte."

So that we may perceive a common denominator in the apparently
incongruous group formed by *Kultura*'s contributors in the early
years (ex-communists and Pilsudskiites, liberal conservatives and
leftists, members of the nobility, the gentry, or the bourgeoisie—
often Jewish—but rarely of the peasantry, and more rarely still of
the working class), a brief "archaeology" of the Polish intelligentsia
is necessary. Sociologists all agree that for a long time this intellectual
elite carried on many stereotypes derived from the *szlachta*, that
nobility which so little resembles its Western equivalents, if only
because of its large proportion of the population: twelve percent at
the end of the eighteenth century. It was a nobility that cultivated
libertarian and egalitarian myths (wasn't the kingdom of Poland a *res
publica* of the *szlachta*?) and became receptive to left-wing ideas during
the nineteenth century, for only the leftists of the West supported
the Poles in their struggles for independence. Ruined, exiled, or
deported to Siberia after successive insurrections, torn from their
lands, countless members of the gentry merged into the intelligentsia,
which functioned according to an implicit principle of co-optation.
This principle extended even to the inclusion of communists (admit-
tedly few in number), so that one might trace the uninterrupted
filiation of a Polish establishment (with common bonds between

"those in power" and "the opposition") from at least as far back as the failed insurrection of 1863 and continuing well beyond the communist takeover. Only Gierek's emergence as Party leader in 1970 breaks with this pattern at last, marking as it does the predominance of a "new guard," a new class—homogeneous, rising in the social scale, educated in Party schools or on the job, uninterested in ideology, hostile to intellectuals—which tries to base its legitimacy on "reasons of state" and a vague concept of the "moral and political solidarity of the nation" (this term will resurface with a vengeance in the 1970s and be used, through the irony of fate, by the workers of Gdansk in their struggles against the authorities). *Res Publica*, the review ("uncensored," of course) of those young Polish intellectuals who claim spiritual kinship with Tocqueville and Raymond Aron, describes that "frozen image of the past" still projected until quite recently (because things will never be the same after the events of the summer of 1980) by the regime's rhetoric: "It's a vision of the noble history of a country whose past leaders often failed and which only now has been blessed with suitable leadership. A vision of society in which everyone—atheists and believers, leftists and rightists—has supposedly never wanted anything except the good of the nation."

There were many differences between the Polish left and right on the eve of World War II, but the "emotional" dividing line ran between the right-wing nationalists, the heirs of Roman Dmowski (Jozef Pilsudski's chief adversary), and all other political groups, whether on the left or on the right. This chauvinistic and anti-Semitic right, which made up the large National Democratic Party, had two faces: one was the face of the masses, the "Polish-Catholic" (pronounced as one word), the petit-bourgeois incarnation of Sartre's "just man"; the other face was even more sinister—the fascist bands of the ONR–Falanga, whose leader, Boleslaw Piasecki, gave his support to the regime after the war by founding PAX, an organization of Catholics who collaborated with the new rulers. The death of old Marshal Pilsudski in 1935 left his successors somewhat at a loss, and there were those among the mafia of "colonels" who directed a few come-hither looks in the direction of the extreme right, but on the whole there remained countless personal and intellectual ties between the Pilsudskiites and the leftists, ties that were profoundly rooted in the past, since the veteran supporters of Pilsudski had come for the most part from the Socialist Party, like their leader. (It should not be forgotten that Pilsudski's coup d'état in May 1926 against the parliamentary regime was supported by the Polish Communist Party.) In his fascinating conversations with Czeslaw Milosz (in two big volumes entitled *My Century*), the poet Aleksander Wat, founder of *Miesiecznik Literacki* (*Literary Monthly*), the intellectual review of the prewar Communist Party (Wat will of course become a contributor to *Kultura* when he leaves Poland in 1963), humorously describes this *chassé-croisé* between communists and Pilsudskiites: "When left-wing writers came visiting from the West, from France or Germany—like Priacel, for example, Henri Barbusse's secretary—they were astounded to see us sitting like that with the colonels in a café such as the Ziemianska . . . One day, the secretary of the interior sat down at our table . . . You see, we had curiously idyllic relations with the government, and that enraged the petite bourgeoisie, whereas the upper levels of society found this quite acceptable." Wat also remembers an incident verging on the grotesque. After the government had closed down *Miesiecznik Literacki*, Wat and his comrades were arrested and consigned to prison, where they received two cases of "premium quality vodka, caviar," and other delicacies sent from Hirszfeld's (the Fauchon's of Warsaw) by Wieniawa-Dlugoszowski, Pilsudski's confidant and aide-de-camp.

This general outline has no historical or sociological pretensions, of course, and it is surely marked by the passions of youth, for I left Poland in 1939 when I was seventeen. A young Polish friend of mine (a "neo-conservative" of the opposition) said to me recently: "One of the misdeeds of the Endecja (the National Democrats) was to have permanently frozen so many Poles of your generation into a left-wing sensibility." I hope, however, that I've been able to bring to light the one common denominator in the "*Kultura* milieu": its hostility to that nationalist aspect of the Polish tradition, whose resurgence in Poland I so feared—before the events in Gdansk—and which this time would have proved to be one of the principal misdeeds of the communist regime. And I hope I have also explained the "extra-ideological" nature of so many social relations in prewar Poland, where almost every "right-wing" family had "left-wing" cousins (and vice versa). I myself was raised by a grandmother, a famous beauty of the 1900s who dressed in Paris creations and divided her time between Karlsbad and Biarritz. I often dined at home with her and her brother, Stefan Czarnowski, a Marxist anthropologist who strongly influenced most of the Polish communist intellectuals. Jozef Czapski, one of Giedroyc's closest friends and associates, comes from an aristocratic and cosmopolitan family and is himself the nephew of Chicherin, the first commissar of foreign affairs in the U.S.S.R.

It is thus understandable that bonds between émigré Poles and their country were never broken. Contacts were rare during the height of the Stalinist period, for only those in favor with the regime were authorized to travel abroad, and everyone was of course afraid that any initiatives of this kind might be held against them (particularly if they were Party members) at the slightest change in the political line of the Soviet bloc. There were exceptions, though, and several childhood friends or family acquaintances, at one time or another officials in the government, had always come to see me when they were in Paris. October 1956 was a turning point after which these bonds were completely reestablished, and no subsequent pressure from the regime has succeeded in severing them. It isn't surprising that most of the Polish writers destined to leave their country later on (from Milosz to Marek Hlasko and Leszek Kolakowski) immediately published work in *Kultura,* nor is it surprising that one of the most gifted communist intellectuals, Andrzej Stawar, went to Maisons-Laffitte when gravely ill so that he might die there after leaving his last book in the hands of *Kultura.* For several years now, a dozen well-known writers living in Poland have published their books under the *Kultura* imprint and their articles in the review, signing them with their real names (most of these works were banned in Poland, of course), while many other writers—especially the younger ones—publish their work under a pseudonym.

It must also be said that *Kultura* refused from the start to ostracize Poles released from internal exile who find themselves a place in the new cultural, economic, or social structure, or émigrés who decide to return to Poland—an ostracism initially preached by the majority of émigrés. *Kultura* also refused to recognize the decision of the Union of Polish Writers in Exile forbidding its members to publish their works in Poland.

Rereading old issues of *Kultura,* one notices that the review has reflected the realities of the moment in a precise and often premonitory fashion. It should be obvious by now that aside from shared opinions concerning the principles of democracy and social equality, as well as an extremely vigilant attitude toward even the faintest hint of chauvinism and (above all) anti-Semitism, neither Giedroyc nor any of his colleagues was encumbered by ideological considerations, a fact that allowed the review to take some often astonishing twists and turns. Thus, after having initially supported the American policy of "liberation," *Kultura* was the first intellectual journal in Europe to denounce the "objective" complicity of the United States and the U.S.S.R. and to interpret the Cold War as a feint designed to perpetuate the division of the world decreed at Yalta. One of *Kultura's* contributors at the time (a person of sparkling intelligence but somewhat inclined to get carried away by his own imagination) was even completely convinced that a secret agreement existed on this point, an agreement known only to the first secretary of the Party in the U.S.S.R. and the president of the United States and passed on to their astonished respective successors, who find the whole thing hard to believe. In a more serious vein, *Kultura* had envisioned an "Alternative Club" that would establish a bloc of "nonaligned" nations even before the "neutralist" ideas put forward by *Le Monde* at the time.

As far as the situation in Poland is concerned, from the very beginning *Kultura* opposed any return to a capitalistic society and tried to encourage ideas based on self-management, involving unions and cooperatives. This point of view was tirelessly expounded by Juliusz Mieroszewski, who lived in London and advocated the transformation of Poland into a socialist welfare state. Naturally enough, an alliance was soon reached between certain Polish revisionists and *Kultura*, which wholeheartedly supported Gomulka in 1956.

Without historical and archival research (for which I have neither the skills nor the time at present), it would be difficult to establish whether the changes in *Kultura's* opinions on Poland's internal affairs preceded or followed changes in the political agendas of opposition movements within the country. Of course, most of these new directions are perfectly understandable. For instance, although *Kultura* supported Gomulka at first, the review turned against him for good in 1957 when he liquidated *Po Prostu*, a dissident weekly of that time, whereas some revisionists continued to support Gomulka simply because there was no other realistic alternative. *Kultura's* immediate reaction against the anti-Semitic campaign disguised as anti-Zionism that was unleashed in Poland in 1967–68 was obviously rooted in one of *Kultura's* most basic political convictions. An émigré review is more or less fated (on condition that it be truly disinterested and independent, of course) to be right ahead of anyone else at home, but also at less cost, because it functions outside of all social gravity, free of the sticky grip of political involvement *in situ*. Giedroyc might argue that he paid a high price for that indispensable independence and accredited impartiality when he waged his first battles against the Polish establishment in exile, against "his own people" in a way. That is also how I interpret his constant and often unjust war against powerful Radio Free Europe in Munich, without really knowing whether this was a perfectly lucid strategy on his part or a "trick of the unconscious mind." This war earned him the hostility of the Americans and of a large number of Polish émigrés, on the one hand, and, on the other, the incomprehension of his readers in Poland, for whom this radio program was their chief source of daily news. In any case, there was something about this stubborn chipping away at his opponents that made it seem like a "test" he must have felt he had to pass in order to establish his credibility. It was certainly risky business, and *Kultura* undoubtedly reaped a sheaf of canceled subscriptions after each violent outburst of this kind, but new waves of emigrants brought new subscribers to replace the disgusted traditionalists, while others remained faithful to the review in spite of everything. After all, the nonconformity of *Kultura* has its roots in a long Polish tradition—a minority one, it's true, but one with such impeccable social, cultural, and political references that most staunch Polish conformists hesitate to disavow it, for one never knows what the future will bring. They have only to think back on the Romantic poets Mickiewicz, Slowacki, and Norwid, for example, who all blasphemed while they were alive but wound up embalmed as sainted relics in the nation's school books.

Finally, there is the fact that fortune smiled on Giedroyc during *Kultura*'s beginnings. "The history of peoples," writes Czeslaw Milosz in *The Land of Ulro*, "has its own mysteries; such a one is the life the Polish language has forged for itself outside our borders." In the nineteenth century, the greatest Polish poets lived and published their most important works in Paris during the dark years following the failed insurrection against czarist Russia in 1830. The situation was the same after the last war, and it was in *Kultura* that the two greatest contemporary Polish writers, Witold Gombrowicz and Czeslaw Milosz, published their masterpieces. Such works also reinforced *Kultura*'s adversarial and innovative stance with regard to submissive communist Poland and rigid Poland-in-exile. The one thing Gombrowicz and Milosz have in common is precisely this denunciation of Polish cultural stereotypes, which are equally valid (although interpreted in a diametrically opposed fashion) in Poland and in exile. And both writers base their critiques on their claims on behalf of a fundamental "Polishness" that is shamefully repressed in the culture of the Polish establishment, which stubbornly insists on trumpeting its ties to an idealized "West" in the manner of a rich man's poor relation. "It's not art for art's sake, it's art for the West's sake," wrote Gombrowicz defiantly. "One day I will show that the most anachronistic of men, the Polish country gentleman, can become the most modern of beings, as long as the problems are framed in modern terms." As for Milosz, he was better than anyone else at denouncing Polish provincialism, always feverishly sniffing out the "very latest thing" from the West. Both these men set themselves up as rivals to the West and demanded their rights to autonomy: Gombrowicz by defending the individual he was ("The individual is more important than the nation. I come before the nation"); Milosz, in the name of his own vision of the world and Polish history. The angry reception accorded both writers, as much by the majority of Polish émigrés as by "official" Poland, played an enormous role in defining *Kultura*, which later came to bask in the reflected prestige which these two writers now enjoy in their homeland, a prestige confirmed even by the official Polish media. Before Milosz was awarded the Nobel Prize in 1980, Gombrowicz came within one vote of receiving this honor in 1968 (he died the following spring), which went to the Japanese writer Yasunari Kawabata that year. The fact that these two distinguished Polish authors had been published in the same émigré review gave added luster to *Kultura*'s truly exceptional record of achievement.

In a letter I received from Giedroyc in June 1980, he cited as one of *Kultura*'s most important contributions its struggle in support of the idea that Poland should normalize relations with the "ULB" (Mieroszewski's term for the countries once united in the Grand Duchy of Lithuania: the Ukraine, Lithuania, and Byelorussia) and its constant efforts to distinguish between Russia and the U.S.S.R. (its regime and imperial vocation).

The credit due to *Kultura* for having opposed from the very first the irrational hatred of the Russians that is so widespread in Poland is all the greater in that four of the six people who formed the "initial core" of the review had been deported to the U.S.S.R. after the annexation of the eastern section of the country: Jozef Czapski, Gustaw Herling-Grudzinski, Zofia and Zygmunt Hertz. The first two, by the way, wrote excellent accounts of this experience at a time

when most Western intellectuals were busy denying the existence of
the Gulag. It was only by a miracle that Czapski himself escaped
dying in the massacre at Katyn.

For the editor of *Kultura*, Russo-Polish relations and the future of
the nations that lie between these two countries are indissolubly
linked. As he wrote in his letter to me, "Our greatest success, which
I would describe as historic, was in my eyes the common declaration
which we persuaded the foremost Russian dissidents in exile to sign,
a declaration that recognizes the principle of independence for the
Ukraine and the other non-Russian republics in the Soviet Union."

During these last few years, whenever I met a young Polish intellectual
of the opposition I would ask him about a paradox that baffled me.
How could it be, I wondered, that under this shameful regime Polish
culture had reached a level of excellence—in all domains—quite
superior to its accomplishments before the war? The answer was
always that I attached too much importance to what a very small
artistic and intellectual elite had managed to achieve in spite of huge
difficulties, that I didn't realize how badly off the entire population
really was: an incompetent and opportunistic professional class, an
alienated peasantry, a demoralized and shattered working class. Ever
since the electrifying events of the summer of 1980, however, it
should be clear to everyone that such pessimism is groundless.
Although an analysis of these events is far beyond the scope of this
introduction, I would like to point out a few things that are relevant
to my argument.

In 1972, *Kultura* celebrated its twenty-fifth anniversary with an
article taking stock of its past actions and current situation: "It is
sometimes said that Poland doesn't need a *samizdat* because it already
has *Kultura* and its publications. We don't agree with that idea.
Kultura's ambition would be to serve as added reinforcement to a
Polish *samizdat*." Further on in the article, we read: "For a long time,
Kultura reached only a limited circle of intellectuals. Today, after the
events of December 1970 . . . the review would like to extend its
sphere of readers to the professional classes, which might then secure
us some contact, however tenuous, with the working class."

The Polish intellectual opposition came up with something even
better than a *samizdat*: a Workers' Defense Committee (KOR) created
after the events of June 1976; a publishing house as well as at least
forty-four reviews and periodicals "free from censorship" (most of

which refuse anonymity and claim the rights guaranteed them in theory by the Polish Constitution and the Helsinki Accords); and a "flying university." *Robotnik* (*The Worker*), the review brought out by the KOR in 1977, took its name from the newspaper founded by the Polish Socialist Party in the early part of this century and had a circulation ranging between ten and twenty thousand copies.

In an article dated August 27, 1980, published in the October issue of *Kultura*, Kisiel—a famous author and journalist who writes under the same pseudonym for *Tygodnik Powszechny* (*Universal Weekly*), the major Catholic weekly in Cracow—writes: "Full justice has not been rendered to the unsung heroes of our present troubled times: Kuron, Michnik, Lipski, Chojecki, Litynski, and the others. They are not—as has been insinuated by various interested parties—the protagonists of some political intrigue (that kind of intrigue is the province of others elsewhere). They have simply been the first to sow the indispensable seed of spiritual freedom." The fact that these "unsung heroes" close to the KOR have on several occasions publicly stated what they owe to *Kultura*, both morally and intellectually, would in itself be ample justification for the work accomplished by Giedroyc and his review. Finally, it is highly significant that in 1980 the strikers at Gdansk demanded as the third point in their charter (accepted by the government) "that freedom of speech and publications be respected, as guaranteed by the Constitution of the People's Republic of Poland." Elaborating on the implications of this third demand in its declaration of September 9, 1980, the Polish Writers' Union called for "the restitution, in compliance with the Constitution, of the presence in public life of those works and writers who have been excluded therefrom. Polish culture is an integral whole, whatever the ideas, opinions, and residence of its creators."

Solidarity has freed the great majority of Poles, if not from oppression, at least from the lies on which it is based, and once such lies have been discredited, then even though this oppression may still hold people firmly in its grip, it has nevertheless been unmasked for what it is: the same old tyranny of ages past. This is an achievement of inestimable importance, not only for Poland, but for the whole of Eastern Europe. "Today the muse of history speaks Polish," announces *The Polish Revolution*, a book published by Russian *samizdat* in 1983.

The distinguished reputation earned by *Kultura* throughout almost half a century, along with the fact that this journal has become a kind of venerable national institution, has entailed certain drawbacks. *Kultura* is probably no longer as lively, surprising, and nonconformist as it was in its early years, but its uncontested authority has at least one advantage, and one that is particularly precious these days: *Kultura* has long exercised complete freedom of judgment, a freedom that is now simply taken for granted, which cannot be said for any other publication of the Polish opposition.

Translated from the French by Linda Coverdale

I

Where We Live

Jozef Szrett

THE VALLEY BETWEEN
THE MOUNTAINS

THE VIEW RESEMBLES a landscape painting covered with icing: a peaceful green valley in sumptuous blossom between the steep slopes of snow-capped mountains. One can watch it in the glare of the midday sun, at dawn, in its evening illumination, in the shades of the seasons. A romantic landscape. And a metaphysical one, for it is nature that endows us with the graces of good harvest, calm, and beauty.

The Polish landscape, despite the Poles' constant claims to romanticism, is not at all romantic. The mountains that surround our valley are not the mountains of nature but of history. The Poles have had their share of historical success, first in transforming themselves from a small and rather uncouth tribe into a European power, and then—after they collectively spoiled this power—in remaining a large and cohesive nation that would not allow anyone to erase it from the map of the world. But the nations that settled on the two sides of the Polish plain have been even more successful. Although the Germans spent entire centuries unintegrated, within the loose structure of the Holy Roman Empire of the German Nation, when they were finally unified there came into being a major European power, based on a multimillion-strong and well-organized people. In its current divided condition Germany's importance has not diminished, despite the fact that West Germany was cut off from important, primarily agricultural, territories, along with more than fifteen percent of its population.

On the other side of our valley, Russian expansion became so dynamic that the territory Lenin had inherited from the czars was only marginally reduced in the West and remained the size of a subcontinent stretching over two continents. Lenin and his successors inherited something else, too: an enormous mass of different nations forced into a subjugation against which only individuals can revolt. And so, between the mountains—the ethnically monolithic one in the west and the astoundingly diverse one in the east—the valley of the individualistic Poles has been wedged between two expansionistic pressures, between two hostile empires. It has been small consolation that the two powers would clash against each other, since their battles took place in this very valley. What was meant to be a European retreat, an oasis flowing with milk and honey, was transformed into a firing range or, at best, a corridor for the use of any and all Europeans.

In our reflections we must, by necessity, go back incessantly to those mountains that cast such a portentous shadow on our valley. No one can tear them down or eliminate them. We must always remember that the two shadows are the only existing reality. But, at the same time, we cannot constantly let them dominate our thinking. The Pole is curious about the world, he likes to travel, to get to know other countries and nations, and then to compare these experiences with his own Polish experience. Unfortunately, he always makes these comparisons in an aura of complexes and self-compensation. And the closer and more direct these contacts become, the greater are the complexes and the more vulgar the self-compensation. We are focusing on the German and the Russki, the Russki and the German, as if no other states and nations existed, as if beyond these mountains stretched out something boundless and unclear, a sea of darkness.

The Poles, with relatively few exceptions, never loved either the Germans or the Russians. It was actually difficult to communicate with the former; hence, their bizarre name in Polish, which imputes them muteness.[1] The Poles' inability to communicate with the latter was different—the similarity of our languages meant that, while we

---

[1] The Polish word for a German, *Niemiec*, stems from the same root as the word *niemy*, or mute.—Trans.

could understand each other's words, we could not understand what the other meant. Or we did not want to understand. The exceptions, however, were numerous enough to be used by the mountains for their own purposes. Unfortunately, one has to question our myth that ours has been a country without a Quisling. It was the Nazis who did not want one and did not look for one, but we know that there were potential candidates. After all, it was not the Italians, Portuguese, or Indians who signed Targowica,[2] concluded the Warsaw Pact, or imposed martial law in December 1981. The most bitter aspect of this is that such acts were committed with pompous claims of "saving the Fatherland."

Ever since the mountains gained political supremacy over the valley and began to overpower, darken, and even bury it, they have had a guilty conscience toward us. But a bad conscience can affect people's behavior very differently in different circumstances. Very often the desire for revenge is directed against those who are the cause of the guilt, something of which we really have experienced an overdose. Today, among the Germans—the "Germanic spirit" has been rinsed out of them by nearly forty years of democracy—this guilty conscience is frequently expressed in a peculiar embarrassment and demonstrations of goodwill. It is indeed no paradox that most of the recent Western humanitarian aid for Poland has come from West Germany.

The Russians have held on to an unchanged feeling of ill will strengthened by suspicion (and directed not only at us but at all the nations they cannot control). Envy also plays a role here: this unruly, ungrateful *privislansky kray*,[3] which is so carefully guarded, therefore de jure owned by "big brother," in spite of everything has preserved its individual prosperity as well as its cultural superiority. This cannot be forgiven!

Let me explain that by cultural superiority I mean both collective and individual (or perhaps individualized) superiority. It would be presumptuous as well as pathetically moronic to deny the Russians their enormous contribution to world culture. This contribution, however, is the result of the actions of prominent individuals, while

[2] A confederation formed by a group of Polish nobles in 1792 at Targowica invoked the help of Catherine the Great, the Russian empress, against the Polish government and the program of reforms accepted by the Great Diet of 1791 (Constitution of May 3, 1791). This appeal, which had been carefully drafted in Petersburg, provided Catherine with an excuse to invade Poland that same year. To the Poles, Targowica became a symbol of high treason.—Ed.

[3] Russian for "country on the Vistula."—Trans.

the Russian and Polish collectivities represent a very different standard—different in our favor. We have far fewer geniuses but many more—in relation to the whole nation—individuals with a very high intellectual capacity. And this hurts the Russians perhaps more than the fact that the average Pole dresses better, until recently has eaten better, and has dealt with a more technically advanced civilization of daily life. When the Russians sarcastically call us "those Polish *pany*,"[4] this has no class coloring, but only a cultural shading. There are no "masters" in our country in the old sense of the word, but we are "*pany*" because we have not allowed anyone to force us to be equal and turn us into comrades, and the "*wy*"[5] form has not caught on. In today's Poland, the only people who can be contrasted with "*pany*" are the communists, who are commonly called "them."

In a situation where the pressures of the mountains against the valley can be so very easily and directly felt and the collective feelings of the mountains toward the valley so devoid of objectivity, our own collective feelings have also long lost the clarity of the "glass and eye of the wizard." It is not because the Poles have inherited from their great poet an antipathy for those optical instruments which make things look objective, but because they have allowed themselves to be convinced that romanticism is an element of their national character. Meanwhile, an important part of this alleged romanticism stems from neurotic reactions to bias or hostility. And romanticism is not and probably should not be our destiny.

The Poles' bias and hostility toward the Germans has been significantly blunted in recent years. It is not only the assistance I have already mentioned that gives rise to feelings of gratitude (one could look for analogies to the help and kindness of the Germans in the period following the November 1830 Polish uprising against Russia). West Germany has also become a Mecca and a kind of El Dorado for those who feel not so much endangered as impoverished in Poland. A recent monstrous anecdote dressed it up in the form of a riddle: What is the difference between the German and the Soviet occupations? The answer: Under the Soviet occupation they, unfortunately, no longer take you away to forced labor in Germany. Let's omit the whole national-ethical problem of the new wave of emigrants who go to the West for mostly illegal seasonal labor. After all, preferring to

---

[4] The Polish word *pan* means both "sir" and "master." *Pany* is its plural.—Trans.

[5] The supposedly egalitarian second person plural is used in the Soviet Union.—Trans.

be a *Gastarbeiter* to being a citizen of one's own country is anyone's own business, and Catonism is of doubtful value here, especially coming from the Polish communists, who have long established themselves in Poland and will not have to spend years waiting for their own apartment, their own nook (but not a cozy nest) for the family they would one day like to have.

The most important point here is that the material proof of German prosperity (Germany's humanitarian aid to Poland) and the somewhat mythologized vision of the West German El Dorado are to some extent a reaction to the Polish regime's usual clumsy propaganda. The people of communist Poland have too long, too insistently, and too primitively been "threatened with the German." Even if the propaganda that touches on history parallels people's—especially the older generation's—own real experiences, wounds, and scars, all these threats with spies and revisionists have not caught on in Poland; on the contrary, they have evoked the opposite reaction. The following anecdote illustrates the Poles' attitude to official propaganda. An old peasant woman comes to the office of ZBOWID [Association of Combatants for Freedom and Democracy][6] and asks to join. "What did you do during the German occupation, ma'am, how can you justify your application?" "I helped the boys from the woods, from the Resistance." "Do you have witnesses?" "Of course not, they all got killed." "Well then, tell us at least how you helped them." "The usual way. I cooked soup, baked bread, and took it all to the woods. Oh, the boys were so happy, they would always say: *Danke schön!*" "But they were Germans!" "Well, yes, but the good ones, from East Germany."

I would like to venture the following thesis: the contemporary Pole has not learned to love the Germans, but he has also not stopped admiring them for their sophisticated civilization, and—what is more important—he has liberated himself from his fear of them. It is a small step forward, although much, very much, remains to be changed. The Poles are under-informed on the subject of Germany, the history they hear every day is full of deceit, and even on special occasions truthful information about contemporary Germany is lacking. I am not saying that we should all at once stop talking about the issues which cast a very poisonous shadow on our common past, but that instead we should write up a sensible, more general balance

[6] A regime-sponsored association of former combatants and agents embellished with such names as Sikorski and Moczar.—Author

sheet. We must speak and write about the Germans without hang-ups and in a sophisticated enough way so as to avoid giving the average Pole the impression that the German nation has been made up exclusively of Teutonic Knights, proponents of *Kulturkampf*, Nazi butchers, and grotesque shadows from the past, the "revisionists" from associations of ethnic Germans resettled from Poland to West Germany after World War II. We also ought to devote some time to the issue of German participation in the history of our country, since the same average Pole who has heard so much about the Teutonic Knights does not know that the majority of the inhabitants of some towns in Poland's First Republic were Germans, some of them Polonized, others not, who still remained loyal to the Polish state and built up its modern trade and crafts.

It would be nice if a Pole could deal with a German on the same level of economic development, on the same level of material civilization. But this is not possible, not even with a citizen of East Germany, the pseudo-stateling which West Germany has for years been patiently pumping up economically. But we can talk on the same cultural and social levels. And who knows, perhaps a German worker, or even a German intellectual, could learn a few things from us. But to talk on the same level, it is essential that we learn to know and understand each other. We have carried on our bent backs equally large and heavy bundles of historical and cultural experiences, traditions, *modus vivendi*. It is this baggage that should help us arrive at an understanding, liberate ourselves from unjustified self-depreciations and equally untrue self-aggrandizements.

Today the average Pole's attitude toward the Soviet Union, and therefore toward the Russians, is different. I think that for a long time now, since the nineteenth-century uprisings, the collective bias has not been so widespread and so hateful. Even while Stalinist–Bierutist terror raged in our country there was no such consensus, and the proponents of Poland's submission to the U.S.S.R. were not as isolated as they are today. In those days, there were actually quite a few of those who served Soviet interests in Poland, and most of them believed in what they were doing. Today this decimated "elite," which of its own will has removed itself from society, if it believes in anything, believes in power, in participating in power, and in the personal gains connected with it. There is also no point in denying that the great majority of today's dissidents once cooperated, or at least identified, with the regime. They were accompanied in this passive collaboration by numerous "average Poles" who did not belong to the Party, who "were not interested in politics," were exhausted by years of war and occupation and dreamed about one thing only: peace and quiet at any price.

Today the group of non-Party collaborators has shrunk significantly, the divisions have become clearer, and even those who "are not interested in politics" allow themselves the luxury of cursing and swearing at the "Russkis." This anonymous "Russki" has become the reason behind all kinds of evil: the empty shops and the militia's brutality, the captivity of minds and the system's economic oafishness. In individual assessments, these abominations add up to the popular notion of today's typical Russian "Red." The "Russki" is a godless ignoramus and a boor, a drunk, a thief, and a cop, an informer, an Asian and a muzhik, mentally blocked by the most vulgar of propagandas, dangerous in his greed and his craving to rule the world. In other words, a cannibal and a born slave, all in one. Even apart from the extreme simplicity of this notion, what we have here is a classical example of shifting responsibility for the flaws of a system on to a whole society.

In the years of war and occupation, every German was a henchman and a criminal—hence the great surprise when, after a few decades of the democratic West Germany, the new generation of Germans looks to us like a completely normal society. In the Soviet Union, where the regime has not changed or evolved in any significant way, where totalitarian police muzzling still rules, we lightheartedly shift the responsibility for all the repulsive shortcomings of this contemporary *ancien régime* onto the man in the street. It is precisely as if we were blamed and burdened with the defects of Jaruzelski's junta.

But there is another reason: the Pole does not like to admit his own flaws and always finds it more convenient to put the blame on someone else. Hence the Poles' anti-Russianism does not come from reason but from emotion, not from objective reflection but from reawakened old prejudice. The regime's propaganda plays a separate role in this wave of moods. An analogy can be drawn between the anti-German and the pro-Soviet propaganda. They have a similar effect of shifting popular attitudes in the opposite direction to the one intended by the regime. Because the Polish Communist Party is so terribly afraid of Moscow, its overzealousness spoils things that inherently work badly anyway (just like everything else in socialism). Television and radio programs; magazines, including the phenomenal

Country of the Soviets, which no one reads; the surrealistic fictitiousness of the Association of Polish–Soviet Friendship; the morose grotesqueness of the "friendship trains"—all this is a creation of this enthusiastic and therefore all the more clumsy propaganda. By glorifying the "Soviet man," the propaganda simply insults the Russians and creates new waves of antipathy in the Poles. By their fearfulness and servility, the members of the Polish Communist Party are transformed from colonial governors into a *Gauleiter* of their own country. All in all, in the shameful history of the Polish People's Republic, Gomulka alone managed at times to act independently, even courageously, vis-à-vis the Kremlin. If only he had been intelligent.

Obviously, in any culture or civilization, the political system leaves a lasting mark on the collectivity, and through the collectivity on the individual. The Russians, over centuries of their rather gloomy history, have developed some very bad qualities, but—permanently weighed down by misfortunes—they also retained many good qualities. The Zinovievian *homosos* is a lampoon which, like a magnifying glass, reveals the "Soviet man" with his worst characteristics, which have been formed by despotism and the Soviet regime's ever-present pressure. But let's look in the mirror, let's look inside ourselves: don't symptoms of affliction with Sovietism (a Sovietism that is, of course, lightly colored *à la Polacca*) crop up in us, too, again and again?

It seems wrong to encourage the Poles to love the Germans and the Russians. In relations between nations, love is a dispensable, even harmful, emotion, since it can never be consummated. One cannot imagine the lovemaking of nations, and platonic emotions cannot be transformed into a stream of erotic poetry, since a collectivity cannot collectively perform eroticism either in deeds or in words. What is more, the Poles, who are usually quite impulsive and not very constant in their emotions, would rapidly transform unfulfilled love into hatred.

This calls for an explanation. There are other nations living in this valley between the mountains. Our relations with those nations are for the most part not very good, at times simply bad, and it is unquestionably a major achievement of *Kultura*'s that for years it has consistently taken up the "irritating" Ukrainian, Lithuanian, and Byelorussian concerns, even if they were unwelcomed by many of its readers. Since this is not the place to discuss our closest neighbors, our neighbors from the valley, let's simply point out one issue: we are not allowed to forget that virtually none of our closest neighbors has ever been in our situation, none of them has had mountains on both sides, but only on one side. The Ukrainians and Lithuanians will probably protest that, for them, that other mountain, in the west, has been Poland. But they will be wrong, because they will be seeking out analogies in the distant and already closed past. Furthermore, Polish expansionism never adopted the same brutal forms as those once used by the Germans and still used by the Russians.

Another conclusion can be drawn from all this: we should not and cannot count on these neighbors to be any sort of a "buffer" between us and our enemies. The "buffer" concept has proved a pure fiction in politics, and in the interwar period we became an "experimental guinea pig" of post-Versailles Europe. Therefore, we should understand that by establishing the best possible relations with our neighbors we will bring security to the whole valley.

Polish prejudice against the Germans is based on memories of German occupation and the so-called threat to our western frontiers. Anyone who knows history understands that the Germanic nations have frequently experienced powerful eruptions of aggressiveness. *Furror teutonicus* manifested itself in the era of the migration of nations, in the Teutonic Knights' conversions with the sword, and most powerfully in the two world wars. Does this mean that Germany continues to be a nursery of militarism? East Germany, yes, definitely: General Hoffman has been training hosts of "European Cubans," while East German kindergartens and schools are tasked with the mass production of athletes who rake in armloads of medals in all international competitions. But West Germany? The country in which "peaceniks"[7] form the most powerful mass movement and where even soldiers demonstrate against American missiles?

We should also not forget that Poland suffered enormous material losses not only in both world wars but also during the Deluge. In Poland, next to the ruins from 1914–18 (and 1920) and 1939–45, there are plenty of ruins from 1655–57. And is anyone today afraid of an invasion by the Swedes, by those bellicose and ruthless ruffians who under Carolus Gustavus were the terror of half of Europe, while today they clumsily "battle" with mysterious (maybe to some!) Soviet

---

[7] Of course, not all the organizers of the peace movement are Soviet agents, and certainly the great majority of demonstrators have the honorable intention of defending human life, but they have learned nothing from the fate of pacifism before World War II. They are simply demonstrating against the self-defense of the West, forgetting that *si vis pacem para bellum*. So they probably deserve the nickname of peaceniks. —Author

submarines and are prepared—according to Zinoviev—to go along with "Scandinavization" (*per analogiam* to Finlandization), so as to preserve their prosperity at any price?

The once most bellicose nations lost their courage when they came into contact with prosperity and democracy. This is why West Germany ceased to be a threat to the Poles and Poland's western frontiers. The German revisionist leaders with "typical" ancient Germanic names such as Hupka or Czaja are receding further and further into the past.

Thus, the landscape of our valley has undergone very important changes in the last decades, and the mountains that surround the valley are no longer homogeneous. On the one side are soft slopes whose forests and pastures conceal its erosion; on the other side are sharp, inaccessible rocks, glaciers, and perpetual snow. The threat to the Poles from the east is more direct, since it is also a threat to their national character and identity. In his dealings with the Germans, the Pole has only two choices: to remain himself or to become completely Germanized. With the Russians, the problem is more difficult, since the Russians have become specialists in different methods of meting out patriotism to the nations they control while keeping a tight hold on the reins of "internationalism," the duty to obey Moscow headquarters. Russification within the confines of manipulated pan-Slavism (or whatever other name is chosen for it) does not necessarily mean that people lose their national character, or even their language; it suffices for it to take place in the minds of individuals. There are quite a few alternatives, and this is why the idea of Slavic Christian brotherhood promoted by John Paul II is very important, albeit not very popular in the West.

In the West, we repeatedly hear that the Pope is too involved in politics. The Pope simply cannot avoid getting involved in politics, since everything that concerns humanity is ipso facto politics—the defense of the rights of the individual, the principles of fair employment, and the catechization of nations and social groups. Hence the idea of Slavic Christian brotherhood is political, if we agree that reaching the hearts and minds of human communities, not through machinations, terror, and corruption, but with teachings about God's mission, is also politics.

"Spiritual" and "ideological" Russification does not currently pose much of a threat—the majority of the Polish people have long been immune to this danger. But the Poles' immersion in their current anti-Russianism is hardly better. In the long run, it threatens to drag along absurd hostility which can only lead to the extermination of one of the two nations—clearly, of ours, because we are weaker, less numerous, and currently also sufficiently disarmed.

But we do not want to build bridges between our nations out of sheer calculation. For them to become truly meaningful, we must get to know each other better and understand each other. We view the Russians as a throng of humble slaves who obediently follow every order from above or as the macabre masks of the cruel old men of the Kremlin and their unfailing butchers. Polish nightmares about the Russians take on the figures of the Georgians, like Stalin and Beria, the Ukrainian Khrushchev, and . . . the *"Polachishek"*[8] Dzerzhinsky.

Mickiewicz's Muscovite friends have been forgotten, and we do not quite think of the magnificent contemporary dissidents as Russians. But, as J. J. Lipski[9] noted in his valuable study of patriotism, these dissidents deserve much greater respect than do ours, because ours are risking much less—we have no labor camps or forced exile. By risking a hundred times more than we do, the Russian dissidents have saved the honor of all Russians. And not with any theatrical leap into a river, but by stubbornly demanding political freedoms and civil liberties. It is with equal stubbornness that we would like to vilify them.

Apart from this—and it really is necessary to bring up this truism here—the Russians have made an enormous contribution to world culture. This was never easy and at times they had to pay a high price for it (Dostoevsky). They deserve great respect, if only because of this.

And finally, and this will be a surprise to many Poles who have not had the opportunity to have deeper and more direct contact with the Russians, the Russian people are for the most part gentle, warm, helpful, hospitable, and peacefully inclined. The collective qualities which we impute to them come either from the lack of freedom in their country or from the hypocrisy and isolation in which their system has cornered them. It seems that the Russians' greatest sin is their patriotism, which has two faces. It is, in Lipski's assessment,

---

[8] Condescending Russian diminutive for Pole.—Trans.

[9] Jan Jozef Lipski, writer and literary critic, founder-member of the Workers' Defense Committee (KOR). His essay "Two Fatherlands; Two Patriotisms" appears in this collection.—Ed.

exuberant, steeped in messianism, and can be transformed into ruthlessness. In fact, this Russian messianism is completely different from our own, which is tearful, over-angelic, and full of martyrdom. Their messianism is the messianism of leadership and therefore an imperialistic one. Let us hope that one day everyone, both in the mountains and in the valley, will wake up and realize that the Poles are not a Christ and the Russians are not the Moses of nations (not even of the Slavic nations).

It makes no sense, as I have said, to try to convince nations that they ought to love one another. One should not even try to encourage them to be fond of each other. The collectivity, by adopting from individuals the sum total of certain individual features, does not become a different individual but remains a collectivity, and can be observed quite objectively only from this perspective. Therefore, not love but respect that evolves from getting to know each other better and being able to understand each other better must form the foundation of international relations.

So, what can come of the respect that the most outstanding individuals have for another nation, if the two great communities, our valley and their eastern mountains, have genuine contempt for each other, mixed with—and this makes it even worse—envy? We are envious of their size and numbers, of their political and military might, while they envy our more sophisticated culture and civilization.

Let's go back to patriotism. After all, neither they nor we can be called unpatriotic. But how many times have we, and especially they, misused this lofty sentiment? It may be useless to add up how much different people have done for the common good of other nations, but it is worth recalling that we have very often fought for that community of great nations which is Europe. Someone will say that we wrote the lofty motto "For Your Freedom and Ours" on our banners at those times when we were suppressed, crushed by the mountains surrounding us, and seeking help from any source, appealing to other peoples with our own solidarity. But the anniversary of the rescue of Vienna,[10] which was celebrated in 1983, reminds

[10] When the Turks under Kara Mustafa attacked Vienna in 1683, the Pope and Leopold I, the Emperor of Austria, appealed for help to the Polish king, Jan Sobieski. Sobieski took command of the combined European rescue forces and scored a spectacular victory over the Turks. Vienna was saved and the Turks were pushed out of Central Europe for good. German historians draw attention to the role of Charles of Lorraine in the Battle of Vienna; Polish historians stress the role of the Polish artillery and Sobieski's winged hussars.—Ed.

us how much many of our old warlike initiatives resembled the Crusades. We must not lose sight of these symptoms of chauvinism which we did not lack in the past and do not lack today. But, again, we should not compare our chauvinism with Russian chauvinism. One can conduct negotiations—which are usually pointless anyway— only between states. Nations do not need to eliminate rockets, tanks, and airplanes, but only their phobias, complexes, and bad feelings. And here even a unilateral "disarmament" has a chance of being effective, of "disarming" the other side.

The mountains, even the western ones, will not erode and disintegrate. Although it is not true that in our era miracles no longer happen—we deal with them every day, often without noticing them, going about our business, exhausted by our daily existence. Sometimes miracles have a collective character. One such miracle is the birth of Solidarity. In our era, saints do not travel on little clouds over the sites of battles, especially the battles taking place within societies. People need to be summoned to create individual and collective miracles, to find courage in their dailiness, to declare themselves on the side of miracles. Can we bury Solidarity under a mound with our collective resignation, our collective dislike of exerting ourselves— Solidarity which has been broken only on the organizational level but "has not yet perished"?

As for relations with our neighbors, we must, through collective goodwill, do everything to transform yesterday's and today's enemies into tomorrow's friends, or at least honest partners in the coexistence of free nations. Kisiel[11] is right when he stubbornly repeats that we— as a nation and as a state—must reach an agreement with the Russians. He is only wrong to address his plea to the Soviet *verkhushka*,[12] to those icy crags of the *ancien régime*. His mistake lies in the fact that one cannot negotiate with the Soviet "power elite," which is as isolated from its people as the Polish Communist Party is isolated from the Polish people. Such negotiations would be impossible without the mediation of our own *Gauleiter*, and in any case there is nothing to negotiate about, because to negotiate one needs a partner and not a liar!

The Poles must not negotiate but talk with the Germans and the Russians—with the former without the demeaning awareness of

---

[11] Stefan Kisielewski, a well-known Catholic publicist and novelist.—Ed.

[12] Russian for "top Soviet leadership."—Trans.

economic inferiority, and with the latter without the feeling of cultural or civilizational superiority. This does not mean that all the descendants of Piast Kolodziej[13] should become great buddies, get drunk together, and kiss each other on both cheeks. Conversations between nations should be understood metaphorically, as the collective conversation of individuals with each other. This kind of dialogue must necessarily begin with the basic question: Who am I in the contemporary world? This is the first, basic step toward an understanding of and a respect for strangers.

It is not at all strange that *Kultura*, which is located outside Poland, has chosen to build bridges between the nations of Central Europe. Many Poles do not like this, but we should not look for easy and immediate approval. The only right way of looking at these problems is from the perspective of a free conscience.

Poland and its people will stay on this plain next to the Ukrainians, Byelorussians, Lithuanians, Slovaks, and the other nations. But they cannot become their political leaders, nor can they become dependent on them economically. And no one is going to crumble or move the mountains which surround this valley. It is in our interest to liberate ourselves from oppression by others, and at the same time liberate ourselves from resentments and complexes. And we should not reject any hand that reaches out to us. The mountains do not have to be stern barriers which only cast a shadow on the valley. This vision is almost childish in its naïve kindness, like a landscape painting from a church fair, but it is not as unrealistic as it might seem at first glance.

(January–February 1984)
Translated by Maya Latynski

---

[13] The legendary forebear of the first dynasty of Polish monarchs, the Piasts.—Ed.

Juliusz Mieroszewski

IMPERIALISM: THEIRS AND OURS

WE FEAR THE RUSSIANS. We fear the Russians not on the battlefield, because we recently scored a serious victory over them. There are still some people living among us who took part in the Battle of Warsaw of 1920.[1] We fear Russian imperialism, Russia's political designs. Why do the Russians prefer satellite states—Poland, Czechoslovakia, Hungary—to friendly, relatively neutral neighbors? In the current situation there is no logical answer to this question. If West Germany today had a powerful army, atomic weapons, and professed the idea of retaliation, then the role of the satellites as a bulwark for Russia would be understandable. But, as we know, today's Germany has nothing to do with militarism. In my book on Germany, I ventured the opinion that German tanks would never again appear on the outskirts of Moscow. Some alignments and patterns do indeed

[1] A turning point in the Polish–Soviet War of 1919–21. In August 1920, advancing Soviet armies were stopped by Polish troops on the outskirts of Warsaw. As a result of the Polish victory, the Red Army began to disintegrate. Lenin sued for peace with Poland and offered as much territory in the borderlands as the Poles cared to take. According to many historians, the Battle of Warsaw was one of the most important battles of the twentieth century. Polish victory prevented Soviet military intervention in Germany and possibly other countries of Western Europe.—Ed.

repeat in history, but in most cases history never repeats itself. History is fascinating because "the same thing" is never "the same thing," and nearly identical situations bring about different results.

Still, historical conditioning makes us attach too much importance to the so-called imponderables and too little importance to change. Older people—and the author of these words is one of them—especially tend to say that nothing has really changed. Russia is imperialistic because it has always been imperialistic. Our instinct tells us that the Germans, too, have not really changed, and when the right circumstances occur they will arm themselves to the teeth and reach out for our western territories.

Seventy or perhaps even eighty percent of politics is an interpretation of history. None of us knows exactly what the members of the Kremlin Politburo talk about during their secret sessions. None of us knows what they are thinking or plotting. But we do know about their predecessors' thoughts and designs from the history of the past two hundred years. We therefore deduce that they think much like their predecessors did, because, "basically, nothing changes."

Historical conditioning may in a given situation stand in clear opposition to reality; but, in general, history has more power of suggestion than does the present. History towers over the present the way a father towers over his young son.

Looking at Russia, we are weighed down with a historical ballast. But are the Russians also weighed down with a historical ballast when they look at Poland?

Edgar Snow in his book *Journey to the Beginning* cites a long conversation he had with Maxim Litvinov in Moscow. The conversation took place without witnesses on October 6, 1944.

It is worth remembering that Litvinov was married to an Englishwoman, knew the West well, and spoke fluent English. At that time his career was coming to an end, and he knew it perfectly well.

When Snow asked him about Poland, Litvinov replied that the Russians can under no circumstances agree to the return of the "Beck" group (Litvinov's name for the Polish government in exile in London) to Poland.

Interestingly, Litvinov had no objections of an ideological nature. He did not talk about Polish reactionaries, capitalists, or landowers. He did say, however, that the Polish government in London, especially Sosnkowski, represented the concept of Polish historical imperialism and aimed to rebuild the Polish empire of the sixteenth and seventeenth centuries. In Litvinov's opinion, Beck was prepared to form an alliance with Germany in order to reach this goal, while other London Poles were ready to make a deal with the Americans with the same aim in mind.

We were reaching the end of our biological reserve, and having been exhausted by Hitler's occupation and the underground struggle, we dreamed about a bit of Polish roof over our heads and not about an empire. But to Litvinov we were a potential rival.

I was astounded when I read Edgar Snow's account, because it seemed tragicomic to me that in 1944 Litvinov, a seasoned politician, could be accusing us of imperialism. It was as if someone in all seriousness warned a beggar who is barely keeping alive about the dangers of overeating and overdrinking.

And yet . . . on rereading Litvinov's opinions, I came to the conclusion that there was nothing comic about them. Litvinov saw Poland the way the Poles see Russia: from a position conditioned by history.

To the Russians, Polish imperialism is still a living historical current. One does not have to look too far into the past to find witnesses of the Polish presence in Kiev.

When Mikolajczyk told Stalin that Lwow had never been a part of the Russian empire, Stalin replied: "Lwow did not belong to Russia, but Warsaw did." A moment later, he added: "We remember that the Poles were once in Moscow."

Many of us believe that the Poles have been cured of imperialism. But the Russians think differently. They fear that if the Poles regained independence they would march on the imperial path with which they had always identified.

Has the imperialist tendency really died down in us, has the Russians' historical "Polish complex" no base?

I don't believe so. Many Poles today dream not only of a Polish Lwow and Wilno but also of a Polish Minsk and Kiev. Many of them think that an independent Poland should be federated with Lithuania, Ukraine, and Byelorussia. In other words, the only alternative to Russian imperialism is Polish imperialism, and this is how things have always been.

Let's use this occasion to analyze a certain typical phenomenon in Polish émigré circles. After my article "The Polish *Ostpolitik*" appeared in *Kultura*, I received many letters from Poles living in many countries which expressed their full support for the program I proposed. I also got letters from writers and journalists. A few of them remarked that they had long reconciled themselves to the idea of losing Lwow and Wilno, although they admitted that the real reason they no longer wrote about this was to avoid irritating public opinion.

There are two kinds of people who refuse to listen to all arguments or discussions of this issue. The first group includes mostly people from eastern Little Poland and the Wilno provinces. Because of their emotional attachment to these lands, these Poles cannot accept rational reasoning.

In the second group are people who, in order to retain the notion of legality if only in name, reduce the ideal of independence to the absurd goal of restoring the Second Republic. To them, there can be no Poland without the pre-September 1939 constitution with a president, a Sejm (parliament), and a senate. Only a restored and independent Second Republic could choose to give up Wilno or Lwow through a resolution of the Sejm and with the president's endorsement.

What is wrong with such a position is that, insofar as we can accept as a given that, if not we, future generations will live to see an independent Poland, we should also accept as a given that the pre-September 1939 constitution will not remain in force on Polish territory for a single day. The liberated nation will elect a Sejm that will vote on a new constitution to fit in with the new political, social, and economic conditions. The great majority of Poles, both at home and in exile, know this perfectly well.

In effect, even though no one believes in incorporating Lwow or Wilno into Poland, the myth is officially maintained. Furthermore, most people believe that, because a government in exile cannot be involved in any real politics, it is equally unimportant whether it claims Lwow and Wilno or Minsk and Kiev.

But in fact this is not unimportant. As long as we are in exile, we cannot put into practice any territorial changes, but we can and should establish some principles. A new Russian emigration is forming in the West. We should open a dialogue and seek an understanding with these people. The first item on our agenda must be the issue of nationalities.

The new Russian émigrés are anti-Soviet. But we know that people who have nothing to do with communism or even socialism could be Russian imperialists. This is why the test of the political views of every new Russian émigré ought to be his attitude toward the problem of nationalities.

Of course, we must submit ourselves to the same test. We must not believe that every "Great-Russian Program" equals imperialism, while the Polish "Eastern Program" is not imperialistic but only a lofty Jagellonian idea.

In other words, we can demand that the Russians renounce imperialism on the condition that we, too, once and for all give up our traditional historical imperialism in all its forms and manifestations.

It is only in our own minds that the Jagellonian idea is not related to imperialism. But to the Lithuanians, Ukrainians, and Byelorussians it represents the purest form of traditional Polish imperialism. The Polish–Lithuanian Union resulted in the total Polonization of the Lithuanian nobility, and the most passionate declaration of love of Lithuania ("O Lithuania, my country, thou Art like good health") was written in Polish. A Pole cannot even imagine an analogous situation. Is it conceivable that a Polish poet, let's say Slowacki, would have written only in Russian? The Russians made an attempt to Russify us but did not succeed in taking away from us a single poet or writer. On the contrary, in the nineteenth century, the pressure of Russification stimulated an unusual blossoming of Polish literature and language.

It is nice to say to oneself that Polish culture is attractive—to some, much more attractive than Russian culture. But this very fact, viewed from a Lithuanian or Ukrainian perspective, means that the Poles are more dangerous as assimilators than are the Russians. Given the proper conditions, the Poles will fully spread out their assimilators' wings.

The Russians use the attractiveness of Polish culture as a trump card in their perfidious policy of nationalism. In Wilno, a Polish-language daily comes out, theater groups from the Polish People's Republic visit, and so on, and so forth. The target of this operation is not the Poles who live in Lithuania and yearn for their native word. The target of this operation is Lithuanians, and only Lithuanians. From the Russian point of view, the influence of Polish culture—even in its current version—halts the process of reemergence of an authentic Lithuanian nationalism and culture. Of course, Moscow views favorably anything that slows down the process of crystallization of Lithuanian national separateness.

In Eastern Europe—if it is to be not only peaceful but also free—there is no room for any imperialism: Russian or Polish. We cannot clamor that the Russians must give Kiev back to the Ukrainians and in the same breath proclaim that Lwow must be returned to Poland. This is the double standard that in the past prevented us from overcoming the barrier of historical distrust between Poland and Russia. The Russians suspect that we apply our anti-imperialist principle to them, and that what we really want is to substitute Polish imperialism for Russian imperialism.

If, to simplify things, we call the area of Ukraine, Lithuania, and Byelorussia ULB, we must say that in the past—and to some extent also today—the ULB region was something more than a bone of contention between Poland and Russia. The ULB issue determined Polish–Russian relations and condemned us either to imperialism or to satellitedom.

It would be madness to think that by treating the problems of the ULB as a domestic Russian affair Poland can have better relations with Russia. The rivalry between Poland and Russia in that region was always aimed at establishing domination and not good-neighborly relations.

From the Russian point of view, annexing the Ukraine, Lithuania, and Byelorussia into the Russian empire is an essential condition for reducing Poland to the status of a satellite. From Moscow's perspective, Poland must be a satellite in one form or another. History has taught the Russians that a truly independent Poland always reached out as far as Wilno and Kiev and strove to establish its predominance in the ULB region. The realization of these historical Polish aims would be equivalent to the termination of Russia's imperial position in Europe. In other words, Poland cannot be truly independent as long as Russia maintains its imperial status in Europe.

From the Polish point of view, the problem is analogous. We tried to dominate in the ULB region, whether by military means or by pursuing a federalist policy. History has taught us that a Russia which is dominant in the Ukraine, Lithuania, and Byelorussia is an invincible rival. And one can expect nothing but captivity from a victorious adversary.

I would like to stress two points. First, the Polish–Russian relationship cannot be discussed without taking into account the ULB region, because Polish–Russian relations have always been a function of a current situation in that area.

Had there been no Hitler, had there been no Second World War, had the Germans been peaceful and good Europeans, Poland's independence would have been threatened by Russia anyway—in 1920 we scored a victory near Warsaw, but *not near Kiev*. After Stalin's death, the purges and elimination of the best officers of the Soviet Army would have ended and Russia would have entered an arms race that Poland would inevitably have lost. Sooner or later Russia's military superiority over Poland would have been so great that Moscow, with or without Germany's help, would have imposed its protectorate over us. This has simply been in the cards, and many political writers in Poland realized it long before World War II. Adolf Bochenski, an excellent political writer who later died in battle near Ancona, recommended that Poland come to terms with Germany. Bochenski first presented his thesis in a book published by Jerzy Giedroyc at the outset of the era of the "New Germany" when no one in Europe realized yet who Hitler was and what his designs were. The aim of an agreement with Germany would have been to take the Ukraine away from Russia. It always comes down to the Ukraine, Lithuania, and Byelorussia because the situation in those lands dominates the Polish–Russian relationship.

And the second point. It seems to me that even though the Russians have always underrated the Ukrainians and still underrate them, they have always overrated and continue to overrate the Poles. They have always seen us as active rivals or potential rivals—in any case, always as adversaries. Khrushchev did allow the *Panorama Raclawicka*[2] to be taken out of Lwow and returned to Poland, but he also advised against exhibiting it to the Polish public. He contended that the *Panorama Raclawicka* would remind the Poles of their armed insurrection against Russia. The famous episode with the theatrical production of Mickiewicz's *Dziady* (*Forefathers' Eve*)[3] had the same background.

It seems to me that large-scale workers' protests are much more likely in Poland than is armed revolt against Russia. There is not a

[2] Polish historical painting depicting the Battle of Raclawice, where on April 4, 1794, Polish troops led by Thaddeus Kosciuszko scored a victory over the Russians. The significance of this battle lay in the participation of Polish peasant troops, which fought Russian guns with scythes.—Ed.

[3] A play by Adam Mickiewicz, the renowned Polish Romantic poet. Part III of *Forefathers' Eve* is a powerful political allegory with references to Polish–Russian relations in the 1820s. In the beginning of 1968, the National Theater's production of *Forefathers' Eve* was closed by the Polish government. This incident, among other things, led to widespread student protests in March 1968.—Ed.

single politician living in exile who would call on the Poles in Poland to rise up. But the Russians fear a social revolution in Poland less than a nationalist uprising. They also believe that a workers' revolution to overthrow the Party's leadership and its regime would lose its economic and social characteristics and in a matter of days be transformed into a national revolt against Russia.

We must also remember that it was the Poles—and not the Russians—who lived through the shock of the Warsaw Uprising,[4] the shock of the abandonment of Poland by its Western allies, the shock of the occupation of the country by the Soviet Army. We lost the war totally, because it did not leave a shred of independent Republic. Our traditional concept of Poland as a bastion of Western civilization collapsed in ruins. We had been betrayed by our own history, to which we had built altars in literature, in painting, in music. We made the most horrifying discovery that a nation can make; namely, that history is a notepad covered with scribbles. It is the "house of the dead" and not a living past reaffirmed by the present. That is why it is difficult for a Pole not to become a historical revisionist. No wonder that even Catholic writers and noncommunists, even those who have repudiated socialism—standing on the rubble of "exotic alliances"—argued that an alliance with the Soviet Union must be the cornerstone of Polish politics. They deliberately gave up being rivals and assumed the position of vassals.

But we must remember that those traumatic experiences were strictly one-sided; they concerned the Poles and not the Russians.

The subject to which we attribute the optimistic name World History does not exist. There is no such thing as world history, or even European history. There is only Polish, Russian, French, German history. The Battle of Vienna with King Jan Sobieski in the forefront, as it is seen through Polish history, barely resembles the Battle of Vienna related by German history.

History is politics interrupted in midcourse. This is why the political writer must know how to look at history from a bird's-eye view. As for the subject that we are currently discussing, the politician must know how to see the course of events both through the eyes of the Pole and through the eyes of the Russian. For politics is a continuation

[4] The Warsaw Uprising, which lasted from August 1 to October 2, 1944, was organized by the underground Home Army against the Nazis. Soviet troops stood on the other side of the Vistula River and waited while the uprising was crushed by the Germans, leaving about 200,000 Poles dead and Warsaw almost completely destroyed.—Ed.

of history, and it is impossible to understand Russian politics without understanding the Russian reading of history. The Polish nation has always played a serious role in Russian history, and it is absolutely necessary that we become very familiar with the perspective from which the Russians look at us.

The last years of the Second World War resembled the situation that existed in Europe after the Battle of Jena. Napoleon reigned over all of Europe, and only two countries remained unconquered, Russia and England. Napoleon got to Moscow; Hitler got as far as the outskirts of Moscow. In both cases the Russians' principal allies were climate and vastness of territory. The spaces of Russia have an effect on people from Western and Central Europe which is hard to describe. In France or Germany, one hundred kilometers is an enormous distance—in Russia, one hundred kilometers is nothing. In the diary of a German officer, I came upon the expression that Russia is a country without a horizon. Beyond the horizon are new fields, hills, and rivers; beyond this new horizon are more fields, hills, and rivers; and so on, without an end, week after week, month after month. The German officer I quote writes that even in the summer, after many weeks of walking, the never-ending Russian space brings out a feeling of powerlessness in the hardiest man.

The Russians have suffered enormous losses. But history has not betrayed them—that is, the present has reaffirmed the past. Hitler's armies, much like Napoleon's armies, were overcome by the Russian climate and space, defeated and pushed far beyond the borders of the Russian empire.

In Poland, the technological revolution, airplanes and tanks, knocked out of our hands our traditional weapon, the cavalry. We had had, without doubt, the best cavalry in Europe, but in our case the present has not reaffirmed the past. On the contrary, tradition turned out to be a toothless old woman facing columns of motorized German tanks which defeated us in seventeen days.

All that I have written here is intended to illustrate the fact that history has not betrayed Russia; on the contrary, it has reaffirmed traditional Russian assumptions. In effect, the Russians—unlike the Poles—believe that nothing has changed since the Battle of Jena. Russia has a different regime, but one that is also imperial and invincible. The bottom has fallen out of our Polish world—as one would graphically say in English. In Russia, even the Revolution did not knock the bottom out of the Russian world, because Russia remains historically identical to what it always has been; that is, imperialistic and predatory.

Let's take another example. The revolution and catastrophe that took place in the Ottoman Empire as a result of the First World War deprived Turkey of its historical identity. Turkey ceased to be an imperial power. Indeed, contemporary Turks think completely differently from the way their grandfathers and great-grandfathers thought even a few dozen years ago. But the October Revolution did not result in the fall of the Russian empire and it did not change a thing in the Russian historical disposition. Stalin after the Second World War behaved like the Czar and Autocrat of All-Russia, symbol and exponent of the Russian imperial idea.

We all know this, but few of us realize that Russian historical conservatism also encompasses a view of Poland and of the Poles. Litvinov spoke about reconstructing the Polish empire of the sixteenth and seventeenth centuries, which seems comical to us, but to Litvinov, unlike us, the twentieth century is a continuation of the sixteenth and seventeenth centuries, with the same traditional problems, including the Polish problem. Like the czars, Stalin, Litvinov, and Brezhnev believed that it must be either the Poles or the Russians who rule the Ukrainian, Lithuanian, and Byelorussian lands. For them, there was no historical third solution—there was only a choice between Polish or Russian imperialism.

The Russians overestimate us because they look at us from the Russian historical perspective. On the other hand, the Poles, who are proud or, even more often, sentimental about their history, believe that this Polish imperial glory has nothing to do with today's reality.

We behave like the nobleman who lost his fortune. Because of clumsy management, adversity, and especially a bad neighbor, we lost our "fortune," which we thought we deserved by divine and human right. We console ourselves that "historical justice" has punished the Ukrainians, Lithuanians, and Byelorussians for exchanging their good Polish masters for bad Soviet masters.

We were in a position of preeminence in the East for three hundred years. If we take the Grzymułtowski Treaty[5] of May 3, 1686, as the turning point in the history of Polish–Russian relations, we must

[5] Peace treaty signed in Moscow, also known as the Eternal Peace Treaty. The treaty ceded Smolensk, Kiev, and the so-called left-bank Ukraine to Russia. These territories were de facto annexed by Muscovy in 1654. The treaty, which accepted the previously signed Truce of Andrusovo (1667), brought about the partition of the Ukraine between Poland and Russia.—Ed.

admit that Russia has been dominant in the East ever since. This "either us or them" attitude prevents the normalization of relations between Poland and Russia. It causes the Poles, much like the Russians, to have no faith in a third solution. Consequently, we accept our current satellite status as a gloomy state of affairs but the only feasible one.

But there is a difference between the Poles and the Russians. History has confirmed the Russians' supremacy. Our battles, insurrections, even victories have been shattered by history. The "either us or them" attitude prevails because we know no other. But the majority of Poles no longer believe that we will ever be able to dominate the Russians. The satellite mentality and servilism are the consequences of this lack of faith.

I also do not believe in the "us or them" alternative; I do not believe that we will ever be able to push Russia away from the outskirts of Przemysl to, say, Smolensk or Kiev. And I also believe that today the "us or them" mentality, despite its deep historical roots, is an anachronism, a barbarian anachronism. In the twentieth century, the Ukrainians, Lithuanians, and Byelorussians cannot be pawns in a historical game between Poland and Russia.

I have attempted to show that the "us or them" mentality, despite the fact that it draws its strength from a centuries-old tradition, is essentially a poisoned spring. We must seek contacts and an understanding with those Russians who are prepared to recognize the full right to self-determination of the Ukrainians, Lithuanians, and Byelorussians. What is equally important is that we, too, must forever renounce our right to Wilno and Lwow. We must also give up all designs that would, when the opportunity arises, aim to establish our predominance in the East at the expense of those three nations. Both Poles and Russians must understand that only a nonimperialistic Russia and a nonimperialistic Poland would have a chance of straightening out relations between them. We must understand that imperialism is bad, be it Polish or Russian, real or only potential, awaiting more favorable circumstances.

For the reasons analyzed above, the so-called nationalities issue is not only a Russian but also a Polish problem. Only a radical solution to this problem can reshape the relationship between Poland and Russia.

It seems to me that more and more Russians are aware of this. I would like to stress once again that the "us or them" mentality must be extinguished not only among the Russians but also among the Poles. It is a two-sided process. Those Poles who patiently await the moment of retaliation for the Old Poland as the "bulwark for Christianity" are consistently feeding Russian imperialism.

Finally, one last point in these reflections. Poles today are ill-disposed toward lofty mottoes and slogans, toward all types of romanticist phraseology. But the politics of a captive nation must unite people of different convictions, and for this reason it must be based on a moral ideal which would give our program for independence an ethical dimension. All contemporary designs for independence are missing this moral, supranational dimension.

No one will be enraptured by the idea of economic growth or the slogan "A color TV in every home and a car in front of every house." Although everyone wants to have a car, no one is prepared to die for cars or color television sets. In Vietnam, Cyprus, the Middle East, Northern Ireland, Angola, or Mozambique, people often die for ideas that are misguided but passionately believed.

Poles today, both at home and abroad, believe in nothing, literally nothing, passionately. Unidealistic people ("Nothing is worth dying for") are completely defenseless when confronted with force. They are the best material for the mass production of slaves.

On reading *The Gulag Archipelago*, one can only conclude that those gigantic, multimillion-man camps would have been unthinkable without the cooperation of their inmates. The philosophy of "Death to fools" to which the great majority of prisoners adhered, combined with the force of the Soviet state apparatus, made the Gulag Archipelago a very prosperous enterprise.

Of course, the greatest fools are those who believe in the slogan "Death to fools," and the Gulag Archipelago monumentally confirms this thesis.

The ideals of self-determination and freedom for our brotherly nations that separate us from Russia, together with a pledge to abandon all imperialistic plans—which include the hope to make a deal with Moscow at the expense of the Ukrainians, Lithuanians, and Byelorussians—would add to our programs for independence a moral dimension, which today is missing.

Rabid anti-communism, present among the émigrés, produces nothing but an animalistic hatred toward Russia. This anti-communism lacks a moral dimension and it is fused with nationalistic egotism, at times even with chauvinism. We are interested in the

Gulag only insofar as we can see in this pyramid of martyred bodies and souls a heralding of Russia's disintegration, which in turn would allow Poland to win back Wilno, Lwow, and maybe something more.

(September 1974)
Translated by Maya Latynski

Jan Jozef Lipski

TWO FATHERLANDS;
TWO PATRIOTISMS

A FATHERLAND EXISTS only because there are also alien lands and, consequently, there can be no concept of "us" and "ours" where there is no "them" and "theirs." It is the attitude toward "them," more than the attitude toward "us," which defines the notion of patriotism. Love for one's own country and for one's nation can only be understood, perhaps somewhat paradoxically, by one's attitude toward other countries and nations, but this paradox is intrinsic to all intellectual and emotional individuation.

Who are "ours" and "theirs"? What distinguishes "my" country from one that is not mine, "my" nation from one that is not mine?

The answers to such questions are not affected by the various kinds of descriptive characteristics of nations: the fact that we speak Polish and "they" speak their own language or that we live according to a different cultural pattern from "them" is not in itself a crucial factor. The formation of our culture was produced by a synthesis with Christianity, adopted from the West in the tenth century and the percolation of the Renaissance, the Enlightenment, and Romanticism. Even if some of us believe that the greatest poet ever was Goethe, Dante, or Shakespeare, Mickiewicz and Slowacki mean something very different to us. The experience of years of tyranny and struggle for liberation has probably been forever ingrained in the Polish national consciousness. Perhaps, although this can be disputed, most of us are marked by something which could be called the Polish national character. The issue is not concerned with objective descriptions but with value judgments: Do we consider ourselves better or only different? Do we believe that there is some kind of special worth vested in this difference? And, if so, how is it defined? Do we believe that by some prerogative we are entitled to special rights and privileges and, perhaps, have certain obligations to others? Depending on the answers to these questions, we lay claim to different patriotisms. In extreme cases we in fact belong to different fatherlands, if a fatherland is defined not only by membership in one exclusive ethnic group but also by a unity of spiritual wealth and values.

The system of values against which it is necessary to view the question of a fatherland is, above all, the system of moral values. We belong to that cultural orbit whose ethical concepts were shaped primarily by Christianity. Whether or not we believe, we were molded by the commandment which orders us to show love for our fellowman, and this is the basic moral guideline of our culture. However, I do not wish to diminish the importance of the moral contribution of other religions and world views: Judaism, out of which came Christianity; Islam; Buddhism; Hinduism; and Confucianism, the most secular-oriented ethical culture, all achieved much that is worthy of respect in the sphere of ethics. Philosophers of our cultural ambit, who represent a nonreligious, secular current, also enriched our ethical development and consciousness. Nonetheless, it was Christianity above all that gave us our moral nourishment, and it is within the fundamental concepts of this ethic that we wish to remain.

I believe that chauvinism, national megalomania, xenophobia (or hatred of everything foreign), and national egotism cannot be reconciled with the Christian commandment to love our fellowman. On the other hand, patriotism can be reconciled with it. Just as the special love for one's own family need not, and should not, create an obstacle to love for one's fellowman, so the special love for members of one's own national community should be subject to the same higher moral order. Patriotism issues from love and should lead to love; any other form is an ethical travesty.

"Love for everything Polish" is a common formula of national "patriotic" stupidity: after all, there were some rather shameful manifestations of prewar Poland, such as the fascist ONR (National Radical Camp), the pogroms of Lwow, Przytyk, and Kielce, the Bereza camp, and similar aberrations which are also "Polish." Patriotism is not only respect and love for tradition; it is also the relentless selection and discarding of elements in this tradition, and an obligation to this intellectual task. The burden of guilt for making fallacious judgments about the past, for perpetuating morally false national myths which serve national megalomania, for remaining blind to the blemishes in our history is, from the moral point of view, not as great a sin as committing evil against our fellowman, but is the premise of evil and the path to future evil. Every time we romanticize our past and obscure the facts with omissions and half-truths, every time silence is kept and the atrocities our nation has perpetrated are glossed over, the fires of national megalomania are fueled. It is an illness. Every evasion of acknowledging one's own guilt is a defilement of the national ethos.

We have two traditions in Polish literature regarding the treatment of historical themes. One serves the interests of national megalomania, and the other is the bitter tradition of reckonings, the tradition of Zeromski. According to him, Saragossa is both a national tragedy and a disgrace; the Austrian partitioner provided legislation which carried a measure of social progress, and the Polish peasant of the January Insurrection (1863) is portrayed with naturalistic verisimilitude—a far cry from the usual "patriotic" sketches. His novel *Early Spring* (1924) is a frightening and cautionary indictment of independent Poland and its ruling bureaucracy. The paradoxes of the Polish People's Republic in the 1960s had to exist, to allow for attacking Andrzej Wajda from a "patriotic" position for precisely the sentiments he found in Zeromski, and for Zeromski's work to become the subject of historical and literary based texts in the period of the Moczarist offensive.

Every new "patriotic" offensive must be viewed with suspicion when it manifests itself as an uncritical echo of the beloved slogans of national megalomania. Behind the phraseology and *maquillage* which Poles find generally acceptable lurk cynical technicians of sociology who watch to see whether the fish has bitten. Which bait from its national history does it like best? The uhlan's shako, the hussar's wings, the combat jacket of the Uprising? In his poem "A Moral Treatise," Czeslaw Milosz says:

It is not unlike a quagmire,
Once entered it pulls one in more deeply.

For many years, the nationalistic and patriotic phraseology used in the press has been accompanied by a campaign against anyone who dares to spoil the views and panoramas portrayed there for the consumption of fools. The attack against Kazimierz Brandys's *Postal Variations* is particularly vivid in my memory. It is one of Brandys's wisest and most ambitious works. A whole pack of "patriotic" journalists and critics set upon him as someone who ridicules and mocks our past. This was astonishing. Brandys poignantly tells the story of a Polish family which with each successive generation, together with the rest of the nation, goes to battle to fight for the independence of the fatherland; each generation suffers defeat and the vanquished fighters are cast into the pit of destitution, illness, social and psychological derangement. This is the tragic truth of the fate, if not of the entire nation, then at least of its elite, which is the bearer of the nation's consciousness. I read this novel as one would read a historian's account of the disasters befalling a nation, and I became ill from it. Once again I relived the tragedy of our history only to learn later from the critics that Brandys was ridiculing and mocking. I suppose it depends on one's sense of humor—and on the subject.

This and similar campaigns were conducted as a rule in the same periodicals and by the same journalists whom we came to know in the memorable year of 1968. Soviet lackeys had donned the uniform of an uhlan.

Pause for reflection: What purpose did these masquerades serve? Whom were they supposed to fool? Whom were they trying to lure with their "patriotic" bait? Whom were they trying to poison with their chauvinistic venom? What has all this to do with love for the fatherland? And which fatherland?

If this concerned the official press only, if no one had been ensnared by this "patriotic" lure, if such strains were absent from Polish tradition, there would be nothing to write about or with which to polemicize. But, unfortunately, this is not the case. Refrains of national megalomania and xenophobia can also be found in the uncensored, and therefore genuine, press. There is an enormous social gulf between the "official" and the "uncensored" expression of "patriotism," and the abyss is filled with people over whom the battle is being waged. Which fatherland will they choose? We must not, on any account, forsake those people, suffocated by xenophobia and national megalomania, whose thoughts and feelings have not yet been irreversibly mutilated by hate and pride. The form that Polish patriotism adopts will be decisive for the fate of our nation and for our moral, cultural, and political future.

Xenophobia and national megalomania nourish and support one another. We know the extent to which Poland suffered at the hands of the Russians and the Germans, but this does not vindicate overstepping the boundaries of stupidity and hatred with regard to those nations. An individual and a nation harm only themselves through such stupidity and hatred. The extent to which xenophobia is enmeshed with idiocy is apparent from the fact that they combined in August 1968 to prompt some of our compatriots to agree to an invasion of Czechoslovakia, which was an affront to our morality and contrary to our national interests.

Let us consider the attitude of the majority of Poles toward the Germans and the Russians. It is morally corrupt not to acknowledge the existence of moral problems just because it is more convenient not to. For centuries we have held grudges against the Germans. The Prussians, together with the Russians and the German-speaking Austrians, partitioned the First Republic. The dispossession of Polish peasant lands and the national and religious persecution under the Prussian partition were the first signs of what was to come during the Second World War. There is no point in dwelling on the enormity of Hitler's crimes committed on Polish soil. However, if we wish to remain in the fold of Christian ethics and Western European civilization, there must come a time for us to say: "We forgive and ourselves ask forgiveness." We were able to express this sentiment at the time of the ascendancy over our nation of the Polish Church, the greatest independent moral authority still remaining to us. We must affirm this as our own; its moral content alone is sufficient cause for its adoption. But there is also a national and cultural element: as a nation with a sense of membership in Western civilization and culture, we dream of returning to our larger family, to Europe. Therefore, there is a need for reconciliation with the Germans, who form part of this Europe and will continue to do so. The boldest and most prescient act in postwar Polish history took place when the Polish Episcopate extended their hands to the German Episcopate. The words spoken to the German Episcopate, however, represented a problem which cannot be circumvented if one wishes to remain faithful to the precepts of the Christian religion: the question of our guilt with regard to the Germans. Even to pose such a question in Poland is quite unacceptable and one can understand why: the apportionment of guilt is strikingly unequal. Nonetheless, we must not be satisfied with viewing our own guilt lightly, even if it is immeasurably less than theirs. Evil is evil, even when it is a lesser or unavoidable evil. Committing evil creates a moral responsibility, even though the victim of that evil may have committed an evil one hundred times greater against us.

A large number of myths and false inventions about our historical relations with the Germans have been amassed in the Polish consciousness. These must someday be rectified in the name of truth and in the interests of our national sanity. Such historical illusions are a sickness of the national spirit and serve permanently to sustain our xenophobia and national megalomania.

Virtually every Pole today (even educated Poles!) believes that after the Second World War we returned to the lands that the Germans had stolen from us. In pursuit of historic Polish claims to the areas that constituted Poland after the war, we have muddled and distorted the facts. Many of these regions and territories—in East Prussia, for example—were never Polish and were gained by the Germans at the expense, not of the Poles, but of the Prussians. Western Pomerania, ethnically Slav but non-Polish, stubbornly threw off Polish suzerainty several times and created its own state apparatus, which survived until the seventeenth century, when it was destroyed by the Swedes: the Russians took these lands, which were not even inhabited by the Poles, from the Swedes and not from the Poles. The Germanization of Western Pomerania followed a natural, nonviolent course. Silesia had been a vassal state of the Czechs since the Middle Ages and, together with Bohemia, became part of the Austrian monarchy. The Prussians annexed Silesia from the Austrians, not from the Poles, in the eighteenth century when the Germanization of Lower Silesia and Upper Silesia preserved their Polish ethnicity. The organized, and to some degree successful, pressure of Germanization did not become a factor in these areas until the latter half of the nineteenth, and during the course of the twentieth, century.

We also ignore the fact that German culture had flourished in these lands for several hundred years. We read wistful articles about the Silesian Piasts, about their castles and palaces, but no mention is made of the fact that "our" Prince Henryk Pobozny (1258–90) is known in German literary textbooks as *"Minnesanger"* (their "troubadour") and composed his poetry in the language of Walter von der Vogelweide and Hermann von Aue; it was not until two centuries later that Polish anacreontic verse was to develop and blossom. Henryk is a symbolic figure in the history of Silesia.

The centuries of German culture which evolved alongside our own Polish culture in Silesia, Warmia, Mazuria, Gdansk, and the Lubusz territory, and the exclusively German culture of Western Pomerania, have given us a rich inheritance of architecture and works of art. We are the custodians of this achievement for mankind, and are obliged consciously to guard this German cultural achievement without hypocrisy and silent omissions, and to protect these treasures for the future, which is our future, too.

We do not care to write about or recall our debt to the Germans in terms of culture and civilization. The Polish words for roof (*dach*), brick (*cegla*), stonemason (*murarz*), printer (*drukarz*), painter (*malarz*), woodcarver (*snycerz*), and hundreds of others testify to the debt we owe our western neighbor. The splendid architectural achievements, the sculptures, paintings, and examples of other arts and crafts in Cracow and many other Polish cities and towns, which were executed from the Middle Ages until the nineteenth century, are to a great extent the work of the Germans who settled there and enriched our culture. Practically every Pole has heard of Wit Stwosz, but not everyone knows that he was an ethnic German. No one, other than art historians, knows the names of the hundreds, perhaps even thousands, of German artists who left an indelible imprint on our culture.

History should be a gateway to the past. Which symbols would we like to choose for the future? Should the decimation of Polish culture by the Hitlerites in the Second World War dominate our consciousness, or should the enrichment of our culture by Wit Stwosz and hundreds of splendid lesser-known artists predominate? Do we wish to remember only the German flesh-skinners of Auschwitz, or also that handful of Germans, both prisoners and in the garrisons, who fought against evil? Jozef Garlinski, the émigré writer and historian, wrote about this in his work *Oswiecim Walczacy* (*Fighting Auschwitz*), which is based on firsthand accounts and was published some fifteen years ago in London; nowadays, Polish customs officials have instructions to confiscate this book. In our consciousness, can Germans only be members of the Gestapo or SS? Were not the heroes of the "Weisse Rose" in Munich also Germans who in the pit of darkness took up the most difficult of struggles, the struggle against "their own" in time of war?

The "Weisse Rose" was a somewhat eccentric group of true Christians whose actions, such as could be achieved, bore witness to the fact that, unlike the majority of their compatriots in those years, they were Christians not only in name but were prepared to accept martyrdom in order to live according to the precepts of truth and goodness. Their credo, although it had nothing to do with Poland directly, should live with us: in the first place, because they were Germans, of the same nation as the murderers of millions during the Second World War, and second, to remind us of the ethical imperative which affirms the moral obligation to go against one's own nation and state when they assume a criminal course of evil, even when the nation and the state are fighting a war. Are the heroes of the "Weisse Rose" unworthy of the name of German patriot? Were they traitors to their own nation? On the contrary, it was they who saved the remnants of their nation's moral dignity and created values indispensable to the future of Germany. In their souls, they cherished a fatherland different from the one in which they had the misfortune to live and die like martyrs.

The fear and distrust harbored by a substantial number of Poles toward the Germans is understandable. It would be foolhardy and absurd to assume that the effect of nationalism, which has increased steadily since the age of Bismarck and Wilhelm I, if not from earlier times, has disappeared without trace from the Germans, both in their attitude to us and in their mentality generally. There is no shortage of information, exaggerated out of all proportion by our official propaganda, concerning life in modern-day Germany, which offers proof that we should observe with caution a segment of the German population which could potentially lapse into recidivism. At the same time, however, we must do the maximum possible to create the optimal atmosphere for reconciling our two nations. For this to be possible, we must above all change many things within ourselves and in our historical consciousness.

The typical Polish attitude toward the Russians is different. A great deal of hatred mixed with fear, but also much respect, has accumulated with regard to the Germans. Besides hatred (less deeply rooted than toward the Germans, and milder) and fear (nightmares about

Soviet tanks shooting down rebellious Poles), the prevailing attitude toward the Russians is now mixed with a feeling of superiority. The devil only knows from where this stems, but generally the Poles are convinced of the inferiority of Russian culture to their own. The cultural "superiority" and "inferiority" of nations is a delicate and dangerous subject. In many respects, nations resemble individual human beings. Just as a person who is raised according to the Christian ethic, and accepts it cognizantly, understands that every human being, Christian or not, has worth and dignity to no lesser degree than another human being (although one may be wise, another foolish, one good, another evil), so every nation has its worth and dignity regardless of whether at any given time it is possessed by Hitlerism or some other abomination, or whether it has a wealth or poverty of art, etc.

To have a sense of cultural superiority over a nation which produced Dostoevsky and Tolstoy, not even taking into consideration at least twenty other writers who could be the pride of any European literature, a sense of superiority over the nation of Rublev, Mendeleyev, and Stravinsky, must indicate some great misunderstanding. This is the nation which had created the *byliny* (epic songs) and great church paintings while ours was still an impoverished national literature and our painting was in its infancy. No Polish writer has exerted such influence on the literature of the West (that West to which we belong) as have Dostoevsky, Tolstoy, Turgenev, and Chekhov. Nor is there any indication that the traditions and culture of the Polish peasant are richer than those of the Russian peasant. They are just different. Our megalomaniacal sense of superiority over the Russians is both grotesque and pitiful.

This attitude receives legitimation from another perspective. Since the Romantic period, certain concepts have gained currency in Polish ideology, according to which, supposedly, Russian culture was negatively affected by the hybridization of Byzantine and Mongol–Tatar influences. In simple terms, one could say that the result of this Byzantine–Mongol hybrid is a culture in which the subordination of the individual to hierarchical authority is apparent, that collectivism dominates over the individual, that the ethic of the horde dominates over the ethic of the individual.

As is usual with such generalizations, some things hit the mark and at the same time much of it does not tally. The traditions of Muscovite despotism certainly bear generic relation to the model of Chinese rule, and the position and role of the czar and his court certainly were modeled on Byzantium. But countering this tradition is another Russian tradition—that of spiritual independence, which began with Prince Andrei Kurbsky (1528–83), if not earlier. It is a tradition of dissent and the search for ideological support in the West. The Russia of the Decembrists, Herzen, Bezkishin, and the other supporters of the January Insurrection of 1863, "Zemlya i Volya," the *narodniki*—this is not Byzantine–Mongol Russia. In our own time, the Russians coined the word *samizdat*, which has also come into Polish usage. They were the first. They showed the way and paid a heavy price. Furthermore, resistance there is more difficult and requires more courage.

Let us not forget that the liberation of all of Eastern and Central Europe from Soviet totalitarianism depends largely on emancipatory movements within the U.S.S.R. The Russian nation, which is numerically the largest and plays the most important role in the empire, is still far from demanding its democratic rights. As an oppressed nation, it is, consequently, particularly demoralized. But there now flourishes a new phenomenon: Soviet "patriotism" (unfortunately, one comes up against this phenomenon not only among the Russians). It is not difficult to find among these "patriots" proponents of a policy of interventionism and pacification which keeps a tight rein on the satellite states. Any mention of the possibility of self-determination for the nations which constitute the U.S.S.R. provokes anger. Greater respect, purged of a grotesque and foolish sense of superiority, and a more vital fraternalism should align us with the Russians who are struggling for freedom. The number of Russians who opposed the totalitarian police system, considering the degree of repression they encountered, can only fill us with awe and admiration compared with the few courageous individuals in Poland who dared to take such action.

Although the U.S.S.R. is heir to the aspirations and even the style of czarism, and although Russian nationalism plays an enormous role in Soviet expansionism, when we speak of the Russians we do not wish to remember that while Sovietism attempts to destroy the national identity of the Lithuanians, Latvians, Ukrainians, Georgians, Armenians, Poles, etc., it is also forcefully destroying the national identity, traditions, and culture of the Russians. Sovietism is as deadly for the Russians as for the Poles.

The Lithuanian, Byelorussian, and Ukrainian nations should occupy a special place in our appraisal. These nations have shared a common fate with us for centuries. Little do we realize, however, that they celebrate this common fate far less than we do. The Polonization of the nobility of Lithuania and Rus' propelled these nations into the ranks of "nonhistorical" peoples who did not begin to produce their own new elites, the intelligentsia, until the latter half of the nineteenth century, and then only with difficulty. Although the Polonization of these nations occurred as a natural process, achieved without the use of force, it was nonetheless a disaster for these nations and retarded their own development. This is not easily forgotten.

The Ukrainians also well remember the seventeenth and eighteenth centuries; that is, they remember the terrible, barbaric Polish pacification of the Cossack rebellions and peasant insurrections; on the other hand, the Ukrainians choose to ignore their horrifying slaughter of Poles and Jews in 1648 and the massacre in Human. The Poles' memories of these events are just as selective.

The Polish–Lithuanian conflict over Wilno was a truly difficult issue to settle. Both nations had emotional links with this city. To this day, the Lithuanians harbor a bitter grudge against us for Wilno; to this day, we bear a grudge against the Lithuanians because there were groups of collaborators from among their ranks during the Second World War whose acts were particularly harmful to the Poles (and even more so to the Jews). We must break this vicious circle.

The register of guilt, according to which the Ukrainian and Polish nations reproached one another, received a further debit during the Second World War. This time there was little for which the Poles could be reproached: immediately after the war, the Ukrainian Insurrectionary Army (UPA) suffered defeat at the hands of the Soviet Army—they were pushed into the southwestern perimeter of the Polish protectorate and fighting flared up in the Bieszczady Mountains. The solution to the problem of the Ukrainian partisans was to turn the area into a desert, an idea certainly conceived by the mind of an NKVD "adviser." Members of this organization were talented practitioners of the Roman principle of *divide et impera* and were familiar with such precedents, but on a far grander scale, in their own native country.

I wish to add some thoughts on our relations with the Czechs. The unilateral solution by means of military force to the problem of the Silesian territory on the Olza River in 1920, at a time when the very existence of the Polish state hung in the balance, is not a point of honor for the Czechs. Nonetheless, Poland's participation in the partition of Czechoslovakia by Hitler was an ignominious deed. Thirty years later, Polish troops took part in the occupation of Czechoslovakia. The Polish nation cannot be held accountable for the rule imposed on it from outside, which relies mainly on power from outside, but the frightened silence kept by all but a few Poles,[1] with their glorious tradition of struggle for "your freedom and ours," is a shameful fact of our recent past. One even came across people so naïve that they accepted the invasion and senselessly churned out absurdities about a German threat or about Czech enmity toward us . . . National megalomania and xenophobia merged again to conspire against a nation which is particularly close to us, especially now. What petty lack of solidarity we showed our brothers from beyond the Carpathians!

We must understand that, for moral and political reasons, our traditional xenophobia and megalomania toward all surrounding nations is suicidal for Poland. We are already deeply imbued with Sovietism, which threatens us with the loss of spiritual ties with our past, ties with Western culture and with the ethical traditions of Christianity. We must recognize that either all the nations of the U.S.S.R. and her satellite states will be free from the threat of death and decomposition (moral *and* political), or none will be.

Anti-Semitism, so distinct a manifestation of xenophobia with so different a function and role in history, demands separate discussion. Is anti-Semitism indeed a product of xenophobia?

When there was a community of Jewish people living in Poland who differed from Poles in every way (language, national consciousness, religion, customs, manner of dress, etc.), the anti-Semitism directed at them certainly constituted xenophobia. Yet even when it was not a question of language or dress, and the victims of anti-Semitism had long parted with the religion of their forefathers, they were also discriminated against, because of their true or presumed affiliation with the Jewish community: this was still xenophobia. However, when this xenophobia was extended to people who had been Polonized for generations, and who often professed the same

---

[1] The only voices of protest raised against the occupation of Czechoslovakia in 1968 were those of Jerzy Andrzejewski and Zygmunt Mycielski in letters to their Czech and Slovak "brothers." A small group of students in Warsaw also attempted to distribute leaflets against the Soviet action.

religion as the majority of Poles, who were saturated with Polish culture and even fought for the freedom and independence of Poland, this was no ordinary show of xenophobia, a demeaning and undesirable phenomenon at the best of times, but not necessarily bordering on the socially psychopathological. The only possible explanation for such anti-Semitism is racism, often subconscious and not loudly professed. However, to believe that a people has less worth because of its biological and racial determinants is irreconcilable with our Christian ethical heritage.

One justification for anti-Semitism is based on religious and pseudo-Christian premises. The rejection of Christ by the Jews, and the attribution of guilt for His blood to their descendants, is made analogous to the Original Sin of mankind and is therefore supposedly a proof of their inherent evil. This theory is more obscurantist than theological: a model of anti-Christianity. Christianity does not recognize collective guilt, or collective responsibility for guilt. In Christian theology, Original Sin is not a matter of hereditary guilt but of the contamination of human nature. Moreover, after centuries during which this pseudo-religious justification for anti-Semitism was tolerated, it was finally rejected by the Second Vatican Council. An essential element of the Christian ethic is the conviction that a person may be judged only by his actions; every person is equal and no judgment of his actions can abrogate the commandment to love thy neighbor. Nevertheless, anti-Semitism is rooted in the centuries-old Christian–Polish nation in a manner that should raise our concern.

Anti-Semitism or anti-Semitisms? A sense of superiority over and contempt for a nation which discovered (or invented) the single, omnipresent, omniscient, purely spiritual God, a nation which has bred so many great scholars, artists, writers as proportionately no other nation on earth, a nation which has shown superhuman perseverance, has safeguarded its religion, culture, and identity for millennia in hostile conditions, generates the most grotesque form of xenophobia. The spectrum of anti-Semitic behavior is broad: it ranges from superiority and contempt to a sense of feeling threatened, which can prompt various acts of discrimination right down to liberation through mass murder. The differences are enormous, but they are all irreconcilable with the precept to "love thy neighbor."

In the Middle Ages, various despicable acts of anti-Semitism took place in Poland, but nothing comparable to, or on the scale of, the dreadful pogroms in Western Europe at that time. It was not until the latter half of the nineteenth century that "modern" anti-Semitism made its appearance. By "modern" I mean the feeling that Jews should not be permitted to cross certain barriers of status; an aversion to other religious denominations spread beyond the *szlachta*. The process of "modern" anti-Semitism in Poland had begun; its only restraint was the continued tradition of Jewish participation in the Polish struggle for independence, but even this brake was prone to failure. The anti-Semitic mood penetrated ever more deeply into the Polish bourgeoisie, incited as it was by the provocations of the *Okhrana* in other parts of the czarist empire and in the Kingdom of Poland. Later, anti-Semitism entered the ideology and the practices of the Endecja (National Democrats), and some publications of the ONR even advocated the extermination of the Jews in Poland.

Unfortunately, social resistance to anti-Semitism in Poland was weak. The main party of the Polish left, the PPS (Polish Socialist Party), was strong in workers' circles, but weak in educational institutions, from where the goon squads of the ONR were recruited. The left and liberal intelligentsia expressed solidarity with the Jewish victims of the goon squads, but, on the whole, these were individual acts of courage. The authorities, who gravitated more and more toward the fascist right after the death of Pilsudski, did not attempt to intervene too energetically. The Church viewed it with indifference, and a segment of the Catholic press (e.g., *Maly Dziennik*) even supported anti-Semitism.

The war and the occupation, the horrifying extermination of the Jews by the occupying German troops, followed. In the West, mainly in Jewish circles crushed by the extermination of millions of Jews, irresponsible accusations were made, which had virtually no basis in fact, regarding the complicity of the Polish nation. Such anti-Polish feeling should be regarded as no less shameful a phenomenon than anti-Semitism.

They called us a "nation of extortioners" (*szmalcowniki*). The phenomenon of *szmalcownictwo*—that is, extortion from Jews in hiding or collaboration with the Gestapo in the extermination of Jews—was committed by a marginal group. Every society has its criminal element. This marginal group was so menacing to the Jews that it poisoned their attitude to Poland as a whole. One cannot blame a people who has been hunted for years for such a display of irrationality. But one must not forget that the Gestapo knew how to make use of traitors not only to trap Jews but also to uncover entire units of the Home

Army. Thus, *szmalcownictwo* was not only a matter of anti-Semitism but a diabolical exercise aimed at everyone whom the Gestapo pursued.

By no means all Jews professed anti-Polish sentiments, and it was gross misrepresentation on the part of the Polish People's Republic to put out propaganda to the effect that most Jews in the world shared this attitude. This lie was itself of an anti-Semitic cast based on wrong information. Anti-Polonism among a section of Jews in the West cannot be attributed to all Jews, just as anti-Semitism cannot be attributed to the entire Polish nation.

However, one must recognize that the truth is not as simple and clear as it is sometimes presented. It was not the persecution and tracking of Jews in hiding that sealed the Poles' guilt, but their indifference. It is true that it took an act of heroism to save Jews. I know of people who were armed when they were captured by the Germans and who managed to survive the concentration camps, but I know of no person who hid a Jew and survived being discovered, nor have I heard of such a person. Moreover, a soldier in the Home Army knew that if he was arrested he would certainly be shot, but his young children would survive. The Pole who hid a Jew could not be so sure. The French and the Dutch never had such a price to pay, nor were their endeavors to save Jews so impressive. Polish society's efforts to save Jews were great, worthy of respect, paid for in blood, and not without success. Apart from the individuals and families who saved their friends, and often chance persons unknown to them, institutions such as Rada Pomocy Zydom (Council for Aid to Jews) were in operation and received support and aid from the Polish Underground. The position of the Polish authorities was clear on this matter. However, I believe that a substantial section of Polish society was indifferent to the extermination of the Jews and the blame for this must be attributed, among other things, to the rampant anti-Semitism which existed before the war.

The history of anti-Semitism in Poland does not end there. Immediately after the war, the country was shaken by news of a pogrom in Kielce. There is indication that this was a provocation of the NKVD and the Polish security police; there was a need to present Poland to Western public opinion as a country that was basically Hitlerized and to which only the communists could bring order. There is no conclusive proof of this, but such provocations can succeed only when they fall on fertile ground.

The Stalinist years stimulated anti-Semitism in Poland and had predictable results. Before the war, as often happens with nonterritorial minorities subjected to various forms of discrimination, the extreme internationalist left was popular among Jewish youth and intellectuals. Subsequently, there were a significant number of Jews or persons of Jewish descent in the apparatus of the new ruling authority and particularly in the apparatus of oppression (the security police). Who knows, perhaps this was a Machiavellian order issued from Moscow headquarters? Minorities are well suited to such a role because they are peripheral (compare the bloody role of Poles, Jews, and Latvians in the Cheka); they also perform well the role of sacrificial goat.

October 1956 demonstrated that the motives for anti-Semitism, though they smolder to this day, were not so strong, despite isolated excesses. Several years later, an organized attempt was made to exploit these motives in a political struggle. A group which aspired to power under the leadership of Mieczyslaw Moczar raised the banner of anti-Semitism (under the pretext of a struggle with Zionism) at first in a somewhat clandestine fashion, then overtly in 1967, and with fanfare and drumrolls in 1968. Theirs was an array of propaganda tricks. It would be an embarrassment to term such devices an ideology, although this was precisely the way in which they were used; "patriotism" beat the drum of national megalomania. Certain successes were achieved, but not in the campaign of anti-Semitism. The very fact that it had been instigated from above condemned the campaign to mediocre success. Only the apparat and its activists were interested in this issue. As before the war, it had been the Polish petit bourgeois who despised his Jewish competitor, now it was the Party blockhead who vied with his Jewish competitor for an available desk. In 1968 this was still a reality. It was the young people in particular who reacted to anti-Semitism with hostility.

The expulsion from Poland in 1968 of thousands of Jews and Poles of Jewish descent is one of the ignominies of our country's history. The policed anti-Semitism of the Soviet Union has been grafted onto us. It is no coincidence that the "March" [1968] elite of Party journalists was decorated with the Golden Insignia of the Association of Polish–Soviet Friendship. Besides the irreparable moral damage which these people and their apparatchik allies caused, the calculable losses must also include the exodus from Poland of all those who could not withstand the anxiety; there was a loss of experts and

specialists difficult to replace. I can feel no common homeland with
the "March" journalists and apparatchiki.

Polish messianism bloomed in the hopeless international situation
after the collapse of the November Insurrection of 1830. Our greatest
poets and philosophers immersed themselves in this idea. Their
genius enabled the magnificence of this idea to take flight. I believe
it played a genuine role in carrying us through disasters, but I ask
whether it did not also contribute to those disasters. The legacy of
romantic notions has survived in the mentality of the average quasi-
educated Pole. It gives him a special sense of superiority, often spiced
with religious exultation, just because he is a Pole. There is an
interweaving of religious and national threads in the fabric of this
notion; the positive aspect of it is that the patriotic bombast of the
Party hardly touches Polish society.

Bogdan Cywinski wrote at length (in *The Genealogy of the Unmeek*)
about what it means to be a Catholic Pole. I would like to draw
attention to several aspects of this question, for they are of fundamental importance to our definition of Polish patriotism.

The affirmation of the indivisibility of Polishness from Catholicism
can be interpreted in various ways. Because in its most obtrusive
interpretation this can mean if you are not a Catholic you cannot be
a full-fledged Pole, it is necessary each time to state clearly whether
this is the intended meaning. Recently, an article by Father Sroka
about the indivisibility of Polishness from Catholicism appeared in
the Gdansk publication *Bratniak*. When I questioned him in person,
Father Sroka claimed that he had been misunderstood. What he
meant was that Catholicism exerted so great and various an influence
on Polish culture that the culture as a whole cannot be separated
from Catholicism without the loss of its very identity. This is a
reasonable thesis and should not be an affront to anyone, although
it could well be a subject for discussion. However, I am more
concerned with the first interpretation of the Polish–Catholic equation, which, it seems to me, is rather persuasive wherever we encounter
simultaneously national xenophobia and megalomania constantly fed
on imprecise statements such as this. In this first interpretation is
contained a falsehood which is a disservice to our national tradition
and the state of national feeling today. It excludes important dimensions from our national tradition, as well as excluding from national
life those people who do not consider themselves Catholics.

What in Polish history and tradition is non-Catholic? Passing over episodes which had little impact on the course of our history, such as Polish Hussitism, we can start from the Polish tradition of the Reformation and Protestantism. There is no lack of Protestants among our national heroes, no lack of Protestant ministers among our Polish national activists. It is true that the Catholic Church played a great part in the perseverance of "Polishness," particularly after partitions in the Prussian part of Poland and the distant borderlands of the Russian part of Poland. But in the Cieszyn area of Silesia and in Mazuria, "Polishness" was fostered by the Evangelical Church and its ministers. The final act in this heroic national drama was the martyrdom of the unflinching Protestant ministers and activists during the Hitlerite occupation. The contribution of Polish Protestants to Polish culture and to the struggle for independence is so great that all attempts to exclude them from our Polish national community must provoke sharp opposition.

Similarly, one cannot agree to the omission of a vital and rich contribution to Polish culture from the time of the Enlightenment, and with particular intensity since the era of Positivism, by the nonsectarian laity, often atheistic, sometimes agnostic. It is difficult to imagine Polish culture of the last century without Edward Abramowski, Jan Dawid and his wife, without Waclaw Nalkowski and Ignacy Redlinski, without Stefan Zeromski and Andrzej Strug, without Stefan Czarnowski and Tadeusz Kotarbinski, without Edward Lipinski or Maria and Stanislaw Ossowski, without Antoni Slonimski and Maria Dabrowska, without Leszek Kolakowski. These are names which often represent whole schools and currents of Polish thought, the hundreds of names of Poles who have made an indelible contribution to the achievements of Polish culture.

Another variant of xenophobia is the cult of the "home-produced" as opposed to anything which comes from outside (mainly from the West). The strangeness of such an attitude is all the more striking when one learns that its major adherents at one and the same time generally preach about our ties with Western culture. Such a union of ideas will lead to our self-willed isolation; it is as though these people are of the opinion that our ties with Western culture are more than sufficient.

This attitude is ridiculous and nonsensical. Isolation has not yet profited any culture. The Poles have learned this to a substantial degree from experience. We adopted Christianity from the Czechs; it was then ingrained in us by the Czechs, Germans, and other

Western peoples. Poles began to travel to Paris and Prague, to universities in Italy and Germany in search of learning, at first in a small stream and then in large numbers, to the advantage of our culture. Our Western mentors, the French and Germans, taught us to construct Romanesque and later Gothic buildings, which German artists and artisans filled with sculptures and paintings. The customs of West European knighthood took root in Poland. Civilization and culture spread from the West. At the end of the fifteenth century we began to draw heavily from Italy, then undergoing its Renaissance, and later from all of Renaissance Europe. The entire Polish elite studied at West European universities, primarily in Italy and Germany. From Germany came the Reformation, which enriched Polish intellectual life. From the Turko-Tataric Near East, the Polish nobility took its style of dress, the furnishing of its rooms, its weaponry (and, unfortunately, its custom of human impalement). The influences on Polish literature from Italy, Germany, France, and Spain have been apparent since the sixteenth century. It was not until the eighteenth century that these ties weakened and the importation of this culture slackened, with tragic results for Poland. But fortunately these ties strengthened again in the mid-eighteenth century. Polish artists again traveled to Italy in search of learning, a section of the aristocracy sought not only dress coats and wigs but also enlightened thought, which gave flower to the Commission for National Education and some major reforms. And we have continued to draw heavily since that time: from the West came Romanticism and Positivism, Symbolism and Impressionism, Expressionism and Futurism.

However obvious, these things must serve as a reminder. Polish culture always flourished symbiotically with these stimuli and not in opposition to them. Rarely did we draw so bountifully from the West, and with such resplendent success for our national culture, as in the sixteenth century. In the nineteenth century, Mickiewicz was entirely saturated with Western romanticism and yet he is extraordinarily original. Severing our ties with Western culture would be an act of national suicide.

It is painful at times to think that we took considerably more than we gave. We would like to participate in the European synthesis. With few exceptions, our influences have only been regional. The Ukrainians, Byelorussians, and Lithuanians owe much to these influences, but the French, English, Germans, and Italians owe little. The Russians have done much better in this respect—Dostoevsky, Tolstoy, old Russian iconography. I think that, without being a national megalomaniac, one can hold the opinion that Europe loses a great deal through its virtual ignorance of Mickiewicz, Slowacki, and Norwid. On the other hand, it is relatively familiar with Gombrowicz and Mrozek. This indicates that original artistic values, able to cross the boundaries of our national culture, continue to arrive at the junction which leads from the world to us and back again into the world.

The thoughts expressed here are certainly not revelations, yet many questions that have been raised demand further probing. I imagine, however, that for a rather sizable number of [Polish] readers, these thoughts will be at least controversial and in part unacceptable. It was precisely for this reason that this essay was written, bearing in mind the extent of the spread of national xenophobia and megalomania in Poland, although I do not believe that this is always synonymous with acute chauvinism. I am convinced that one of the most fundamental questions of our present and our future lies in overcoming our national xenophobia and megalomania, or at least in defusing them to the extent that they are no longer dangerous to the destiny of the Polish nation. If this does not happen, any "agent" in an uhlan shako who drapes a royal crest across his chest can lead the nation to wheresoever he wishes, beating on the drum of "national pride" and manipulating our phobias. We will lose any chance at all of cooperating with other nations which, like us, are oppressed by Sovietism. We cannot wait for an easy solution; we must begin to work on building solidarity with the oppressed nations. If not, we will forever close the door to Western Europe, which is our cultural cradle. Each year we are sinking deeper and deeper into Sovietism, which is corrupting our system of values, our social links, and our conception of our own national traditions. Sometimes it seems as though we are rushing toward this of our own volition. Or so it seemed in 1968. But let us hope that our nation will be too wise to fall prey to such manipulations.

(October 1981)

Ryszard Kuklinski

THE SUPPRESSION
OF SOLIDARITY

T HE FOLLOWING INTERVIEW with Colonel Ryszard Kuklinski was
published in *Kultura* in April 1987. It reveals the circumstances
surrounding the imposition of martial law in Poland in December
1981 and sheds valuable light on the *modus operandi* of the Polish and
Soviet military authorities.

Kuklinski served in 1980–81 in the central Polish military apparatus
charged with preparing martial law. He established contact with the
CIA and supplied the U.S. government with the top-secret plans of
the Soviet and Polish authorities. In the fall of 1981, the KGB began
to suspect a leak at the very highest level of the Polish command, but
before it could arrest him, Colonel Kuklinski and his family fled
Poland. Unfortunately, Washington did not take advantage of the
information supplied by Kuklinski at such great personal risk. The
December 13, 1981, coup caught both the U.S. government and
Solidarity by surprise.

In the interview, Kuklinski talks about his former superiors and
colleagues, including the two generals—Wojciech Jaruzelski and
Czeslaw Kiszczak—who have dominated Polish politics in the past
decade. Jaruzelski was elected Poland's president following the June

1989 parliamentary elections in which Solidarity was permitted to run for 35 percent of the seats in the Sejm, or lower house of the Polish parliament, and for all one hundred seats in the newly created senate; Kiszczak, the main architect of the Round Table Talks with Solidarity (the negotiations which led to the June elections), was General Jaruzelski's ill-fated choice to head his first government as prime minister. (He was quickly succeeded by Tadeusz Mazowiecki, a Catholic intellectual and one of Lech Walesa's principal advisers.)

In view of Solidarity's renaissance, Kuklinski's insightful observations about Jaruzelski and Kiszczak—men who continue to play key political roles in the unfolding drama that is today's Poland—are of special value and interest.—Ed.

You were one of the very few who knew that martial law was going to be imposed in Poland.

I had worked on preparing the plans to impose martial law for more than a year, or, more exactly, 380 days, and sometimes nights as well. I already knew by rote the various alternative actions. It sufficed to consult my memory to realize that:

First, the decision to impose martial law in Poland, made under pressure from the Soviet Union, was in early November 1981 virtually irrevocable. Were General Jaruzelski to reject it at the last moment, the radio and TV address to the nation would be made by General Eugeniusz Molczyk, or by another general.

Second, martial-law operations were to be conducted exclusively by Polish police and army forces. If, however, they were to prove incapable of crushing any resistance they might encounter, then fully combat-ready Soviet, Czech, and German divisions waiting at Poland's frontiers would march in.

Third, on November 7, 1981—that is, at the moment when I was leaving the General Staff of the Polish Army—preparations for imposing martial law were so well advanced that pressing the proverbial button would have sufficed to mobilize that entire police-and-army machine. The only remaining problem was preparing a pretext acceptable at least to a part of our society for commencing confrontations and choosing the optimal time for striking the blow.

Fourth, the main variant provided for a surprise imposition of martial law on a night between Friday and a nonworking Saturday. But should the domestic situation not permit this (for example, were

Solidarity to undertake some preventive action), martial law could also be imposed in various operationally unfavorable circumstances, such as during a nationwide sit-in strike.

Those who had paid attention could detect the quite explicit signs of the coming coup. The authorities also were aware that an insider among themselves was sending out alarm signals. On September 13, 1981, for example, at an emergency session of the Committee for National Defense on aspects of the imposition of martial law, General Kiszczak revealed that a large number of Solidarity activists knew in detail about the plans to impose martial law, including the internment plan, the list of persons to be interned, and the code name of the operation.

From your early years, you were conditioned by military discipline and a total submission to orders. What triggered your decision to free yourself from this discipline and to side with Solidarity? What made you do it at such great risk to you and to your family? Any specific event? Or perhaps a specific order?

There is no doubt that that event was the Polish August [the emergence of Solidarity during the Gdansk strike in 1980], and also the order which I had to execute nearly from the beginning of the eruption of strikes on the coast, and which I thought to be in conflict with the interests of the country and the nation which I served. But even earlier personal experiences probably influenced my ultimate choice.

One of these experiences occurred in August of 1968—almost exactly twelve years before the Polish August. At the time, the government-controlled mass media had informed the population about the machinations of imperialism in Czechoslovakia and the attempts to wrench that country away from the community of socialist countries. Mentions also were made of Warsaw Pact troop exercises conducted in accordance with the plan, but they were not particularly publicized. These exercises had already been under way a full year when I received a completely innocuous order directing me to proceed immediately to the command post for the exercises in Legnica, established there by the Supreme Commander of the United Armed Forces of Warsaw Pact countries, Marshal of the U.S.S.R. Ivan Yakubovsky, where I was to take part in planning operational exercises of units of the Polish Army.

When I reported to the staff of Marshal Yakubovsky, I found there representatives of all the armies of the Warsaw Pact, with the exception of Czechs and Romanians. The atmosphere was rather calm. No one uttered the words "invasion," "armed intervention," or "aggression." Such terms were proper for characterizing the activities of Western imperialism. We were merely engaging in exercises. But there was something unusual about these "exercises," foreign to my experience. Some stages of the exercises which we were planning, and which were given the code name Danube, were to be held on Czechoslovak territory but without the participation of the Czechoslovaks. Operational exercises were, to be sure, conducted in the defense of socialist Czechoslovakia, but this time not against any aggressive NATO forces, that supposedly being the purpose for which the Warsaw Pact had been formed, but, strangely enough, against the Czechoslovak People's Army, which after all was part of the armed forces of the Warsaw Pact, but which as of that time began to be designated on staff maps with the color blue, the color reserved exclusively for the enemy. In a word, there could be no doubt as to what this was about, so long as it was not called by name.

Once the plans were ready for a lightning envelopment of garrisons of the Czechoslovak People's Army and their neutralization through persuasion, and the invasion troops only awaited a signal to cross the border of our southern neighbor, I tried to orient myself concerning world opinion on this matter. I had thought that the concentration of such large military forces on the borders of Czechoslovakia could not escape the attention of world opinion. I also had thought that perceiving Soviet intentions would be all the easier, considering the fact that during the final stage of preparations for the invasion on the order of Marshal Yakubovsky, so-called EFIR exercises, which consisted in putting into operation a large number of radio stations, were commenced with the object of demonstrating to the Czechoslovaks the large concentration of Warsaw Pact forces. This demonstration in the ether could not have escaped the West's attention. Certain of this, I began to listen to Western newscasts to confirm my a priori assumption that the world knew of the coming invasion, that the world was resolutely opposed to it and protested it, and that perhaps we could succeed in avoiding the worst.

I felt helpless and deeply disenchanted. That world on which I had counted so much was preoccupied with the war in Vietnam and with the mass protests against it that were then surging across nearly all of Europe as well as the United States. Some mention of Czechoslovakia also was made, but it was of an idyllic nature. No one was protesting against the potential invasion of Czechoslovakia. On this subject, both the Eastern and the Western mass media preserved total silence.

Not wanting to participate in the invasion of Czechoslovakia, I telephoned Warsaw and, under some pretext, requested my superior to recall me from Legnica. My wish was immediately granted. My post was taken over by Colonel Stanislaw Radaj. I returned to Warsaw, cherishing a tiny hope that perhaps I could succeed in alarming the world. Unfortunately, in my situation, that was neither simple nor easy.

Nearly a week later, on the night of August 20, 1968, Soviet paratroopers landed at the Prague airport and units of the Polish Army commanded by Chief of Staff of the Silesian Military District Division General Florian Siwicki [today (1989) Minister of National Defense] had, together with other Warsaw Pact armies, crossed the Czechoslovak border.

I could not escape participating in the invasion. Once it started, I was appointed to the Special Command Center of the Polish Army in Czechoslovakia, established at the General Staff of the Polish Army in Warsaw. Later I did not regret it. By maintaining direct contact with the operating troops, listening to live reports from their commanders, and preparing special reports on the subject for the Minister of National Defense, General Wojciech Jaruzelski, and Wladyslaw Gomulka, first secretary of the Party, I had a unique opportunity for gaining insight into this chapter of our postwar history.

Once the invasion was over, attempts to sum it up and infer conclusions for the future were made within the Polish armed forces.

Along the official line, upon the initiative of the Minister of National Defense, General Wojciech Jaruzelski, and under his auspices, a scientific symposium on Operation Danube was held at the General Staff of the Polish Army. That was a gala event, attended by nearly the entire leadership of the MON [Ministry of National Defense], the commands of the armed services and military districts, Polish participants in the invasion, and, of course, the main authors of the invasion—representatives of the Soviet Supreme Command. The participants in the symposium vied with [but did] not surround the Czech garrisons as rapidly as did Soviet units, the world's best, but they subsequently compensated for it by their exceptional success in persuading Czechoslovak commanders to support changes at the highest level of their Party and state. It was viewed as an outstanding accomplishment that, despite the hostile attitude of the Czech population, which formed living barricades in front of tanks and armored vehicles, it was in principle possible to avoid any major loss of lives and property, and only one child, and by accident at that, had died under a Polish tank. In sum, the symposium viewed Operation Danube as a major military and political success of the community of socialist countries, to which the Polish Army had contributed significantly.

Along the unofficial, that is, semi-official, discussions as well as in conversations between friends and among colleagues, Operation Danube was viewed less enthusiastically and the conclusions were diametrically opposite. The participation of Polish Army units in the invasion of Czechoslovakia was viewed almost everywhere as an unforgivable mistake of the political and military leadership of Poland, a mistake for which a high price would have to be paid once Poles claim their inalienable right to a life of dignity, and clamor for social and democratic changes which the U.S.S.R. will not accept.

My assessments and conclusions were rooted precisely in this undercurrent, and that was probably when it all began.

I did not have to wait long for additional sociopolitical and civics lessons. I had learned them in December 1970 [a time of worker riots], and from its tragic harvest. When the alleged counterrevolution on the coast was already in its death throes, the bodies of forty-four "disturbers of order in the people's state" were buried in cemeteries. They included thirty workers and seven trade-school pupils in their early teens. A total of 1,164 wounded, including a large number of young people, were treated at hospitals.

The meaning of these numbers was and is terrifying, but to me personally the most terrifying thing was the ease with which the authorities, which dub themselves the people's power, had resorted to the armed forces and had directed them, in a manner contrary to their calling, against their own people, and the fact that someone had issued the orders "Blockade," "Stop them," and "Fire!" without anybody—beginning with the Minister of National Defense and ending with the lowest-level commander—declaring that he would not obey these orders.

I was continually bothered by these thoughts. When ten years later, in 1980, history began to repeat itself, when this time Polish armed forces were mobilized on Moscow's order with the object of using them against Polish workers, intelligentsia, and youth, I simply said to myself, no. I believed not only that a soldier is not bound to carry out orders contrary to his conscience and beliefs but also that he should not carry them out. What is more, I believed that the Polish people had no chance to overcome the confrontation, and therefore something extra should be done to counteract it.

The United States had been warned about Soviet preparations for the invasion in December 1980 and March 1981. Both times, the United States government publicized the warnings internationally. Did these warnings come from you?

It seems to me that assessments of military operations of the type represented by the preparations for invading Poland in 1980 and the following spring could not have been based solely on the warnings of a single individual. Nevertheless, I am justified in assuming that my appeal to halt Moscow's drive had at least partially reached Washington and was properly appraised there.

In your opinion, was Solidarity doomed from the outset, or do you believe there was a chance for its survival?

Had the Kania–Jaruzelski duumvirate said no to the Russians from the very beginning, then, under the pressure of overt attacks and threats from Moscow, Solidarity would have had to alter its front of struggle and primarily champion the country's sovereignty and integrity. I am certain that it would have been more inclined toward compromise and that the Soviet Union would have retreated, had the Party-army leadership and the nation created a united front.

Even Stalin did not attack Yugoslavia militarily. This also happened with Albania, and in recent years with Romania when Ceauşescu refused to obey Moscow and to subordinate his armed forces to the Soviet Union.

While observing Soviet military moves from a privileged position, and even being in direct contact with them, I never had any doubts that, though the Soviet Union could have afforded and was ready for military action such as the invasion of Czechoslovakia (and, in principle, without material or human losses), Moscow certainly would not have wanted and could not have afforded war with Poland had it been opposed by a united front of the Polish high command, the army, and the nation. Even if such a war had been of very brief duration, the price to the Soviet Union would have been too high.

Aside from the moral and political cost to Moscow in the area of international relations, it seems to me that it had weighty reasons for assuming that a Czechoslovak-style military action against Poland would not be as smooth. To crush the eventual resistance of the Polish Army alone, the Russians would have had to commit a majority of their armed forces from the European part of the U.S.S.R. and even to throw in part of the troops from Czechoslovakia and East Germany.

The Russians were aware that spitting at tanks, which they had encountered in their sneak invasion of Czechoslovakia, is not in the style and character of Poles. They also were aware that Polish society was the richer by Czech experience and by its own experience in 1956 and 1970, and that the population not only was not intimidated by tanks but had learned how to burn and destroy them effectively when they were directed against them. They also realized that, from the beginning of the crisis, Poles were reacting to the appearance of new, small, Soviet sub-units or installations and probably judging correctly that this was just a game. At that time, an aide to the Permanent Representative of the Supreme Commander of the United Armed Forces [of the Warsaw Pact] at the Polish Army, with whom I had been in working contact, complained to me that Poles were already saying officially that "Soviet tanks burn better than Polish ones."

Hence, were the U.S.S.R. to meet with the open resistance of the Polish leadership supported by the people, or even with symbolic defense gestures (for example, deployment of troops around the nation's capital), the outcome would certainly have been a war of nerves, and if the Polish side were to withstand that kind of war, Moscow would have had to retreat in the end.

However, a totally different situation arose once, in the course of the internal Polish conflict, the Party-army leadership—that is, Kania and Jaruzelski—took the side of the U.S.S.R. and agreed in principle with the Russians that they were facing a counterrevolution, promising them that they would deal with Solidarity on their own by means of political-administrative measures, asking merely for more time.

Given this attitude on the part of our leaders, Moscow was not facing the organized might of a sovereign state ready to resist; it was facing a defenseless society.

Suppose we now try to re-create the course of events in chronological order. What came first—the threat of invasion or the idea of martial law?

Unfortunately, martial law.

When did this idea first surface, and who proposed it?

From information sent in writing to the Soviet leadership, which I had personally prepared with the cooperation of the Ministry of Internal Affairs upon the recommendation and according to the directives of General Jaruzelski, it is clear that the idea of imposing martial law on Poland had been conceived as early as the peak period of the August 1980 sit-in strikes; that is, nearly sixteen months before martial law was imposed by General Jaruzelski.

The collective originator of this idea was the so-called Party-state leadership staff headed by the newly appointed prime minister Jozef Pinkowski and promulgated on August 24, 1980 (immediately following the Fourth PZPR [Polish United Workers' Party] Central Committee Plenum, which had expressed its support of negotiating with the striking workers). The members of that staff included the Central Committee secretaries Kazimierz Barcikowski and Stefan Olszowski, Deputy Prime Minister Mieczyslaw Jagielski, and probably Tadeusz Grabski, and also, most certainly, the heads of the principal ministries—National Defense, Wojciech Jaruzelski; and Internal Affairs, Miroslaw Milewski.

To delude the mutinous population, the leadership staff agreed to sign a rather imprecisely worded social accord to extinguish the conflagration of strikes that had spread across nearly all of Poland, and in the ensuing more favorable conditions to switch to a counter-offensive by means of administrative measures, including, as a final resort, the imposition of martial law.

Since the initial attempts—made in September 1980—to outmaneuver people by means of various administrative measures had produced the opposite results, the leadership staff adopted the general decision to commence preparations for imposing martial law.

Within the Polish Army these preparations had begun on October 22, 1980; that is, two days before the proceedings for registering Solidarity at the Warsaw Voivodship Court were instituted. On that day, at the instruction of the Minister of National Defense, General

Wojciech Jaruzelski, the General Staff of the Polish Army began urgently to draft a plan for imposing martial law.

General supervision of the planning was done from beginning to end by the chief of the General Staff of the Polish Army, General Florian Siwicki. Participation in the initial stage of the planning at the General Staff of the Polish Army was confined to the deputies of the Chief of Staff; namely, General Tadeusz Hupalowski, General Jerzy Skalski, General Antoni Jasinski, Brigadier General Mieczyslaw Dachowski, and I myself, Colonel Ryszard Kuklinski.

The preliminary draft (or rather an assessment study) of the plans, including drafts of certain martial-law decrees, was completed early in November 1980 and, the same month, presented for consideration to the National Defense Committee, chaired by Prime Minister Pinkowski. The plans were offered in general outline, without details, because, in the view of the military leadership, some of the members of the National Defense Committee had been among the so-called *Smoncesy* [Yiddish for "nincompoops"]; that is, persons of doubtful loyalty who showed an inclination to remodel Poland's political system and who were merely temporary members of that body.

The initial concept of martial law—with regard to postulates, to what should be suspended, prohibited, ordered, militarized, and delegalized, where the army should be dispatched and where the security forces, who should be protected and who interned—was not too different from the law as finally implemented thirteen months later.

The plans for imposing martial law were temporarily shelved. Was that the reason for the threat of a Soviet invasion in early December 1980?

Basically, yes. As seen by the Soviet leadership, the delay in imposing martial law was not only promoting the organizational strengthening of Solidarity, which the U.S.S.R. had opposed from the outset, but also opening the way for the formation of new independent social structures in Poland.

All this had strengthened the Russians' suspicions that the Polish leadership, and primarily Kania, was employing delaying tactics and may even have been playing a double game.

Against this background, at the end of November 1980 the Soviet leadership began to organize a new leadership team, with the active participation of its embassy in Warsaw and the Supreme Commander of the United Armed Forces of the Warsaw Pact Marshal Viktor Kulikov and its representative in the Polish Army, General Afanasy Shcheglov.

The seizure of power by the hard-liners, who even then were ready to crush Solidarity, was to be preceded by the introduction of large military forces of the Soviet Union and other Warsaw Pact countries into Poland. The related discussions, as well as discussions concerning the eventual neutralization of the Polish Army, which was viewed as demoralized, were conducted between the Russians and General Jaruzelski. The details of these dramatic conversations are unknown to me. General Jaruzelski alone can and should disclose them. As for me, I only know their results. Immediately after these discussions, upon the personal recommendation of the utterly devastated General Jaruzelski, on January 1, 1980, First Deputy Chief of the General Staff of the Polish Army, Division General Tadeusz Hupalowski, and Colonel Franciszek Puchala flew by special aircraft to Moscow to familiarize themselves with the details of the Soviet plans to bring military intervention forces into Poland.

Judging from the information they had received on the same day, that is, on December 1, 1980, at the General Staff of the U.S.S.R. Armed Forces in Moscow, and also judging from the registered blueprints of the final invasion plans taken from Soviet maps, three Soviet armies, totaling fifteen divisions, one Czechoslovak army consisting of two divisions, and one division of the East German National People's Army were to be sent into Poland under the guise of conducting Soyuz 8 [81] exercises. All together, eighteen Soviet, Czechoslovak, and German divisions were to participate in military operations in Polish territory. The invasion forces were to be ready to cross Poland's frontiers on December 8, 1980. According to plan, Soviet forces were to operate in central and eastern Poland and Czech and German forces in western Poland. The invasion was to be accompanied by a tight blockade of Poland by the Soviet Baltic Fleet and the East German People's Navy. In the initial stage of the intervention, units of the Polish Army were to remain at their regular deployment sites (as had happened in Czechoslovakia). It was only following dramatic bargaining by General Jaruzelski that the Russians agreed to the participation of a few Polish units in secondary tasks. Thus, two armored divisions (5th and 11th) were to be attached to the Czechoslovak Army, and two mechanized divisions (4th and 12th) to the German Army.

What you are saying now, six years later, is depressing. How did these Soviet preparations affect the Poles on Jaruzelski's staff?

The ruthless and uncompromising attitude of the Russians, who in their conversations with General Jaruzelski refused even to consider the eventual exclusion of the East German National People's Army from the intervention forces, and who had even questioned the possibility of any participation by the Polish Army in the military operations, completely paralyzed the top leadership at the Ministry of National Defense. General Jaruzelski was in shock and stayed behind locked doors in his office, completely inaccessible even to his closest associates. Not much better off was General Siwicki, and also General Hupalowski, to whose lot it had fallen to bring the invasion plans from Moscow. This paralysis lasted throughout November 30 and December 1. Everyone was waiting for a miracle. But there was no miracle. The blueprints of the invasion plans brought from Moscow by General Hupalowski and Colonel Puchala had confirmed the general outline of what was known even earlier from the discussions between the Russians and General Jaruzelski.

A detailed analysis of the Soviet plans, made by the General Staff of the Polish Army after the plans were brought to Warsaw, led the General Staff to conclude that the Russians totally misunderstood the situation in Poland; that they were unaware of the mood of the people and were underestimating the strength of Solidarity, and, last, that, instead of having a calming effect, the invasion might result in still greater social unrest and even in a nationwide uprising.

Against this background, on December 12, the chief of the General Staff of the Polish Army, General Florian Siwicki, made another attempt to persuade General Jaruzelski to renew talks with the Russians to eliminate this worst-case scenario. At the suggestion of his aides, General Siwicki proposed presenting various other options to the Russians, especially the option of imposing martial law in Poland without waiting until conditions became more favorable. But General Jaruzelski's apathy was such that he did not even tolerate any discussion.

A new element appeared a day later, when General Eugeniusz Molczyk entered the picture. General Molczyk, who on December 1 and 3 was at the Bucharest session of the Committee of Defense Ministers of the Warsaw Pact countries, upon returning to Poland and familiarizing himself at the General Staff of the Polish Army with the plans brought from Moscow, made another attempt to persuade General Jaruzelski to intervene in Moscow, to present a specific plan for an immediate crushing of Solidarity and the opposition by Polish forces alone. He had supposedly told General Jaruzelski, "History will never forgive us if they do the job for us."

In your opinion, what had influenced the Soviet decision to abandon the already well-advanced invasion plans? Pressure from the West, or the offer of General Jaruzelski to settle the matter without an invasion?

Both. As we well recall, the preparations for invading Poland did not escape the attention of the Western world, not as in the case of Czechoslovakia. Thus, here the Soviet Union not only was deprived of the important surprise factor but, with the warnings emanating from the Western governments, and even from Third World countries, it had to realize that intervention would end the political detente in Europe, disrupt economic cooperation between the East and the West, and, in all likelihood, accelerate open military cooperation between the United States and China.

Consider that in the first days of December, at a time when the military high command responsible for Poland's national defense was sunk in total apathy and desperation, the reaction of the United States was unusually sharp. On December 3 President Carter sent an urgent dispatch to Brezhnev in which he demanded that the Polish government and nation be allowed to resolve their own problems independently and warned about the negative consequences of a decision by the U.S.S.R. to use force against Poland. On December 4 the same declaration was made publicly by President Carter.

In sum, considering the firm pressures and explicit warnings by the West that the invasion would prove very costly to the U.S.S.R., Moscow was now more inclined to let the Poles handle the problem on their own, even if it took more time.

On February 16, 1981, a group of forty-five higher officers from the Ministry of Internal Affairs and two functionaries of the Propaganda Department from the Central Committee gathered in the auditorium of the Inspectorate of Territorial Defense and Internal Defense Troops on Aleje Niepodleglosci to play a war game, with the object of refining and finalizing the plans for imposing martial law.

Everyone present in the auditorium was asked to sign a pledge of secrecy. The proposed actions could not be put down in writing and were merely presented orally. Only the game's scorekeepers (on one side, Colonel Jan Wasiluk and Colonel Jan Czyzewski, and on the other side, Colonel Czeslaw Witt and I) were authorized to take notes.

During the discussion, the players had reached a consensus that imposing martial law might be the beginning of the greatest drama in Poland's history, but the final conclusions they came to after that appraisal merely brought that drama closer.

Thus, the idea of General Tadeusz Tuczapski that the government should submit for consideration to the Sejm emergency martial law decrees was ultimately rejected. The players concluded that eliminating the multimillion-member Solidarity was possible only with the element of total surprise. It was determined that the most favorable moment for commencing the operation would be a day of leisure, preferably a Saturday night.

So-called Operation Springtime, intended to intern approximately six thousand activists from Solidarity and other independent occupational and social organizations, was regarded as the most important move. It was determined that this operation would produce the expected results only if carried out twelve to six hours prior to the official imposition of martial law.

During the game, final agreement was also reached on the division of roles between the army and the security forces and their cooperation during expected confrontations with the populace.

It was agreed that only security forces would operate near industrial plants, work establishments, and higher-education institutions. As for the army, it would act more cautiously, at most as a supporting force, deployed in the cities and blockading industrial centers.

The war game concluded the so-called spring period of planning. On February 20, 1981, the conclusions of the game were presented to General Jaruzelski. On the following day, on Saturday, February 21, the chief of the General Staff of the Polish Army, General Siwicki, informed me that the report had been approved by General Jaruzelski. The prime minister had made a few minor revisions and recommended that the name of the report be changed to "On the Status of the State's Preparations for Imposing Martial Law," so he could present it to the Soviet leadership during the 26th CPSU Congress.

Only a few persons knew that during the meeting in the Kremlin on March 3, 1981, while presenting the program of his government to the Soviets, Prime Minister Wojciech Jaruzelski had also submitted the detailed report "On the Status of the State's Preparations for Imposing Martial Law" and given assurances that the Polish leadership, "being aware of the support of the Allies, is resolved to resort to this measure to defend the country against the counterrevolution."

From what you have said, it appears that in the spring of 1981 the government was ready for a confrontation with the people, and that the Soviet Union was well informed of this. Why, then, did another attempt at armed intervention by the U.S.S.R. take place in March and April? Could you present at least the basic facts surrounding that event?

Your comment that in the spring the government was ready for a confrontation with the people is imprecise. The government had plans for imposing martial law, and it had a plan for destroying Solidarity, but in the circumstances at that time it simply did not seem possible to translate these plans into reality. Aside from any other motives prompting General Jaruzelski, he saw no chance for imposing martial law, out of purely pragmatic considerations. For the point was not only to institute that operation but to complete it victoriously for the "people's power." In the spring of 1981 this was not realistic, or even possible, because what the authorities had at their disposal was a partially disintegrated Ministry of Internal Affairs, an army of doubtful loyalty, and a handful of hard-liners in a disintegrating Party, while they were opposed not only by millions of Solidarity members but also by a hostile society. Given such a ratio of forces, the coup was doomed in advance.

General Jaruzelski continued to assure Moscow, both before and after March 3, that he was resolved to impose martial law, but in his never-ending talks with the Russians, for which I personally prepared the materials according to his directives, he explained that it was necessary to wait a little, until the ratio of forces improved somewhat, until Solidarity lost some of its popularity and the government gained at least partial support from the people. He also pointed out that time was needed to consolidate the forces that would support the authorities (this concerned the well-known weaknesses within the Ministry of Internal Affairs and the Party.)

The Russians—as usual in all their contracts with General Jaruzelski—heard only what was convenient to them or what they wanted to hear. Early in 1981, they heard only that he had expressed readiness to "defend socialism" in Poland and was resolved to impose martial law. As for his comments that it was necessary to wait until conditions improved, chiefly until the ratio of forces improved, the Russians considered that insubstantial, since they were ready to alter the unfavorable ratio by sending their divisions, and even Czech and German divisions, into Poland.

It was against this background, just before General Jaruzelski became prime minister, that Moscow stepped in with the initiative of holding a previously unplanned large command-staff exercise in Poland and its frontiers, in which some 150,000 troops, including 30,000 in Polish territory, were to take part.

The General Staff of the Polish Army had the worst premonitions in this regard, because the Russians did not conceal that the exercise was closely linked to the situation in Poland and conceived as a form of international assistance to Polish Communists. Given the tactic of calming Moscow that it had adopted since the beginning of the crisis, the Polish Party–government leadership accepted this offer of international assistance. How the Russians interpreted this assistance became obvious soon afterward.

Shortly before the Eighth Polish Communist Party Central Committee Plenum, at which decisions were made to replace the prime minister, a group of eighteen Soviet generals arrived in Poland. They included all the deputies of Marshal Kulikov, and their ostensible purpose was to verify the readiness of the Polish Army for Soyuz 81 exercises. They toured all military districts and services of the armed forces, visiting divisions and even regiments. These generals were not at all interested in the training or combat readiness of the troops; their sole concern was the attitude of the command personnel toward the counterrevolution. What they tried to do in their (sometimes private) conversations with Polish officers was not just call upon them to act but call upon them to fight against their own nation.

At the Mechanized Regiment in Wesola near Warsaw, General Anafasy Shcheglov (one of the nastiest exemplars of Russian chauvinism) had the nerve to ask the regiment's CO: "What will you do in the event that it is necessary to remove strikers from a plant or factory?"

On March 27, 1981, a U.S.S.R. government plane landed on the military runway of Okecie Airport and disgorged about thirty officials of the KGB, the U.S.S.R. Ministry of Defense, and the Gosplan, who had come to familiarize themselves with plans for martial law in Poland. The military group was headed by Marshal Viktor Kulikov and the KGB team by Andropov's first deputy.

Upon studying our plans, the Russians thought them insufficient and presented their demands. According to the Russians, the imposition of martial law was dictated by the need to defend socialism. Martial law should be accompanied by a suspension of the Constitution and by the transfer of all power into the hands of the Supreme Military Command. The Russians also recommended that internment followed by investigation and summary courts-martial be carried out fourteen hours prior to the imposition of martial law. Further, security forces, together with the army, should be used to crush the counterrevolution and the strikes. They recommended that the Polish General Staff and the district commanders accept Soviet advisers.

On the evening of April 3, under the shelter of darkness, a Soviet aircraft brought Kania and Jaruzelski to face Brezhnev himself. The conversation must have been brief, because on the morning of April 4 the same Soviet military aircraft brought them back to Warsaw. I am ignorant of the exact wording of these conversations, but I can reproduce their atmosphere, and even their nature, on the basis of the activities of the Polish General Staff on those days.

On April 3, when Kania and Jaruzelski were getting ready to fly to meet with Brezhnev, the Russians began an air war of nerves with Poland. That day, without any advance warning to Polish air controllers, they transferred from their Czech to their Polish bases thirty-two Mi-6 helicopters and airlifted to Brzeg, by means of ten AN-12 aircraft, unidentified military cargo. On the following days these helicopters made combat overflights to the region of Torun and other parts of Poland. Aside from their terrorizing aspects, these overflights were a major menace to Poland's airspace, since Soviet pilots did not obey our air controllers.

On April 7, while he was at the Congress of the Czechoslovak CP, Brezhnev decided to end Soyuz 81 exercises. Formally these exercises were over, but the military terrorism of the U.S.S.R. against Poland continued.

On April 10, Kulikov, together with his Deputy for Allied Fleets, Admiral Mikhaylin, returned to Poland, to the region of Swinoujscie, and there tried to get an appointment with Jaruzelski. But Kulikov was told that the prime minister was with Kania and could not meet with him until April 13. General Jaruzelski wanted to avoid the meeting, because the Soviets continued to insist on a specific date for imposing martial law. In preparation for the meeting with Kulikov fixed for April 13, General Jaruzelski came to the Polish General Staff to familiarize himself and his close associates with the final plans. He looked clearly depressed, even devastated. After examining the most critical documents, he became even more depressed. He declared openly: "Even in my blackest imagination I could not conceive our doing anything like that. I would rather no longer be prime minister when these documents have to be signed and implemented. But the situation is that bloodying three noses in Bydgoszcz has led us to the edge of the abyss."

As he continued to express his disjointed thoughts, he criticized Rulewski of Bydgoszcz Solidarity and Bujak of Warsaw Solidarity, claiming that "their attitude is typical of social-fascism." General Jaruzelski declared himself in favor of a compromise plan between mass internment of the opposition and a brief and selective detention and arrest of the most extreme activists. Jaruzelski's further reflections were interrupted by the daily TV newscast, which he wanted to view. That day, the newscast was rather gracious toward him, because both the Polish people and the foreign correspondents (of course, only those from the West) generally responded well to his address to the Sejm the previous day. This evidently cheered him up, and after the newscast, he left the General Staff. On April 13, he met with Kulikov, and resolutely opposed fixing a date for the imposition of martial law and signing the related documents.

In mid-April, the threat of armed intervention by the U.S.S.R. began to recede, although it probably never quite disappeared. The Soviet Union has never withdrawn from Poland the wartime system of command of the intervention forces established during Soyuz 81 exercises.

During the crisis in Poland, Marshal Kulikov handled not only the military aspects but also the burden of direct contact and talks with Poland's Party leadership. The contacts between Kania and Jaruzelski on the one hand and Brezhnev on the other were merely occasional. On a day-by-day basis, it was Kulikov who pressured them. Toward the end of the crisis, Kulikov did not even want to talk with everyone or every time. He prided himself, for example, on having ousted Kania from the palace on Sulkiewicz Street where the marshal resided now and then, because Kania had come to see him at a late hour and, moreover, was drunk. That Kania was under the influence of alcohol may have been imagined by the angered marshal, but the fact remains that he was asked to leave Kulikov's residence because he had adhered to the line of the Ninth Extraordinary Polish Communist Party Congress and was opposed to the use of force. This is a historical fact.

What circumstances for the second time restrained the Russians, in your opinion, from resorting to direct armed intervention in Poland? Was it again the West's reaction, which was prompted by your secret reports, or were there other factors?

It seems to me that the reasons why the U.S.S.R. refrained from invading in the spring of 1981 were the same as in the previous December. On the one hand, there was the very strong diplomatic action by the new American Administration of President Reagan and a majority of West European countries, and, on the other hand, the apprehensions of the Russians about the reaction of the Polish people, or even the Polish Army itself, to the use of force.

Given the resolute attitude of the Western countries, and in view of the explicit rise, following the Bydgoszcz provocation, of a kind of national front of resistance against the use of force, which was even joined by a considerable part of the Polish Army, the offer by the Polish authorities, and especially by General Jaruzelski, to accomplish this [the coup] on their own proved more tempting to the Russians than instigating in Poland a conflagration that would be difficult to extinguish or whose cost to the U.S.S.R. would be too high.

General Jaruzelski displayed a marked inclination toward the use of force, even before the "favorable conditions" he was waiting for occurred, probably under terrific Soviet pressure coordinated with the activities of the native Targowica [hard-liner] group and accompanied by domestic tensions of no small magnitude. He was very close to using force in mid-June.

At the same time, transition to a wartime command structure began. The Operation Directorate of the Polish General Staff was to be the main center for directing the state under martial law [the Polish expression *stan wojenny* means both a state of war and martial law]. After the directorate was reinforced with internal-security officers from other military institutions and functionaries from key civilian ministries, two teams were to operate within it: the planning team, to which I was appointed as the head; and the command team, to be directed by Colonel Franciszek Puchala. As of the end of September, work stations began to be prepared and provided with special communications equipment for directing operations under martial law.

The modest premises of my section became crowded, and the atmosphere increasingly tense. The regular operations team which had been on duty since the strikes on the coast in 1980 was augmented with officers from other internal-security institutions. The door to my office, where all the strands of planning had converged, was never closed. After almost a year of preparations for imposing martial law, I became accustomed to pouring plans on paper. Then in September the first collisions between these plans and the human element commenced. I felt sickened, listening to the representative of the Propaganda Department of the Central Committee, who was expounding his vision of shutting down weeklies and newspapers which I read and valued, or when he began to name columnists and journalists whom I liked to read or listen to and whose voices were to be stifled. I was terrified, listening to the names of various opportunistic mediocrities who were to replace my favorite editors.

When on October 31 we, the Polish Army's delegation headed by General Molczyk, landed on the military runway of Okecie Airport, a highly placed military person, one of the welcoming committee, told me what I had been dreading since September 13: "The decision has been made. At this moment Jaruzelski is coordinating the deadline and plan for the operations with the Allies."

On November 2, at about 1400 hours, I was summoned to the deputy chief of the Polish General Staff, General Jerzy Skalski, who supervised the planning for martial law by the Operations Directorate of the General Staff. Along with me were summoned the chief of the Operations Directorate of the General Staff, General Waclaw Szklarski, and his other two deputies, Colonel Czeslaw Witt and Colonel Franciszek Puchala.

General Skalski told us with the greatest gravity about new and highly important factors that would significantly influence our planning. One factor was information from a reliable source that the Americans knew about the latest version of our plans, including the draft decrees on martial law.

The news that our secrets had been leaked to the West and that Solidarity might be warned at any moment was a shock to all present.

A dramatic exchange took place. One after another, we took the floor: General Szklarski, Colonel Puchala, and Colonel Witt claimed that they had no part in it and placed themselves at the disposal of the Security Services. The last of that trio to speak, Colonel Witt, repeated a view he had long voiced, that all the actions of Solidarity since its rise demonstrated that it had a hidden ally at the very center of power.

When all eyes were directed at me, I had regained control of myself and decided to support Colonel Witt's notion and declare that I was one of them and present my rationale. I began by saying that I fully shared the opinion of Colonel Witt and that I placed myself at the disposal of the authorities and was ready to cooperate in the investigation under way. When I began to collect my thoughts in order to continue speaking, General Skalski interrupted me, declaring that he was not conducting the investigation (that was being handled by the Security Services) and that, moreover, the circle of suspects was not limited to us four. Next, he said that we should consider how to organize our work optimally in order to accomplish the tasks before us.

It is natural and human that, in face of a major peril to your life and of eventual repressions against your close family members, you decided to leave the country. Could you describe how it happened?

The peril did not arise suddenly and unexpectedly at the beginning of November. I still had not thought about leaving the country. Even after September 13, when the Security Services began a vigorous search for sources of the leak of our plans to Solidarity, I stayed at my post. Since the revelation of the code name of the internment operation, Springtime, narrowed the circle of suspects to those who had known it, I expected to be arrested at any moment. However, my reaction was confined to writing something in the nature of a political testament. But at that time I still had felt needed. Between November 2 and 7, I increasingly lost that belief.

On the morning of November 7 I attended a routine briefing by the chief of the Polish General Staff. General Siwicki had nothing new to say to us, but actually this convinced me that nothing now stood in the way of the imposition of martial law.

After leaving the small conference room of the General Staff at around noon, I began to collect my thoughts. What next? I got into my Volga and the chauffeur took off at full speed from Rakowiecka Street to take me home, as usual, to Nowe Miasto via Pulawska and Pierwsza Armia Wojska Polskiego Streets and then via the Lazienki route and the Vistula River highway. I told him, "Today there's no need to hurry," and asked him to drive slowly. For the first time in more than a year, I began to watch the passersby, the buildings, and even the trees of my city.

As we exited the Vistula River highway into Sanguszki Street, my likable army chauffeur, of whom I was as fond as if he were my own son, asked me when he was to return to drive me to work. I answered: "Tomorrow, drive directly from your regiment to the parking lot of the General Staff. The car might be needed by the officers in our section. Monday, do the same thing. If I need you, I'll call."

While passing Przyrynek Street, once again I noticed two young men who quickly turned their faces away. The same thing happened at the end of Rajcow Street, directly in front of the vestry of the Church of the Holy Virgin Mary—that is, a little less than fifty meters from my home. They had been keeping watch there day and night for nearly a week. I was perfectly aware that they were not Solidarity extremists, who, according to official warnings from my superiors, intended to kidnap family members of important military persons, to ease or even disrupt martial-law operations by blackmail. I also knew perfectly well that they were not guarding my family against such an eventuality, because the army, rather than the civilian security service, was to be used for that purpose. I guessed that I was under surveillance.

I did not expect an immediate arrest or even arrest within the next few days, because the Security Services had first to sniff out my conspiratorial contacts and links within the Polish armed forces and in my relations with the Soviet Army and other Warsaw Pact armies, with the Party, with the opposition, with Solidarity, etc., which would be essential to their investigation. The situation was serious, however, and my calculations might go wrong. Thus, I began by putting my home in order: it contained not only a large library, which included certain underground publications, but also a large collection of top-secret materials and documents concerning the unequal military cooperation between Poland and the Soviet Union within the Warsaw Pact and all the preparations for imposing martial law, which could readily be considered evidence of espionage.

I regarded all these documents as a kind of elaboration and expansion of the diary I had been keeping with few interruptions since August 1968, or rather of observations jotted down at night with the idea that one day perhaps they would see the light of day. On November 4, 5, and 6, I selected and burned personal papers such as letters, a dossier of telephone numbers, addresses, snapshots of friends, anything that might incriminate innocent people. On November 7, immediately upon returning home, I began to burn my valuable archives. The apartment was full of smoke because, given such a large quantity of papers, the chimney ceased to work. To avoid suffocating, I opened the windows, well aware that the smoke from my apartment might attract the attention of the security agents circling the building and that they might at any moment burst into my home.

On the other hand, I began to realize that I was destroying copies of documents of great historical importance, whose originals would certainly never be made public. Since I would not come to any greater harm if I were caught in possession of them, I decided that I might as well leave the country with the remaining papers. But I think it is still too soon to describe how my escape took place. I believe, however, that in the future this, too, can be made public.

Could you describe the relationship of dependence of the Polish Army to the Soviet command? Is it the relationship of a subordinate and a superior, or is Jaruzelski able to oppose the decisions of the Warsaw Pact or submit them for discussion?

The situation of Poland, whose leaders had begun in the late 1960s gradually to discard Poland's sovereign right to dispose of its own armed forces and national defense as it sees fit, is greatly complicated, although it is not hopeless in all circumstances and in all situations.

It is hopeless only in times of danger of war and in times of war, because, according to the Statute of the United Armed Forces and the Organs for Directing Them in Time of War, which was accepted by Poland sometime between the end of 1979 and the beginning of 1980, in either situation the direction of Poland's defense and the command of its armed forces passes entirely into the hands of the Single Supreme High Command. Poland agreed voluntarily that the Single Supreme High Command would be exclusively the Supreme High Command of the Armed Forces of the Soviet Union, and that its working organ would be exclusively the Soviet General Staff. The Polish side even agreed to the present and future absence of any Polish representative or even a liaison mission at that Supreme High Command.

The Polish Armed Forces will be commanded by the Soviet Supreme Command through the mediation of the latter's lower command echelons. Thus:

The Polish front, that is, all the operational land troops and the air force, will be directly subordinate to the Soviet Supreme Commander of the Western Theater of War.

The entire Polish Navy, including its land bases, will be under the commander of the U.S.S.R. Baltic Fleet, who, in case of danger of war or in an actual war, automatically becomes the commander and his staff the staff of the United Baltic Fleet of Warsaw Pact Countries.

Even the National Air Defense Troops (regarded from the moment of their formation as the core of home defense) will be led by Soviet rather than Polish commanders. A piquant aspect of the agreement was the endowing of the Soviet high command with rights to use Polish air-defense units outside Poland's territory.

In sum, in the event of danger of war or actual war, ninety percent of the Polish Army will find itself directly under the orders of Soviet commanders. Left within the purview of the national military-political leadership will be only domestic logistic units, engineer maintenance units for safeguarding the transit of Soviet troops across Polish territory, and units expected to train reserves to compensate for war losses.

All orders and directives from the Soviet commanders will be addressed directly to their subordinate Polish troops, bypassing the Polish high command. In practice, this means the unlimited right of the U.S.S.R. to dispose of the Polish Army without any prior consultation with Polish authorities.

The role of the Polish high command will be confined solely to supplying matériel to Polish troops fighting under Soviet command, to training reserves, and to compensating for human and material war losses.

The foregoing decisions, in view of their exceptionally sensitive nature, are classified top-secret and no one in the Polish Army apart from a handful has the least knowledge of them. Even the commanders of the armed services and of military districts are familiar only with that part of the decisions which concerns them directly.

In peacetime, Soviet guidance of the armed forces and the defense of Warsaw Pact countries is camouflaged under the so-called United Command of the United Armed Forces. That command is so structured that all the leading posts, from the Supreme Commander through the Chief of Staff and the deputies of the Supreme Commander for Air Defense, Air Force, Navy, Technology, and the Rear, as well as at all levels downward, ending with the section (department) chief at the Technological Staff and the Committee of the United Armed Forces, are staffed exclusively with Soviet personnel. Regardless of the posts they nominally hold, the officers of the other Warsaw Pact armies exercise only communications and liaison functions with respect to their own national armies.

From the moment that General Jaruzelski became Minister of National Defense, the Russians never had any trouble with Poland in the area of politics or military solutions. During 1968–81 they got whatever they wanted without having to go over the head of the Polish high command. In the early 1980s they already had under their control practically everything relating to the national defense of Poland and the operation of its armed forces.

For example, it is Moscow that determines the long-range numerical size of the Polish Army in peacetime and in time of war, its organizational structure, armaments, and facilities, its state of combat readiness and mobilizational readiness, of training instructions, tasks and plans for its use in time of war, etc.

The implementation of the obligations accepted by the Polish Ministry of National Defense in this connection is checked on by the Russians twice a year. There exists a dual reporting system. Some reports are transmitted to Moscow by the Polish Ministry of National Defense, while others, identical in form and content but based on Soviet sources, are dispatched by the Soviet Mission of the Supreme Commander of the United Armed Forces to the Polish Army. Moscow analyzes and compares these reports and expects profuse explanations from the Polish side whenever it uncovers any deviation from the adopted obligations, underfulfillment of plans, or even mere inaccuracies in the Polish reports.

There are also paradoxes such as the fact that the numerical size of the Polish Army made public by Poland during the Vienna negotiations (and of course not consonant with truth) was specified by the U.S.S.R. General Staff in Moscow. Since the incorrect figures were complicating the negotiations in Vienna in 1980, the Polish General Staff intended to bring them somewhat closer to the actual figures. In that connection I accompanied General Siwicki in Moscow during his attempts to do this, and I personally witnessed a two-star Soviet general from their General Staff tell the chief of the Polish General Staff: *Nel'zya* [Impossible]—whereupon he handed us a prepared card bearing data which we could use in our negotiations with the West.

Pursuant to the obligations assumed by Poland, the Polish General Staff has to coordinate with the Soviet high command the peacetime deployment of units of the Polish Army, among other things.

The Russians have a guaranteed right to conduct inspections of and monitor Polish Army units. The absence of precise rules defining what they can control and what they cannot has resulted in, for example, the situation that occurred early in February 1981, when, under the pretext of monitoring the readiness of the Polish Army for the Soyuz 81 exercise, Soviet generals from the United Command checked on the readiness of various Polish units for the confrontation with Solidarity.

The Warsaw Pact does not give any member country or any group of member countries the formal right to interfere in the internal affairs of another member country, let alone the right of armed intervention. This can be attested to by adherents of this principle. I know of instances in which Romania said no on issues of the highest importance to the U.S.S.R. and suffered absolutely no consequences. One such instance took place at a session of the Advisory Political Committee on November 23, 1978, in Moscow. At that session, the Romanian side refused to agree to a resolution containing a general provision to the effect that the Supreme High Command of the U.S.S.R. Armed Forces was acknowledged to be the sole high command of Warsaw Pact forces in time of war. When loyal allies of the U.S.S.R. began to attack Romania because of this, President Ceaușescu got up from the conference table and, with the entire Romanian delegation, left Moscow. Soviet pressures on Romania continued throughout 1979, but in the end Moscow had to give in. President Ceaușescu wants to be a loyal ally of the Soviet Union without being its vassal. His country did not participate in the invasion of Czechoslovakia and, as I noted earlier, it did not sign any agreements placing in doubt the sovereign status of Romania.

The situation of General Jaruzelski, who had in the past provided active support to the Soviet Union in its invasion of Czechoslovakia, thus acknowledging de facto the right of the Warsaw Pact to interfere in the internal affairs of its member countries, and who has caused Poland's defense capability to be so greatly contingent on the Soviet Union, is totally different, and therefore it is difficult for me to imagine circumstances in which, even if he wanted it very much, he could say a resolute no to the Russians.

As is known, there are people in Poland and abroad who view General Jaruzelski as a kind of hero, who, out of patriotic considerations, saved the country from a catastrophe. How do you view it?

My view has been consistently that in Poland there existed a real chance to avoid both Soviet intervention and martial law. At the onset of the crisis, General Jaruzelski was not the top figure in the government. Nevertheless, from August 1980 on his voice had the greatest weight. Had he, together with Stanislaw Kania, proved capable of greater dignity and strength, had they honestly adhered to the existing social agreements, instead of knuckling under to Moscow, present-day Poland would undoubtedly look completely different.

(April 1987)

Czeslaw Milosz

ABOUT OUR EUROPE

I ASSUME there is such a thing as Central Europe, even though many people deny its existence, beginning with statesmen and journalists who persist in calling it "Eastern Europe" and ending with my friend Joseph Brodsky, who prefers to reserve for it the name of "Western Asia." In these decades of the twentieth century, Central Europe seems to exist only in the minds of some of its intellectuals. Yet the past of that area—a common past in spite of the multitude of languages and nationalities—is always present there and is made very real by the architecture of its cities, the traditions of its universities, and the works of its poets. Neither is the present deprived of signs indicating a basic unity underlying diversity. When reflecting on literary works written now in Czech or Polish, Hungarian or Estonian, Lithuanian or Serbo-Croatian, I perceive a tone and a sensibility not to be found elsewhere, in West European, American, or Russian writings.

I have assigned myself an ungrateful task: the attempt to define specific Central European attitudes. The task is ungrateful since, in an attempt of this kind, we do not have at our disposal precise instruments of analysis and must therefore accept in advance a certain unsolicited vagueness.

Central Europe is hardly a geographical notion. It is not easy to trace its boundaries on the map even if, while walking the streets of its cities, we do not doubt of its survival, whether that be in my baroque Wilno, or in the differently baroque Prague or the medieval-Renaissance Dubrovnik. The ways of feeling and thinking of its inhabitants must thus suffice for drawing mental lines which seem to be more durable than the borders of the states.

The most striking feature in Central European literature is its awareness of history, both as the past and as the present. It seems to underlie the treatment of various subjects, not necessarily themselves historical, and can be detected in love poems or novels dealing with love imbroglios. Personae and characters who appear in these works live in a kind of time which is modulated in a different way than is the time of their Western counterparts. Events of the political decade in which the characters live, of decades which formed and marked them, but also those of their parents' lifetime, constantly lurk in the background and add a dimension rarely met with in Western works. In the latter, time is neutral, colorless, weightless; it flows without zigzags, sudden curves, and waterfalls. In the former, time is intense, spasmodic, full of surprises; indeed, practically an active participant in the story. This is because time is associated with a danger that threatens the existence of a national community to which the writer belongs. I suspect that the historical imagination always comes from the collective memory and from a sense of menace. In this respect there is an affinity between Central European and Jewish literature. Nations in that part of Europe, despite the fact that some of them have lived through times of prosperity and glory, have spent long periods under foreign domination, threatened with the loss of their national identity, oppressed by the enemy, whether by the Turks, the Austrians, the Germans, or the Russians. The defeat of Germany in the First World War and the disintegration of the Hapsburg and the czarist empires were followed by the appearance of two names symbolic of any potential federalist tendencies in the future: Czechoslovakia, consisting of the Czechs and the Slovaks, and Yugoslavia, consisting of the southern Slavs. After a short breathing spell, the Russo–German pact of 1939 put an end to the hopes of national independence in that area, while the Second World War resulted in the return to the oppressive situation of the preceding century—the

Soviet empire taking over from the defunct big monarchic powers.

A sad history. Yet it is far from certain that the bigness and might of states are accompanied by fertility in science, arts, and letters. Examples to the contrary abound and it is possible that incredible tangles and mazes of political circumstances are necessary to incite the human spirit, if only to liberate itself from them and to manifest its sovereignty. Anybody who speaks of Central Europe may be reproached with bringing back the phantom of Mitteleuropa, as that whole region must anyway belong either to the Russian or the German sphere of influence. My answer is that, should this remain true forever, the Molotov–Ribbentrop Pact of 1939, which divided territories, has to be regarded as epochmaking, indeed. I recognize, though, that my Europe, the domain of acute nationalism, both resisting external control and turning against one another, may be dismissed for that reason as a potential troublemaker to be kept in check by a guardian—the Soviet empire. If not for Moscow's rule, goes the argument, the nationalities of the area would be at one another's throats. One need look only at the Hungarian–Romanian, Slovak–Hungarian, Polish–Ukrainian, Polish–Lithuanian quarrels. Here I touch upon a problem too complex to be dealt with in a short essay. In any case, I see sufficient reasons to believe that the most energetic minds in those countries successfully resist the temptations of national chauvinism and represent a considerable force working for the unification of Central Europe. At least, they share a perception of its common destinies and of peculiar traits that make it different from its big neighbors, West and East.

Humiliated national pride usually gives rise to delusions, to self-pity, and to mythologies. Observing that, a Central European writer receives training in irony. The very condition of being a Pole or a Czech or a Hungarian becomes an object of his irony, which colors his approach to life. Thus, the brave soldier Svejk, who repeats the pattern of the slave Aesop and his master, acquires a durable significance. Irony finds nourishment in the present international setup, which is an offense to reason. In an era of anti-colonialism, at the very moment the British Empire and the French Empire were crumbling, independent states of half of Europe were converted into colonial satrapies controlled from outside. Those satrapies send their delegates to the United Nations—more correctly, not united nations, but disunited governments. The basic fact is the border of the empire and the garrisons of its army, while the mentality of the masters is felt by the subdued populations as alien, nearly incomprehensible, and barbaric. Russian self-admiration—more than that, self-worship —goes beyond the habitually expected range of national vanity and bears the mark of a nineteenth-century messianism which in that part of the world left no good memories. Similarly, Russian contemporary art and literature, obstinately clinging to clichés, frozen by censorship, seems sterile and unattractive. Yet innumerable soldier Svejks in their dealing with Russians must pretend their reverence and gratitude for Big Brother.

There is, of course, Marxism. The decades of communist rule have radically transformed the whole area by lifting social barriers, urbanizing the populations, and creating a mass society. The process paralleled transformations that occurred in Western Europe owing to technological progress. There they exemplified the general egalitarian tendency of our era. However, what happened in the process of the communist takeover in my part of Europe may be compared to the fairy tale of liberating a genie from a bottle. No longer peasants, who were rather indifferent to national heritage, the industrial workers appear as harbingers of both national and libertarian aspirations. For example, the Solidarity movement in Poland typically combines social unrest and national resentment of foreign rule. A forceful and enforced leap carried those countries in a few decades far from what they were before the Second World War, with resulting new conflicts and new pains.

Now, let us imagine a Central European intellectual in his confrontation with the world at large, with his colleagues from Western Europe, America, or Latin America. As long as he keeps silence or, if he talks, spares the sensibilities of his interlocutors, everything is fine. As soon as he begins to talk frankly, he has the impression that he is regarded as a monster of irony and cynicism. That rift is certainly one of the strangest phenomena to be observed today, and its thorough elucidation would probably lead us to the core of modern man's predicament. The clue is undoubtedly our intellectual's position on Marxism. He perceives a certain aura around that term, a kind of awe and veneration even among people who are far from any political commitment. He himself does not claim to be a Marxist or an anti-Marxist; he just shrugs and smiles, for he knows too much. There are, in his opinion, certain demonic subjects which must be approached warily, as many hidden traps and temptations wait there for the imprudent. Marxism appeals to the noble impulses in man, and thence its force of seduction. It is impossible to communicate the truth about it to anybody who has not seen it at work. However, its product, the totalitarian-bureaucratic state, monopolizing all political and economic power, was prophetically described by a Central European writer, Franz Kafka. Direct experience is responsible for the fact that the most thorough survey of Marxist philosophy ever written comes from the pen of another Central European, Leszek Kolakowski. The adjective "demonic" applied to Marxism is not an exaggeration. First of all, the number of people killed and tortured to death in its name surpasses many times the total number of victims of Hitler's National Socialism. Second, a doctrine promising "the withering of the state" has led to the emergence of an all-powerful state and its omnipotent police. Third, instead of the end of the oppression of man by man and of alienation, a realm of nearly absolute alienation came into being, where the individual does not belong to himself, both literally and figuratively.

And yet a confrontation of my intellectual with his Western counterparts is made even more intricate by the durable influence of this system on his way of thinking. Lifeless and petrified, the Marxist doctrine receives in his countries no more than lip service as a tribute, but some of its practical results are tangible. In the first place, great numbers of people have been liberated from the curse of Adam; namely, work. If, as the Polish saying goes, "the state pretends that it pays us, we pretend that we work," we can speak of a reversal of the capitalist conditions; namely, the economic fear, fear of unemployment, to a large extent disappears, while work time is used for parallel activities, for securing goods and money through private deals, standing in line, etc. This does not apply perhaps to heavy industry, but masses of white-collar workers, often half literate, confirm the pattern, no less than peasants, whether they are collectivized or not, with their private sector of the economy. A habit has been formed regarding the role of the only employer, the state. It is supposed to provide a minimum of subsistence for everybody and is held responsible for empty shelves in its stores. Fear is thus shifted from the sphere of the economy to the sphere of political surveillance. Immigrants to Western countries from the Soviet bloc have great difficulty in comprehending the principles of the self-reliance of the individual, which implies misery, homelessness, or starvation as penalty for failure. All this cannot remain without impact upon the mind of the Central European intellectual. When looking for Western interlocutors open to his views, he notices that only the conservatives take his horror of political oppression and his defense of freedom seriously. The liberals seem to close their ears, for their true passion is breast-beating and a hatred of the capitalist system. Yet the character I discuss cannot be an ally of the conservatives, except perhaps in foreign policy, as he takes for granted that the welfare state fulfills the human need of decency and minimal security. He understands the dilemmas involved in relying on the state and its plethora of bureaucrats but feels they can be resolved without renouncing the free decisions of the individual.

If his thinking appears bizarre to Westerners, it is, I suspect, because of a shade of Hegelianism which has become nearly instinctive with him. He reasons in terms of the movement of history and the life of ideas whose ascendance or decay indicates the direction that will be taken by human societies. The fascination exerted for several decades by Marx upon most creative artists and thinkers testified, in his opinion, to the vigor of the revolutionary trend. But now Marxism has been abandoned at the top, by the elite, both in the East and in the West, while it attracts lower-level minds and spreads among people just emerging from illiteracy. A similar descent from the top down to the layer of everyday myths characterizes the thought of Freud. What, then, is the prognosis? Probably this: the nineteenth-century notion of what is "scientific" has to run its course. Marx wanted to dedicate Das Kapital to Darwin, and though Darwin declined the offer, a link between various scientific or pseudo-scientific theories of evolution is obvious. Since modern man is brought up in the spirit of nineteenth-century science, Marxism still has a large appeal, though it is withering gradually from the top, where its coherence as a philosophy has been found wanting. Exaggerating a little, I would say that my intellectual from Central Europe is inclined to divide people, wherever he meets them, into three categories: proto-Marxists, Marxists, and post-Marxists, to such an extent as he is serious about ideas—forces incarnated as the main philosophical currents of his time.

Is his world apocalyptic? Not in the sense that the minds of many writers in the West are. It looks as if he has rejected meditation on the possible effects of nuclear war as futile and has moved the very possibility of war into the realm of the absurd joke, to a story about a peasant wedding where drunken guests start to fight, using not knives but atomic weapons, or about an intercontinental missile placed by the authorities on somebody's private balcony. But dark visions of the future in a different and perhaps deeper sense seem to be a specialty of Central European writers. Let us not forget that the word "robot," now internationally accepted, was introduced by Karel Čapek and that Stanislaw Witkiewicz's novels and play of anticipation proved to be prophetic. He had already described, before Orwell, totalitarian rule by the Party of Levellers and the predicament of artists controlled by what he called the Ministry of Mechanization of Culture. The future in such works is envisaged in the function of internal disintegration of the bourgeois society which is too weak to present an effective resistance to the Levellers, who would seize power and liquidate their opponents. Here we have the main component of criticism addressed by my Central European to the West, parallel but not identical with anti-Western propaganda conducted day and night by the Levellers; i.e., by the Communist Parties. That propaganda speaks of the decadence of capitalism as opposed to the health of the so-called socialist societies. However, one has no need to be a very perspicacious observer to notice that the word "decadence" may be applied to both sides, if, and this I assume to be correct, it means undermining the notion of good and evil. Complete relativization of good and evil, by making them dependent upon social criteria of a given historical moment, is a major event in the history of the European mind, and in this respect Nietzsche, who foretold "European nihilism," was no less apocalyptic than Dostoevsky, who, in *The Possessed*, outlined the essential features of the Russian Revolution. And the refusal to see the loss of the metaphysical foundation as a great tragedy characterizes people today, just as it was foreseen by Nietzsche. Man loses, however, his subterfuges, which allow him to escape the issue, when he is confronted by the totalitarian state. Scorned by the rulers and no longer protected by the Ten Commandments, a victim, one of expendable millions, discovers, so to say empirically, the unmistakable line separating good from evil. In the geographical longitude I deal with, the experience of Nazism sufficed to prove that one could not relativize the basic values and compromise on them without becoming guilty of connivance with criminals. Yet— and here I return to my question as to the apocalyptic frame of mind in Central Europe—things ceased to be so simple with the advent of communist rule. A long-range program aimed at gradual absorbtion of society by the state means that all clear-cut differences are obliterated and it is difficult to distinguish between baseness and integrity, lie and truth. Everybody is tainted and everybody is a victim. Orwell's *Nineteen Eighty-Four* astonishes by its accuracy, even if he pushes his negative appraisal of the proles' ability to think too far and does not take into account private economic endeavors, that margin without which the system could not survive. All in all, however, an observer of the system is no more optimistic than was Orwell. According to him, it is not impossible that a totalitarian state is a logical outcome of the spiritual deprivation of modern man, a kind of punishment, as in the biblical story of Babel. If such is the case, the future of the planet is gloomy indeed.

But another peculiarity of the human type I describe battles against those depressing predictions. Anybody familiar with the history of the Czechs, the Hungarians, or the Poles knows that certain codes of behavior mandatory for the intelligentsia go back several centuries. A civic commitment, a pursuit of a dream as to what the political and social life of a country should be, animated socioreligious movements of the Czech Hussites, of the Polish Socinians, produced voluminous utopian works on the ideal Christian state, such as Andrzej Frycz Modrzewski's *On the Improvement of the Republic* of 1543, and are visible in the pedagogical, scholarly, and theatrical activity of Commenius. Undoubtedly libertarian and directed against the supremacy both of the Church and of the state, those trends were precursors of a great romantic and democratic élan of the end of the eighteenth century and the first decades of the nineteenth century, a specific confluence of sober Enlightenment ideas and of a Schillerian enthusiasm. All this is far from being forgotten and gives to Central European writings a tinge of nostalgia, of utopianism, and of hope.

There is no reasonable basis for hoping that the present international setup will be changed in the foreseeable future. After the Napoleonic Wars the big powers divided the spoils among themselves at the Congress of Vienna, and the established order lasted, with some modifications, for a hundred years, till 1914. The long struggle of revolutionaries against the villainy of the allied monarchs did not prevent the repetition of this pattern at Yalta. From Moscow's perspective, the newly acquired area is a property to be gradually assimilated and Sovietized, though, until now, their program has to a large extent failed, as the events of 1956 in Hungary, of 1968 in Czechoslovakia, and of the 1980s in Poland indicate. Yet the Russian tanks are there to stay and to teach a lesson. In such circumstances, let me boldly state that the humanistic imagination should be separated from and even opposed to the political imagination, for dealing with probabilities, including that of the survival of the planet, with strategy, with evolutionary trends, etc., is quite a debilitating occupation for a person engaged in the humanities. As to myself (now it is clear that I am also drawing a portrait of myself), I think that Central Europe is an act of faith, a project, let us say even a utopia, but my reasons for adopting it are quite realistic. As numerous Centers for Russian and Eastern European Studies demonstrate, a division of Europe into West and East is accepted by American universities. That acceptance can be objected to on the ground that it confuses a political borderline with cultural borderlines of the past. Those who object advance the argument that a cultural division of Europe into two halves has been for centuries identical with the division into the realms of Rome and Byzantium, and, thus, the Latin language of the Church and of Roman law determined the Eastern borders of the West. Behind that argument we can detect the complaint of nations proud of belonging to Western culture and now Easternized by force. There is a validity in that complaint. And yet let us confront the facts and say that neither had the old religious frontier between Catholicism and Orthodoxy been a very precise indicator, nor were these countries, situated between Germany and Russia, pure-bred Western. Ideas from abroad penetrating these lands, diluted and transformed, acquired a specific quality, local habits were persistent, institutions took forms unheard of in the Western part of Europe, which could only wonder at Hussitism in the late Middle Ages, at a bizarre parliamentary system in Renaissance Poland, or at the "paradise for heretics" (*paradisum hereticorum*) in Poland and Transylvania, to give just a few examples. And even today the average person in France or America is unable to say what the Uniate or Greco-Catholic Church is. Moreover, snobbery and love of things Western notwithstanding, we, from those mostly agricultural marshes, had many axes to grind in our encounters with Western mercantile and manufacturing societies. The present ambiguous attitude toward the capitalist West is nothing new. A hygienic reason behind our choosing the term Central Europe is that it authorizes us to look for the specificity of its culture and protects us from the temptation of misleading analogies. A curious phenomenon could be observed in European literature and the art of the last decades: the Iron Curtain and the differences of two political systems only in part stopped the circulation of ideas and fashions in spite of all the efforts hermetically to close the borders and to impose Russian models. In poetry, in painting, and in the theater, Warsaw, Prague, and Budapest have been more similar to Paris, Amsterdam, and London than to Moscow. And yet it would be rather unproductive to search in Central Europe for echoes of Western Surrealism, Existentialism, Structuralism, or the Theater of the Absurd. If there are influences, they are transposed, often changed into their opposites, under the impact of a unique collective experience. I am inclined to agree with Milan Kundera when he says that at present there is more energy and vigor in the literature of our Europe than in its Western variety.

Another aspect of cultural interchange can be highlighted by the idea of Central Europe, and that is the place of Russian art and literature in the cosmopolitan years before the Revolution, at the time Russian writers and artists took part in the European movements of Modernism and Symbolism. A study of Symbolism may provide interesting examples, for Russian Symbolism did not resemble French Symbolism, but, on the other hand, Polish Symbolism (forgive my referring so often to my own yard) was not like the Russian variety, as the odd theatrical works or plays of Stanislaw Wyspianski or the paintings of Jacek Malczewski so clearly demonstrate. A study of diverging paths within the common trend would be useful for the future, when Russian art and literature again recover their spontaneity.

I do not regard my speaking of Central Europe as just an expression of regret that things are as they are. Much can be done, in literary and art scholarship, in criticism and intellectual history. By delineating how we all who speak the languages within our pale are akin, by making a long overdue comparative investigation of our patrimony, we can help avert national conflicts, even if the day of one or another kind of Central European federation is distant.

(April 1986)
Translated by the author

II
What We Think

Leopold Tyrmand

THE HAIR STYLES OF MIECZYSLAW RAKOWSKI

> *I no longer believe that the revolution should sit in judgment on the world. I believe only in the revolution which transforms us.*
> −Henri de Man, *The Psychology of Socialism*

AND QUITE right, too. However, I shall use de Man's proposition in a sense different from the one in which he intended it. The verb "to transform" de Man uses in its positive and directional sense, as if to say: "Let us, instead of making revolution, transform ourselves, become better people." Fine, but isn't it more interesting to consider how a successful revolution transforms us all, different people that we are? Were I determined to seek out finer details, I might easily run the risk of producing truisms. I propose instead to let the brilliant plurality of metamorphoses, their richness and diversity, spread themselves before us in a startling array like an Op Art painting. This way we shall have no difficulty in avoiding vulgarizations.

I introduce Mieczyslaw Rakowski with a feeling of emotional neutrality. Life has never brought us close to one another. He has always greeted me politely, if without interest, as I have him. What we knew about each other and what we thought has remained unchanged over the years. We were ideological enemies, but there was no hatred between us. I even regarded him with a certain degree of pleasure, despite the general sense of revulsion I felt. There was something vaguely amusing about him which confirmed my more general assumptions, and it is always agreeable to be proved right.

In 1958 the International Press Club asked me to take part in a public discussion of my article in *Tygodnik Powszechny* in which I had suggested that a revision of our concepts of postwar Germany was necessary—the first time this had been attempted in Poland since the end of the war. It provoked a wave of indignant slogans from the communist press, as well as insults from émigré Poles, and *Tygodnik* skillfully dissociated itself from me. I accepted the invitation with the masochistic pleasure of a suicide who becomes ecstatic at the thought of being publicly torn to pieces. In the event, it wasn't quite as bad as that. True, the nationalist-communist coalition sank its teeth into me, but the university students and other youngish people responded with a remarkably pragmatic approach and applauded loudly my most provocative excursions. Rakowski was in the chair, and one had to admit that he performed his duty with the forced but obvious neutrality of a referee who desperately wants his own eleven to win but never for a moment forgets his position as umpire.

Some years later I suggested to Rakowski that he should print the first part of my unpublished novel. It was a tactical move: the publication of my novel in his journal *Polityka* would be a surrealist event and neither of us took the possibility seriously. In my battle for a passport and for the publication of my book, I wanted to be able to say: "*Polityka* is considering publishing a novel of mine." This throw-away remark, skillfully dropped in various offices in the course of various conversations, made a certain impression. Sometime later, Rakowski telephoned and returned my typescript (which he certainly had not read) and we parted with great affability, smiles and *bonhomie* all around. We both understood very well what the game was about. The fact was that Rakowski had also scored a few points in his own game—at that time he was immensely keen to appear as liberal an editor as possible who gave due consideration to every manuscript on its merits. So, even if in his opinion I was too extreme even for a liberal editor, he could not refuse to have a look at my typescript; for then I would have gone around Warsaw with new evidence of persecution, this time from *Polityka*.

Rakowski is a syndrome, like Kott, Comrade Blatmanowa, and Mr. Bolo, about whom more later. You may ask why, when attacking other syndromes, I consider Rakowski with a degree of neutrality. The answer isn't simple. Although they represent a dangerously prolific species, Kott, Comrade Blatmanowa, and Mr. Bolo are just nauseating. Rakowski is a more complex phenomenon. Of course, one could make him into a convenient stereotype, but to what end? Individualization and incarnation better convey the horrors of the transformations which de Man was not himself able to know.

The history of the hair styles of Mieczyslaw Rakowski is the history of victorious Polish communism. Rakowski's social credentials are of the best: he is the son of a Pomeranian peasant. At the beginning, the communists loved nothing so much as authentic peasant progeny; in anticipation, they had prepared little verses about the Slavonic and truly Aryan sons of the soil, who fought bravely against the deluge of German imperialism, in poverty but unswervingly. The product was consequently healthy, well built, fair-haired, and fetching. When I first saw Rakowski, he had on his head what one might call a shock, an enormous crop of blond curls, a veritable thatch of hair. The result was undistinguished, or so it seemed at first, but in fact it was a carefully studied exercise in style. This was the heyday of Stalinism, and Rakowski, together with a pal of his, a certain Wysznacki (later editor of *Stolica*), was apprenticed to learn the trade of communist executioner of the printed word, under the then famous butcher Stefan Staszewski, head of the press section of the Central Committee, and later a rebel. I had been told about Staszewski many years before by Immanuel Birnbaum, of *Süddeutsche Zeitung*, the doyen of European wit. He once remarked, when we were both living in the Warsaw YMCA among the Christian youth: "Staszewski? Take care! A blond Jew—it goes against nature—you can never tell what he'll do next . . ." In the light of the October 1956 events, this proved prophetic. At the time of which I am speaking, Staszewski had not yet become a nonconformist rebel, but was a stooge, while Rakowski called himself an instructor in the press section of the Party's Central Committee— a title whose significance was lost in the maze of communist euphemisms. His appearance was stylized, with discernment and precision: an effect of unobtrusive "ruralness" was achieved by means of the hair style and clothes, while the face was designed to radiate the intellectual ardor of a nascent class- and Party-consciousness. Much, sometimes a career, depended on the adroit use of such devices— Rakowski hit upon the right solution. His hair was flaxen, curly yet wiry, bouffant in effect, and it never failed to produce a feeling of solidarity in those with new positions in the Party and the government, whose birth certificates were to be found in the registries of the smaller towns of the Republic. He dressed neatly, although he wore shapeless anoraks and overcoats, with padded shoulders, which came down to his ankles. Never a tie. From a distance, his appearance was no different from that of the village youth, who looks the same whether in the volunteer militia, a cooperative society, at a Service to Poland meeting in the village hall, in the Corpus Christi procession, or at a village dance, always associated in one's mind with canoes on the Vistula sands, smoked bacon, Double-Double beer, and the slushy tune they play under the paper lanterns which hang among the posters extolling Stakhanovite workers. At that time, the young were thought to personify the beauty of the socialist body; they were much relied upon. It was they who were to Polonize the Russian–Jewish, intelligentsia-ridden Party cadre, and bring it closer to the populist image. The cadre, just then, was engaged in laying the foundations of the system amid dialectical traps. The less gifted among them went into the army and joined the security police as officers; the brighter ones were made to learn about materialism and the theory of surplus value, with much sweating of brow and grinding of teeth. It was very much in vogue to stress the importance of the psycho-physical traits of country bumpkins in the development of the intellect, of culture, and of the new Poland. Nevertheless, a certain smile played over the peasant-fresh lips of Instructor Rakowski, unobtrusively supported by a steely glance, from which it seemed that the instructor knew all too well the theory of the intensification of the class struggle with the progress of socialism. Iosif Vissarionovich could rest assured that the peasant masses of Polish Pomerania would do all that was necessary to raise themselves higher according to dialectical precepts.

At the time of the debate in the International Press Club, Rakowski's hair was shorter but still flaxen, like a golden fleece, and crew-cut so as not to put off the new administration with an excess of dandyism. He was now wearing a double-breasted, off-the-rack suit bought from a big department store, and a tie. He laughed a lot, mostly at the more radical attacks on official policy. He was most charming and carefully avoided causing me any embarrassment. Despite the surface ease, one could detect an underlying anxiety. It grew from years of failure and turned into the pliability of one who realized early on that a different approach was needed now. He, and others like him, still dressed modestly and with sobriety, but now with a socialist urbanity which somehow protected them from shafts of irony, and made it possible for them to laugh at things to which five years earlier they would have taken a gun. In the extreme complexity of the situation, Comrade Rakowski managed to demonstrate, with grace and to the best of his abilities, something which was difficult to grasp but which it was essential to understand in order to survive. And, moreover, he did this more adroitly and with more tact than most. At that time, of course, it was the editor of *Polityka* and the future chairman of the Polish Journalists' Association that I had the pleasure of meeting.

A historical sketch from memory: When Gomulka came to power, he immediately ordered a retreat from liberalism. But he did it so quietly that only the cleverest noticed it. The less clever, with their ears still buzzing with the music of jazz festivals, failed to notice it (some are still vegetating at a table shared with Janusz Minkiewicz in the Actors' Club; others are enjoying great respect in the town of Lomza, where they now hold an extremely useful position in the local library). Rakowski picked up the directive instantly; he has an extraordinarily sensitive ear. It is by no means out of the question, however, that Gomulka himself whistled the new tune to him from close at hand, since at that time, it was said, they were on closer terms than is usual even within a family. I do not know all the details of the steps in Rakowski's career, but the fact is that immediately after October 1956 he found himself in the limelight and at the hub of national politics. Everyone drew attention to the intimacy between the new Boss and the press instructor of the Bierut era. As I said, I don't know for sure how it came about, but I do know that the new job fitted Rakowski to a T.

A very special periodical was needed. And a very special formula to justify the ideological-political swindle which had stripped the Poles of what they thought they had won. It had to be done delicately, with great finesse and with due regard to the latest achievements, in a style which in no way recalled the prehistoric primitivism of a Jakub Berman. This journal would have to forge a new path of novel concepts; it would have to become a super-laundry for old wangles and tricks which have failed so many times in the course of the revolutionary "unfolding" and the building of socialism, and which have still to be constantly cleaned, turned, dyed, and used anew. Who would be able to think up a new version of the old tricks? That was the message, and the prize would be sizable. *Trybuna Literacka* was already in existence; this was a Sunday supplement to *Trybuna Ludu*, in which Putrament, Zukrowski, and a few others busied themselves trying to salvage Things Eternal and Things of Value from the previous era, as if anything other than their own salaries were worth salvaging. The one genuine journal, *Po Prostu*, had been abolished: the only true agent of change and focus of effort to develop something worthwhile in Polish socialist thought since the days of Rosa Luxemburg. The bankrupt stock was there for the taking; all that was needed was a receiver. But why Rakowski? What were his qualifications, his merits, his abilities? Again I must plead ignorance. I know him only by his fruits. He was given quite a base of operations: *Trybuna Literacka* was merged with *Trybuna Wolnosci*, the theoretical organ of the Central Committee of the Polish Communist Party, with a circulation well into the six-figure bracket and much appreciated by the private sector, whose shopkeepers considered its paper ideal for wrapping pickled herring. Apparently no one found another use for it during the twenty years of its existence. Another paper which was incorporated in the merger was a periodical with the somewhat megalomaniac title *Swiat i Polska* (*The World and Poland*), known to have been read exclusively by the editor, the proofreader, and their respective families. The resulting amalgam was accommodated in great comfort in a building which survived the war because the Germans had used its walls as a backdrop against which to shoot Poles, lined up in rows. It took the name *Polityka*.

I do not intend to write a critical analysis or study of *Polityka*. I have not the time, qualifications, or, above all, interest. But I do know, instinctively and for practical purposes, what *Polityka* is. First, it is an attempt at theft which did not come off. It was intended to steal the position of *Po Prostu* and it failed to do so. Nonetheless, it is not an imitation. It carved out its own image, distinctive if not very pretty. Its original purpose was to rescind the ideas of the Polish October, a program terrifying in its simplicity. The Poles, according to this program, had achieved *politically* everything it was possible to achieve; to have gone further would have meant abandoning socialism and that could not have been allowed, not only because the Russians might feel hurt, but because of the incontrovertible fact that socialism was axiomatically a good thing per se. Not yet perfect, of course. Therefore we must improve it. But the theory is okay, to be subjected neither to revision nor to improvement. Practice is another matter, and the main accomplishment of October, which itself was an Enormous and Splendid Achievement, was that we will now be able to discuss it. To discuss, but not necessarily to change. The social model was also okay, there was no question of change there. But in places the implementation was not quite up to the mark, and in such cases we will send our reporters to write extensive reports. The economic model was also okay and correct, but, here and there, there were certain faulty details of implementation which we will bring out into the open and analyze. Our foreign policy was correct, we were on the right side and we will look among our brothers for those whose sentiments were closest to ours, be it even Togliatti, for what he said was true and beautiful, even if it is impracticable from our point of view. We were deeply concerned about social injustice and would expose it without fail. We will pinpoint corruption, dogmatism, nepotism, abuse of authority, stupidity, selfishness, and mutual back-scratching, all of which were covered up in the previous period for the sake of a falsely conceived *raison d'état*. Socialism is openness, light, thought, rationalization, science, sociology, public-opinion polls, modernity, and the inviolably *correct principles* of social existence. From time to time and here and there, these principles have been broken by weak, inadequate, and narrow-minded people, sometimes through lack of understanding and sometimes out of malice. There were occasions when this happened as a result of the complicated interplay of social interdependence and class-conditioning, but the complexity and the mysterious impenetrability of such situations were bound to yield to the rays of the only modern scientific and progressive ideology known to man. That was how, by the circuitous route of the October revelation and enlightened absolutism, *Polityka* returned to the obscurantist intellectual hotchpotch in which, as experience has shown us, it was impossible to build for the future or even to breathe. However, anyone who has lived through the past twenty years, from the village simpleton to Professor Infeld, has it ingrained on his mind once and for all that:

It is the *system* that is bad and rotten, the people who live under it become corrupt, it contaminates anyone within its orbit, while the untainted are condemned to be crushed and go under.

Communism equals humanity deceived. All that generations of dreamers, ideologists, and writers proclaimed about it (before it acquired its earthly form) amounted to the abuse of public confidence. They said, poor innocents:

1. That it would be based on truth. It brought about a sanctification of lies on a scale never known before.

2. That it would be based on justice. It became a gigantic incubator of large and small injustices.

3. That it would bring true freedom. It brought about the best-organized slavery in every walk of life and every social institution to a degree unknown in the tyrannies of old.

4. That it would ennoble man, who would be free from exploitation. It degraded man, placed him under the power of stupidity, cupidity, and the basest of instincts; it led him to destroy others in the most sophisticated way yet invented.

None of these are, however, problems with which *Polityka* would concern itself, even by way of the most recondite allusion. Socialism is a sacred cow; it is not to be eaten. But one must eat to live. Therefore, everyone under the Red Star has to rely on contrivance of some sort in order to survive. As these things go, *Polityka's* contrivance was simple: substitute a mock problem for a genuine one, or a pseudo-solution where no real one was acceptable, and you're off. As with Orwell, everyone is equal, some more than others, so with matters of concern, "objective" concern being superior to all others. *Polityka's* "objective" concerns were wide-ranging: Poland and socialism and the human condition and distribution and hooliganism, traffic regulations and midwives and the quantum theory and the quality of lubricants and the health service and some unknown aspects of Pilsudski's rule. "Objective" concern meant that *Polityka* was not to be concerned with *Ding an Sich* (that would be subjectivism at its worst), only with its place in Gomulka's communism. Viewed from the perspective of fifty years of Leninist–Stalinist communism, it represented a kind of achievement: the cult of the individual and the dogmatism of the past disallowed all such concerns en bloc on the premise that all was for the best in the best of all countries. The simplest empiricism indicates, of course, that morally and socially *Polityka's* kind of concern amounts to one Great Big Nothing, in the words of Winnie-the-Pooh. The men of *Polityka* will read these words with bitter resentment: they alone know how many of their initiatives were stopped, how they had to fight for every word, and how difficult it was to achieve even that which someone like myself ("bastard") can so easily squash, besmear, and make into a mockery. The trouble with their superhuman efforts and their bitterness remains the same: they amount to precisely nothing. They have no moral or social significance. It is an essential quality of communism that everyone struggles, panting for breath, with someone more stupid and more vile than himself, but the very universality of the struggle does not make it of value in itself. It is only its direction and quality that place it in some hierarchy of values and meaning. *Polityka* displays positive concern (already emancipated from the constraints of Socialist Realism) for the man-in-the-street, the gray cooperative, the average machine tool, and the post-October mill girl, a girl who uses Lechia cosmetics and Przemyslawka eau de cologne, a girl who "poses" a problem—is she, in fact, correctly fulfilled sexually and technologically? This pseudo-factual, pseudo-social, pseudo-responsible substitute for involvement in reality led to *Polityka* becoming the favorite reading matter and the mini-Bible of Mr. Bolo. But *Polityka* dreamed of fulfilling another role: it wanted to be the forum and the font of wisdom for the Gomulka-style progressive intelligentsia, the technological new class, and the neo-positivists of the petrochemical industry.

Mr. Bolo presents quite a problem: it is difficult to produce a Bolo synthetic portrait, if only because he comes from such a range of social backgrounds. In the early days of our People's Democracy he walked around in a cashmere overcoat, was scented with lavender, and tended to be involved in Silesian or Cracovian private enterprise. The private-enterprise band is, of course, the most heroic social group in Poland; its superhuman struggle with communism, bureaucracy, and the exterminating effect of the tax system surpasses the Greek myths, the battle of sailors with the elements, the pioneers' efforts to combat the cruelty of desert and forest. Such a proud and admirable stance in the war with Public Enemy No. 1 should, should it not, assure the private entrepreneurs of the love and respect of the rest of society. Not a bit of it! Someday soon I intend to devote more time and attention to the problem. Mr. Bolo must not, however, be identified with private enterprise alone: there are numerous Mr. Bolos among the ranks of doctors, lawyers, technicians, and civil servants, especially those engaged in foreign trade. The beaches of the Baltic and the Tatra resorts were once full of Mr. Bolos, but no longer: they now spend their holidays in other People's Democracies, or, quite simply, in Paris. Mr. Bolo never has any trouble obtaining a passport, foreign currency, or anything else one would need for these occasions. Since October 1956 Mr. Bolo has driven a Wartburg, then a Skoda, then a Fiat, and so on—no public-transport nightmares for Mr. B. Since the Polish October, Mr. Bolo has also changed his style of dress: his inspiration derives from Western films, now more widely available. Mr. Bolo changed to synthetics, nylon, Orlon, and, of course, to suede jackets.

I think Mr. Bolo must, in fact, be a son of August Bec-Walski from the 1940s cartoon, a stereotype of a reactionary, an ex-landowner and bigot; but he was flattened by the Stalinist steamroller and is now a thoroughly reformed and perfectly well-adapted individual. After October, Mr. Bolo became a kingpin in the so-called small stabilization. Ideologically and socially his background is socialist, and it follows that he is an anti-Semite by tradition, but his snobbery has overridden even his anti-Semitism and in his dreams he often sees himself walking arm-in-arm with [the Polish–Jewish writer] Adolf Rudnicki along a crowded resort promenade. In short, Mr. Bolo is a wheeler-dealer, one of those who couldn't care less and who knows nothing because he has no wish to know. He could not care less; he would get on just as well in Pilsudki's Poland as in a communist Australia. People of that type silently ducked down for a time during the [1939–45] war, for it was too risky a game and the price one might have had to pay was too high, but they rose to the surface again in excellent form under communism, and the species is flourishing in numerous varieties. Were one to tell them the truth about themselves, they would feel deeply hurt. They do not do any harm to anyone, they criticize things as much as anyone else, they tell political jokes and get on with everyone, don't they? And if they are friends with one or another notorious member of the apparat, does it matter? What's wrong with that? That's the way it always has been and always will be: the strong get to the top and the wise stick with them. I have been told that I myself infuriated one of the Bolo tribe by openly describing in a book my own stratagems when dealing with the bigwigs of the Security Services. Thus, I apparently "spoiled" the efforts and chances of others. How unethical. Humanism, freedom, and principles are all "bullshit" to Mr. Bolo, but even so he fails to see that crooked dealing is so much a permanent function of a totalitarian system that, even if I tried, I couldn't have spoiled any other "deals." On the weekends Mr. Bolo buys his *Przekroj* and his *Polityka*, slips them both into the door pocket of his new BMW, and drives off to Zalew, the newest spot. *Przekroj* makes him feel "in"; *Polityka* absolves him. Thanks to *Polityka*, Mr. Bolo feels politically involved, socially concerned. Thanks to Mr. Bolo, *Polityka*'s circulation swells.

It is the silent tragedy of *Polityka* that it sees itself as the organ of the descendants of Zeromski's self-sacrificing heroes (now armed with a television set and a motorbike). In reality, it is the organ of the Bolos of this world.

I suspect that the fundamental watershed in the life of Mieczyslaw Rakowski occurred in the early 1960s. As before, he responded instantly to a new variation on the theme of Polish communism. The time of conditioning and instrumentalism was over; we were entering the era of personalities. Everyday history was no longer to be governed by the iron laws of science, by the letter of the Leninist gospel, by the political textbooks, but by a series of trials of strength among the people in power. The personality of the Boss was always dominant, but others were now emerging. There was Kliszko, the Harlequin Confessor; Moczar, the small-town bully who managed to rise to the provincial level and then higher still; there was Cyrankiewicz, the old snooker player and cardsharp who had a way of marking the cards in such a manner that they still looked clean. There was Gierek, the King of Silesia, a specially guarded region, generally known as "Katanga." There were the momentary, short-lived successes of Zambrowski and Strzelecki, but the message was filtering through: in order to get anywhere, you had to be a somebody. This was the present rule of the game. Best of all, you should be someone in your own right, someone unique, an exceptional individual all around. The difficult part was hitting on the right sort of individual characteristics.

I saw Rakowski again, this time at the premiere of the student cabaret STS in Warsaw. The venue itself was significant: a favorite of Gomulka's in one of the few remaining shelters of the surviving revisionists, very much emasculated but still rather dicey. This was a completely new-style Rakowski, and the change seemed, frankly, fascinating to me. All in beige, enveloped in Western wools, suedes, leathers, and olive-toned shoes, the editor shone, distributing smiles, gracious glances, *bon mots*. Instant ripostes made him a full-fledged member of that particular milieu where baroque bitterness and razor-sharp conversation reigned. There was nothing of Mr. Bolo in all this. On the contrary, Rakowski represented Mr. Bolo's natural adversary: a swinging beatnik, a rock 'n' roller, a frustrated Existentialist with a penchant for the chic, and, with sufficient foreign currency, he modeled himself on the style of Saint-Germain de Près and the heroes of New Wave films. But the hair style, the hair style above all! It was the keynote of the whole effect, giving it an absolutely up-to-the-minute slant: the hair was cut short and combed forward at the front, not, however, in bangs, but in the newest French fashion introduced by Maurice Ronet. How impressive it was! I instantly understood the difficulties which had had to be overcome, and the strength of character required to overcome them in the process of straightening those curly ringlets of yore. But the clothes? The clothes! My God, how did he get hold of them? "Quite simple," said the girl I was with. "Through Wilkomirska, of course."

I don't know exactly when Rakowski married Wanda Wilkomirska. I do know, however, that the famous violinist really came into her own at the time I am referring to, when the uniqueness of personality acquired overall importance. The sobriety of village jerkins was left behind: playing the peasant and donning the appearance of a puritan in rustic clothing was now part of the dim and distant past; wealth and its appurtenances became the symbol of achievement. Now it was permitted to have one's own villa furnished with antiques, a small yacht on the lakes, and wallpaper from Hamburg—all this underlined the correctness of development. Obviously, in the circumstances, Wilkomirska was worth her weight in gold. I am told that she is a distinguished violinist, recognized on both sides of the Great Divide. This may well be the case, I know nothing about it, but I couldn't help noticing that no other musician went abroad quite so often, especially during the Stalinist era. It is no secret that Wilkomirska is from a well-known Party family and that from childhood she was the delight of various Komsomols. Under communism, as elsewhere, some are better than others, and a good violinist will be a *better* violinist for being the daughter of old communists, who made her first appearance on stage in a pretty red Pioneer's kerchief; just as under feudalism, a poet who was also a count was a *better* poet than a poet who was only a villein. The Party had molded her, she owed everything to the Party, the Party was proud of her. No wonder, then, that she was so often to be found on the lists of artists representing Polish art in the West, that it was easier for her to travel abroad, to buy a car in West Germany and bring it back into Poland without paying duty on it, to exchange it for another model when the fashion changed, and so on and so forth.

The Rakowski–Wilkomirska marriage seemed to me to throw a very interesting light on the mores of our time and constituted the successful attempt by an individual to become financially independent under communism, an attempt worthy of a character in a Balzac novel. It should be made clear that in the Warsaw of Comrade Rakowski, as much as in the Paris of Monsieur de Rastignac, political independence and freedom of maneuver, the ability to think for oneself and to commit acts of real and not-so-real nonconformism, are a direct function of financial independence and of being freed from the worries of tomorrow's bread-and-butter. And how all this helps in building up the personality! I'm inclined to think that, without the Wilkomirska investment, Rakowski would never have managed that astounding transformation into a *Przekroj* playboy, despite the fact that the sensational new hair style revealed certain attractive features which had been unnoticeable in the past. There he was, quite a lad, an open smile, strong manly features, a kind of Pomeranian Steve McQueen. It is a fact that middle-aged farmers and such-like, suitably emancipated and coiffed, always had a charm of their own, much sought after in the capitals of the world. Some circles in Poland simply adore having Gramsci read aloud to them by just such a product of *Przekroj*, and Rakowski, dressed to the nines, mastered the style to perfection. It is worth noting, just for the record, that in the past Rakowski the Central Committee instructor, Rakowski the editor, and Rakowski the chairman of the Journalists' Association, hated *Przekroj* and all it stood for, and was the first to demand that anyone who followed the *Przekroj* recipe for dress or coiffure be burned at the stake. What caused him to change so? Why such a turnaround? Was this change visceral in nature or cosmetic only?

In the mid-1960s, the situation (very much telescoped) looked something like this: Gomulka and Kliszko were out on a limb, Cyrankiewicz was still available, Ochab was in retirement, and around them bubbled molten magma from which the occasional cry could be heard: "Moczar!" "Gierek!" "the young secretaries!" This last was often interpreted as "Rakowski!," particularly among the Americans, who take with a childlike innocence to anything and everything they are told in Warsaw. The Americans evolved a theory. As the secretaries to the secretaries of the Central Committee were only taken on after thorough testing, and as it was possible to get a lot done with their help, it followed that they probably formed a definite political force, a potential partnership perhaps: the Young Turks, the Young Secretaries. Rakowski was therefore invited to America, where he spent a few months, was given the red-carpet treatment,

and was allowed to talk to President Kennedy. There is no end to
the naïveté of the Americans. It seems they are still living under the
spell of Scheherazade; it is difficult to imagine what they were hoping
to achieve with this visit. In any case, at the beginning they were
charmed by the swinging appearance and hair style number 3, and
swallowed politely the banal slogans about coexistence, which were
slightly adjusted for different audiences (be it the Department of
State or the American left). They got their just deserts when Rakowski,
on his return to Warsaw, published a book with the title *Multi-Story
America*, which he wrote in a style quite different from that which he
had adopted in his conversations in America. The book was essentially
a pack of lies, gross oversimplifications, and an insult to the reader's
intelligence. But it won't do any good to accuse Rakowski of writing
a bad and silly book: he was not, after all, a genuine writer or
journalist, but only a press instructor, an editor and chairman of the
Journalists' Association. However, the Americans will never learn
that it is not important what a political sponger says when he is in
America, that it is what he says at home that matters. They won't
learn, and that is why they may well lose the battle for the world.
Heaven help us if they do. The only beneficiary of the whole
expedition was, of course, Rakowski: his American grant and the bit
of globe-trotting created, in Warsaw and elsewhere, an aura of
tolerance and accessibility about him. And that was just what he was
after.

Social position, a Party post (Rakowski became a deputy member
of the Central Committee), financial security, exotic sex appeal, and
the fashionable appearance of a swinging Marxist are trump cards
in the formation of a personality with a view to a great career. But
there was still something missing, the mixture did not quite gel; the
format, the caliber were not quite there. There was, however, the
tried-and-tested technique: if not quite up to the job yourself, join
forces with others in the same position. Thus a triumvirate was born:
Starewicz, Zolkiewski, Rakowski. They came together, reached an
understanding, and hung up their sign: "Liberalism."

What did this liberalism amount to? Everything and nothing at all.
Each of the triumvirate, until the moment when he revealed himself
to be a neo-liberal, had behind him the beautiful and richly illustrated
dossier of a totalitarian bully, a Stalinist hireling, a cynical hypocrite,
a servile flunky. Starewicz and Zolkiewski need no introduction: their
names speak for themselves, one in the field of administration, the

other in the realm of culture. For twenty years they played out their roles with the ruthlessness of Nazi *Gauleiters*, leaving behind a trail of cruelty by command. The liberalism of ideas, conduct, and principle was the subject of their lifelong contempt. As young men, they prostrated themselves before violence executed against truth and goodness; it had become their lifeblood to worship brute force, which they called reason or necessity, and which they made into an absolute value. In the communist decalogue, liberalism is a mortal sin; the word is a stench to the nostrils, it is associated with mental and physical decay, the putrescence of the body cells and psychological disintegration. What, then, prompted the triumvirs to take such a hazardous step? What provoked their chief instrument, Alicja Lisiecka, to use the term "liberal" in a place as full of malicious gossip as the canteen of the Writers' Association? A term which, if repeated to Gomulka or Kliszko, carried with it the risk of bloody reckonings behind closed doors. They took this risk openly and deliberately. What made them endorse such words? What made them raise the cursed word, like a reptile, above their heads and hold it there for all to see, despite the revulsion they must have felt?

The fight for Gomulka's inheritance was on. There were a number of challengers. The small-town giant Moczar bulges at the security police headquarters (now computerized), the power rooted in the provincial miasma, heading a force of butchery cooperatives, small fruit-growers, allotment holders, and the barmaids from Zamosc, where during the war everyone had someone in the Underground, only nobody now knows what kind of Underground it was. Moczar forges ahead under the banner of patriotism; others fight behind a veil of economics, using truncheons but with the promise of a higher standard of living, fridges for all; some even attack the feudal privilege of the apparat. There isn't much room at the top, it's difficult to get in, yet they have to produce an alternative that will be attractive enough. What about freedom, then? What about liberty and slogans, which always go down well among people in Poland who have lost their political bearings, and among the "wet pragmatists" in the intelligentsia who still believe in barter politics: buy here, sell there, give support to one, put pressure on another. The triumvirs' past is, of course, a bit of a drawback. Zolkiewski, an old campaigner of repression, makes you want to throw up when he starts talking about freedom. Among the non-Party members of the Sejm, Starewicz is known as the Flunky: it is well known that he is prepared to act the

executioner as and when required by the Master. As for Rakowski
. . . How then should they set about it? There is a way, though. If
all else fails, there is always the way of Konrad Wallenrod, who acted
as a double agent among the Prussian Knights. The Poles love it. No
one has written better on the subject than Adam Mickiewicz, and in
no other country do poetry-reading teenagers so admire the biography of a noble double agent. Perhaps it is just because they have
no idea of how to play the double game that the Poles admire it; the
presence of Wallenrod looms large in Polish literature, but Polish
history has no Talleyrand. Yet it is Talleyrand who appeals to many
among the intellectual elite, who prefer him to their own relatively
simple and straightforward collaborators of the past, the Drucki-
Lubeckis and the Wielopolskis. Under communism, with its plethora
of moral imbroglios, tolerance of the double game has grown, and
its social prestige has grown with it. It seems that it is enough for a
Party member to have his child baptized in secret for him to feel that
he is a latter-day heroic little Wallenrod. Communism, particularly
its Polish version, is, of course, ideally suited to Talleyrand-like
practices. That is why so often two members of the Party, who are
as like as twins, can be regarded in a totally different light by public
opinion. In a democracy, people's moral qualities are tested only on
special occasions, but under communism this tired litmus paper never
has a break; it is put to work day in and day out to make new
assessments, always depending on the facts of a particular case, always
from the perspective of other people's interests, filtered through the
sieve of constantly changing norms of behavior. Moral ambivalence
reigns and no universal norms apply. A person is good for a day,
good for a purpose, good for now. Under communism, a politician
is not judged by his political program but by the decency of his day-
to-day behavior. In the eyes of the people, decency is odds in his
favor, which, one must admit, is an odd paradox. Elections under
communism are highly amusing, not because the whole thing is a
sham, but because the voters in all seriousness consider and devoutly
hope that the candidate, if elected, will be a decent enough man *not*
to do what he promised in his manifesto. The variations on the
Wallenrod or Talleyrand theme are infinite, but our triumvirs have
gone one better and have thought up an improved scheme.

Nothing new, however. The magic formula used to justify the
implementation of sixty years of communism in practice—"He meant
well!"—has been tried before. It was first used when it became

necessary to explain away the chasm between what Marx and Engels wanted and what was done in their name in the process of carrying out their ideas in real life. Lenin and Dzerzhinsky also "meant well" at a time when one could have washed one's hands in the blood running down the gutters of Lubyanka. "He meant well," said the cretins collecting money for International Red Aid before the last war, whenever anyone dared to criticize Stalin for finishing off his closest henchmen. After the war, Hilary Minc applied this formula—this dialectical gadget—with consummate skill. Half of Poland was still repeating "He means well" as the economic magician pushed on toward total collectivization, grinding the peasants into the ground. Cyrankiewicz's factotums have been telling us for twenty years that "he meant well," but time passes and the formula is wearing a little thin. Nowadays, they often add that things would have been much worse without him, but of this we cannot be sure: we have never yet been without him. We know all too well, however, what it is like with him. Gomulka managed to keep his popularity up after October, his tired lieutenants whispering "He means well" at the celebratory banquets, while to anyone with a pair of eyes in his head it was obvious that he in fact meant as ill as possible. The tune, then, has been tried out extensively and the triumvirs' acolytes were able to play an even more complicated version of it with all the exultation and wild excitement brought out by careful rehearsal: "They mean well, they cannot show it at the moment, but if you help them and back them in their struggle with the dark butcher from the Lodz security police [Moczar], the boorish illiterate, they will rise to the top and practice what they are now preaching."

The physiology of lying and the function of distortion under communism are governed by their own peculiar laws. The totalitarian lie comes effortlessly, it is resilient and full of life like a toxin; the serum has to be new each time, the difficulties in producing it are considerable. How easily lying came to the SS men at their trials: it was an order, they had to, they did not know. We know that they were turning the truth inside out, but do we know how to disinfect, delouse, filter, and unravel what remains of reality? On Gomulka's orders Zolkiewski liquidated the bestially revisionist *Nowa Kultura*—did he mean well then, just "could not do otherwise, but had to do it"? Why couldn't he have gone away for a slimming cure, giving as an explanation that obesity would shorten his life? Why did he accept the commission, and now hints that he did not want to do it, and anyway that he meant well? After "the protest of the 34," Rakowski wrote an obnoxious article in *Polityka* full of stereotyped accusations taken straight out of the Leninist catechism. Now, courting some of the thirty-four with his supposedly alternative program, he gives one to understand that "he had to, it was necessary, superior force, that he didn't mean it, did not want it, that he meant well," and that the rest was just tactics and rules of the game. The myth of the game is one of the most serviceable devices, one of the better gadgets. An entire machinery of false images and carefully planted rumors serves to create the myth of struggle where there is no real struggle. We witness a game played for high stakes when the stakes are sham, there are no conflicting programs, and not one job will be lost over the whole thing. Of course, it does not follow from this that there is no conflict between factions. There is, but this is a totally different kettle of fish: genuine gangs fighting for genuine power stick genuine knives into their opponents' genuine backs, but in public they hug one another, they bill and coo, providing the press with lovely pictures of brotherly slap and tickle. The more someone whispers into your ear how much he is against something, the greater is the likelihood that he is for it. And if he privately lets it be known that he means well, you can be sure that his plans are very nasty indeed. And, anyway, where are the guarantees that they have changed at all? We have known the three of them for twenty years: is there anything in their past to suggest that they really mean well now? Why didn't they show it before? Why is it that for the last twenty years they meant so very ill? Why have they never, at any time, done anything whatsoever which might indicate an inkling of goodwill? And finally, where are the people to look for the difference between tactics and common sense? The Polish Stalinist school of psychology has considerable achievements to its credit, quite unknown in the West. It has made a very detailed study of the correlation between action, thought, and speech in the "real" man. It appears that the truth about a person bears no close causal relation to his actions, speech, and thought. Moreover, it seems that actions, speech, and thought are not themselves related to one another. Dostoevsky has already shown quite satisfactorily that a person's actions do not reveal the truth about him to any significant degree. Nor is this truth revealed by speech; we all know that an orator speaking from a tribune draped in red does not believe in even a fraction of his own words. Yet the circumstances in which one can carry out a series of wicked deeds, while thinking that perhaps they are not quite decent, or, better still, communicating one's doubts to friends around a café table, no—this doesn't count. No, *this* is no justification. This sensational discovery is a revelation and a triumph for the Polish psychological school of morality. It poses a nice problem for traditional Christian attitudes toward these matters: Christianity was always inclined to absolve those who were unaware of what they were doing; but to be told that someone was innocent because he fully understood the moral error of his ways at the time of committing them, and, even in a state of super-consciousness, discussed them in detail with his friends over a glass of vodka, is really quite a blow. Unfortunately, the cognitive achievements of this particular school of moral philosophy have become part and parcel of the way of thinking of quite a number of Poles. Sufficiently so for our triumvirs and their like to build on them false hopes and use them to diffuse and sublimate their own shabby villainy.

Nowadays in Poland one often hears that So-and-so is "having difficulties." It usually means that a man who, until recently, was our mortal enemy, who was ready to annihilate our physical or spiritual existence with the soulless automatism of a programmed mechanism, who was planning it with cold premeditation, while calling it a public duty, social progress, or historical necessity, now fawns like a dog, gazing into our eyes in search of understanding and an uneasy false camaraderie. We have seen so many of them. They often succeed in winning our compassion, sometimes even a kind of admiration. Only they never manage to convince us that when their difficulties come to an end (for, obviously, "they meant well") they will change, become different, better. For we have also seen those who did overcome their little difficulties, who have returned to grace and favor, to power and influence, to new possibilities of action. Yes, we have seen them, and they remained just as they were before—hypocritical worshippers of abominable iniquities.

I heard lately that Rakowski is having some *contretemps*. Difficult to say. I would have to see him. The hair style would reveal all.

(October 1967)

Postscriptum

I had a brief glimpse of Rakowski on one later occasion, several years after I left Poland. It was in 1973, or thereabouts, and I was living in Connecticut, within easy reach of New York. My friend Jerzy Turowicz, editor of the Catholic journal *Tygodnik Powszechny*, was over from Poland, and I had been invited to the private viewing of an exhibition of paintings by the famous painter Jan Lebenstein, also from Poland. This was opening in one of the more prestigious galleries on Madison Avenue.

Accordingly, I drove into Manhattan with my American wife, Mary Ellen, and after collecting Turowicz from the Kosciuszko Foundation, we walked from there to the gallery. Inside, I saw a crowd of people at the center of the gallery, one of whom held out his arms to welcome Turowicz. Turowicz was pulling me along with him, and so it was that I suddenly found myself face-to-face with Rakowski in the thick of the crowd. The memory of my article, which *Kultura* had published six years earlier, on "The Hair Styles of Mieczyslaw Rakowski," flashed through my mind like a red alert. Without a second's hesitation, however, I held out my hand to him. He wavered, turned red, changed expression, but then shook hands. Immediately afterwards, he turned his back on me, and that was the end of our social encounter.

As we drove back, Mary Ellen asked me why that particular individual had so ostentatiously shown his disapproval of my person. I told her who Rakowski was, explained the whole political, social, and moral background, and gave her an outline of what I had written about him and why. Her comment was: "It's odd, but at this moment I wouldn't be able to describe his hair style. It was somehow neutral and unremarkable. Perhaps you made him into too much of a mythological figure in your article, for metaphorical purposes?"

I thought to myself that I, too, had suddenly become less observant. Could I really not have noticed his hair style, such an important element in my assessments of him? "That is ominous," I said. "The fact that one hour after seeing Rakowski I don't really know what hair style he had, doesn't augur well . . ."

In 1981, when I read in the newspapers that he had been appointed deputy prime minister with the task of negotiating with Solidarity, I remembered my remark. A feeling of sadness and discomfort came over me, as it does on each occasion when I see a glint of sin in people's faces, or the shadow of evil among the events of everyday life.

When Rakowski, on behalf of the government, severed negotiations with Solidarity, it was a preliminary step to General Jaruzelski's coup in December 1981. His subsequent role as the general's right-hand man during the period of repressions and the delegalization of Solidarity confirmed the pattern of his previous behavior. It also confirmed my observation that his hair style is no longer of any significance. He can now afford to be unconcerned about it. And so can we.

(1983)

Editor's Postscriptum

Leopold Tyrmand died in 1985. Mieczyslaw Rakowski was made prime minister in 1988 and later, in the summer of 1989, first secretary of the Polish Communist Party.

(1989)

Leszek Kolakowski

THE STRUGGLE BETWEEN CAESAR AND GOD

LET US NOT DISCUSS the Poles' euphoria at the news that the Pontifex Polonus has settled in the Holy See, a euphoria which is quite understandable but irrelevant to these reflections. Let us also not discuss the immediate effects that this event will have on the cause of the Polish church and on the prospects for the battle being waged in Poland to defend civil liberties and human rights. It is obvious, of course, that this event has universal significance, and from the point of view of the role of the Church in the world, it does not matter that the new Pope has come to Rome from Cracow. What matters is that he spent his priestly career in a hostile political environment and a friendly social environment, that thanks to his experience he is thoroughly familiar with the confrontation between the Church and the communist system of government, and that for these very reasons his voice may be decisive in the dispute between the "integrist" and "progressive" trends in Christianity. One need not spend time proving how pivotal this dispute is for the future of Christianity and of the world.

My opinions on this issue come from my goodwill toward the cause of Christianity as I understand it. I must admit that both the "integrists" and the "progressives" have some good arguments, especially in their mutual criticisms, but the point of view that I favor is not a synthesis of the two or something in between, but a separate viewpoint justifiable in itself. It seems to me that mine is a viewpoint which has quite a few supporters among active and courageous Christians, and that it is not new; still, like everyone else, I am free to try to reconstruct it.

I will discuss the Church as an institution that announces to the world the good news about redemption and conciliation and that does not demand from believers that they flee the world and cultivate their own virtues in isolation, like hermits, but asks that they strive for the Kingdom in the thorns of temporality and, in a sense, makes everyone responsible not only for themselves but also for others. Hence the difficulty, which is unavoidable and permanent, of marking precisely the borderline between what is God's and what is Caesar's. For Christianity (apart from its marginal sects) does not believe that people are capable of building the Kingdom on earth through their own efforts and of ridding it of all evil. The intention of building a temporal paradise with human hands must actually seem the work of demonic pride, like the construction of the Tower of Babel, from which humanity gained nothing but an admonition and the confusion of languages. It is certainly not the Church's task to formulate prescriptions for a good political system or to write constitutions. But, on the other hand, in saying that something is good or evil, Christianity cannot strictly set apart the judgments of people—which are always most important—from the judgments of institutions. In saying, for example, that not paying wage earners for their work or oppressing widows and orphans is a sin calling for revenge from heaven, the Church condemns not only individuals but also institutions. Therefore, in everyday life, moral precepts and taboos must often be understood as social ideas, as positions on politically relevant questions. Similarly, an important part of the Church's work must be subject to the rules that govern lay organizations. This ambiguity cannot be altogether avoided. The head of the Church says, as in Paul, that the Church inherited from Christ mercy as well as the office of the apostle on which it bases its authority. But he also says, just as Peter told the centurion, *Surge, et ego ipse homo sum*—rise up, because I, too, am a man.

Christianity's extreme tendencies which I mentioned—"integrist" and "progressive"—are based on different interpretations of the distinction between what is Caesar's and what is God's.

Roughly speaking, Catholic "integrism" appears to be an anachronistic projection of the situation in which the Church saw liberalism as its main enemy; that is, the situation which found its classic expression in the papacy of Pius IX. In those days, the Church's attack was focused on rationalism, the theory of evolution, and the principle of separation of Church and state. Today's traditionalism, although it does not demand theocracy, inherits its mentality from the era of Syllabus, at least in the sense that it would like to take advantage of lay power to defend faith from criticism and to assure the Church of its institutional right to close supervision of lay matters.

If "integrism" in its ideal form is an anachronistic negation of the autonomous sphere of the *profanum*, then "progressivism," also in its perfect form, is a renunciation of the autonomy of faith and of the Church, an attempt to subordinate faith to the demands of doctrinal political considerations, however these may be interpreted. If the integrists are prepared to ally themselves—and, in the eyes of their adversaries, identify—with the political forces that for whatever reasons of their own can guarantee privileges for the Church, then progressivism is prepared to ally itself or identify with all those who believe in the slogans of egalitarianism, even if, according to experience, the latter are bound to aim—by virtue of their principles—to destroy Christianity (at least if we take Christianity to be more than a collection of political slogans). From the point of view of Christian tradition, both cases represent a blurring of the borderline between the *sacrum* and the *profanum*.

Let's take the simplest example, the question of divorce. For progressivists, this issue virtually does not exist and the Church's ban on divorce no doubt serves as yet another example of the Church's backwardness. To the integrists, on the other hand, it is natural that since divorce is not permitted by the sacramental character of the union of marriage it should also be forbidden by the state. But this is a non sequitur. The Church of course has the right to announce that divorce does not exist in Church tradition, which means that believers are not allowed to divorce and if they do divorce are guilty of breaking Church law. But the Church should not and does not need to demand that the state do the Church's work and resolve this unpleasant problem by legislation. Of course, on many other issues it is more difficult to divide things so clearly. Still, I think that the overall principle of the separation of Church and state agrees not only with common sense but also with human rights and Christian principles.

The confrontation between Christianity and communism is a particularly extreme example of the conflict between integrism and progressivism.

For the traditionalists who see the world in categories they inherited from the era of shock that followed the French Revolution, and which have changed only slightly, the evil and the destructive force of communism come from its atheism. But this is a deceptive way of looking at things. In democratic systems ruled by atheists or by people who are indifferent to religion, the Church is not persecuted or restrained. On the other hand, if we spin out a fantasy that one day a meeting of Communist Parties will announce that it has just been scientifically proved that God does exist and—need we add—God expresses his unerring will through the lips of the Politburo, it is easy to foresee that neither the oppression and anti-cultural character of communism nor the situation of religion and the Church in countries ruled by communism will change.

Despotic regimes, and religious persecution under despotism, do not result from communism's atheism but rather from its totalitarianism, from the fact that it is moved by the desire to destroy all forms of collective life and all expressions of culture other than those imposed by the state. Focusing criticism on atheism—in other words, on communism's doctrinal mistakes—which is characteristic of Catholic integrism, is misleading and ineffective for several reasons. First of all, such an attitude precludes the distinction between the religious indifference of liberal democracy and the Soviet-type ideological state, and thereby gets in the way of freeing the Church from its tradition of viewing liberalism as an enemy par excellence. What is more, attacking communism for its flawed theological or anti-theological theory makes it more difficult to criticize totalitarianism as such, regardless of its doctrinal base. In the meantime, totalitarianism, no matter what its ideological clothes, be they racist, communist, or religious, continues to pose the most evil threat to Christian culture and values. It is a well-tested truth that the totalitarian traces in Christian tradition present no real threat today, but the Christians who are fighting for the right to practice in a totalitarian situation would put themselves in an awkward position if they did not base their demands on a clear acceptance of the pluralistic principles of social life; that is, on a radical rejection of totalitarianism regardless of its ideological content, which may be atheistic but may also be religious (a powerful totalitarian potential continues to exist in Islam). Also, assuming that atheism is at the core of communism's evil makes the confrontation between Christianity and communism into a war of ideas. This is a faulty interpretation of the situation at least in those countries which have been pushed into the cage of Sovietism: the communist idea has no power of its own there, virtually no one believes in it, and the only purpose it serves is the legitimation of sheer force exercised over the people. Integrism reduces the effectiveness of anti-totalitarian resistance by implying, or at least not clearly excluding the possibility, that totalitarianism would not be reprehensible if it defined itself through the Nicean Creed instead of Lenin's *Collected Works*. In this sense, integrism peculiarly coincides with that form of Catholic progressivism which sees nothing bad in communism other than its errors on theological issues. In both cases, it would be easy to say that it is the duty of Christianity to convert communism to the true doctrine, and not to resist the destructive forces of the totalitarian system, which always, regardless of its current ideological façade, must lead to the destruction of Christian culture. Contrary to appearances, therefore, integrism, much like progressivism, albeit for different reasons, is weak vis-à-vis communism. Integrism is weak because it carries the relics of a theocratic mentality, progressivism because it considers communism a perfectly respectable solution to the problems of life.

But anti-totalitarian resistance, if it is to be effective, must accept the undeniable right of all people to spiritual freedom. It must therefore recognize, among other things, the traditional republican principle of the separation of Church and state. This principle involves various legal complications, which I do not plan and would not know how to analyze. But two issues deserve to be stressed in these reflections. The principle of separation of Church and state has never been and *cannot be realized under communism* or in any other ideological state. For this principle assumes that every man's individual right to profess or not to profess a belief, as well as the right of religious communities to proclaim their faith, is protected under the law. It further assumes that the state itself is religiously neutral, and therefore that religious affiliation or the beliefs of individuals have no relevance—be it positive or negative—to their situation vis-à-vis the state.

It is clear that no totalitarian system can adopt this principle, because it would mean giving up its ideological pretensions. The communist state *is not a lay state*: the unlimited power of a single party which, at least in theory, has its own doctrinal sheath (whether anyone takes this sheath seriously or not) cannot be neutral toward religious beliefs and Church organization. Ideological discrimination and the persecution of churches are not communism's accidental flaw or a fault which can be corrected but the inevitable consequence of systemic principles: not of doctrinal atheism but of the form of power which aims to control all spheres of life and of human communication. In effect, the scope of the persecutions, limitations, and discrimination varies and changes according to many factors, but all relaxations and concessions are coerced either by social pressure or during periods of crisis in which the ruling apparatus does not control the situation (during the war with the Germans, religious repression abated even in the Soviet Union). From this point of view, the communist ideal was attained in Albania, where all religious practice is strictly punished, and atheism is the obligatory state dogma. China is close to the ideal, as is really the Soviet Union itself: no such ban is formally included in the Soviet legal code, but the churches are deprived of all political rights, concentration camps are filled with people accused of spreading "religious propaganda," temples are systematically destroyed, the priest commits a crime by, for example, attending to a dying person with the last rites, and it is the *legal* obligation of parents to bring up their children in the communist, in other words atheistic, spirit, under threat of having them taken away by force. If repression never went this far in Poland, it was only thanks to the force of social resistance. If today the Party bosses find themselves in a deep social crisis and are attempting to reach a minimum understanding with the Church (without abandoning the countless restrictions, and still maintaining a permanent muzzle of censorship, without which communism has never held power and cannot even be conceived), it is not as a result of their conversion to democracy but for fear of explosions of popular anger. A true separation of Church and state is not possible under communism, if this word is to continue to be defined both by historical experience and by the unambiguous doctrinal principles of Leninism.

On the other hand, the separation of Church and state does not deprive the Church of the right to speak up on all public matters, even though this right is not the result of any particular privilege but one of the universal rights of individuals and organizations in the pluralistic structure of the state.

Exactly the same weaknesses of integrism and progressivism come into the open in different conditions: in the military dictatorships and the despotic (although not totalitarian) states of the Third World, particularly Latin America. In those countries, integrism tends to identify with the oppressive structures of power, as long as these remain anti-communist and permit the Church to hold on to various privileges on the condition that it remains politically loyal. In these situations, progressivism tends to identify with the communist opposition. Both reactions are equally catastrophic for the fate of democracy and for those Christian values whose survival is most essential for mankind. To identify with integrism inevitably means that one is suspected of shutting one's eyes to violations of human rights in exchange for institutional privilege. On the other hand, it is difficult not to accuse those who identify with progressivism that they contribute to the triumph of those political forces which everywhere and without exception, having mastered the instruments of coercion, destroy both Christianity and human and civil rights. To say that in noncommunist or anti-communist tyrannies Christians should "for the time being" fight for common causes and put off "for later" everything that sets them apart from communism is an indication of an amazing absence of memory or of high hypocrisy, because we all know that under communist power there is no "later." Such experiences are so irrefutable and know no exception that it is a shame that one has to repeat them. Those Christians who recently fought against the corrupt regime of South Vietnam today in large numbers (difficult to estimate) fill the concentration camps of communist Vietnam, something that seems to attract little attention in progressive Catholic publications. Communist police dictatorships were established everywhere with the slogans of democracy and not of communism, and with the support of various democratic forces which were supposed to be and indeed later were crushed to the ground. The fact that the readiness of Christians to take on this role of fertilizer for tyrannies and to call this readiness "liberation theology" grows out of goodwill does not make it a lesser aberration. Christianity which sides with the persecuted, repressed, and poor against dictatorships in noncommunist countries need not disguise its fundamental opposition to totalitarianism. The Church can easily avoid being suspected of identifying with the wrong side because it is not a political party. If the Church speaks not on behalf of the "perfect political system" but of the rights of individuals to spiritual freedom, and if it rids itself of all traces of its own theocratic tradition, it is in its power to keep its own special place in social conflict and not risk the accusation of fighting tyranny in one form and favoring the establishment of tyranny in another form (in this respect, both the integrists and progressives are partly right in their mutual accusations).

What in the progressives' language is called the Christian-communist dialogue is nearly always the product of deception or self-deception. Most often this "dialogue" consists of exchanging unbinding humanitarian platitudes whose principal aim is to prevent the revelation of real contradictions and to use incantations to block out the truth about historical experiences. In those cases the kinds of declarations expected from Christianity are: "Oh, yes, we, too, are in favor of social justice and man's liberation," to which the communists are to respond with assurances that "oh, we respect your goodwill and your readiness to cooperate, even though we are guided by a scientific outlook on life," out of courtesy not stressing that the partners in this "dialogue" are the ignorant victims of medieval superstition. In today's conditions this "dialogue" is a rhetorical shield which hides the murky realities of Christian life in countries ruled by communists.

Regardless of what happened in the past, in today's world the question of Christianity and the question of defending the institutions of representative democracy are inseparably connected. This is obvious, by contrast, in all those places where such institutions are absent; in other words, in most parts of our planet. In all those places, albeit in different ways, Christianity is threatened. It can be destroyed in different ways, according to historical experience: not only through persecution and coercion, but also by becoming internally vapid; in other words, by being reduced either to a bare institutional structure or to moralizing, or, what is worse, to political moralizing. Even liturgical reforms may prove conducive to one or the other threat. The insistence on the immutability of liturgy perhaps reveals a lack of trust in the content of Christianity, which, after all, survives in various and mutable forms of expression. But another, similar danger may loom in the accelerated movement to eliminate the traditional function of liturgical communication: it is possible to forget the content in forgetting the form. It seems that many Catholics ponder this in the depressing coolness of their modernized temples.

(December 1978)
Translated by Maya Latynski

Czeslaw Milosz

DOSTOEVSKY AND WESTERN INTELLECTUALS

P ROBABLY, AFTER ALL, I will not write a book on Dostoevsky, but there is no reason why I shouldn't tell what that book would be about. I would not compete with the multitude of essential monographs and penetrating analyses of particular works; rather, I would assume a certain familiarity with Dostoevsky on the part of my reader, and would try to indicate the writer's position in world literature in a manner slightly different from the generally accepted one. It is possible that precisely this different interpretation is what inclines me to believe that to write a book on him would be a dangerous and thankless task.

While studying Dostoevsky and lecturing about him to American students, I could not help but notice that this writer changes according to who speaks about him. This is not readily admitted by Dostoevskians of various nationalities, as they aspire to scholarly objectivity in spite of the fact that their *Weltanschauung* and their sympathies and antipathies do not fail to influence their method of research and their argument. The history of Dostoevsky's critical reception in the course of the hundred years which have elapsed since his death exemplifies intellectual fashions succeeding each other and the influence exerted by various philosophies upon the minds of the scholars. Leaving aside for the moment the Russian critics, we may distinguish a few phases in the reception of Dostoevsky in the West, beginning with *Crime and Punishment*, which was read in translation in the nineteenth century. Though this novel was greeted with acclaim by Nietzsche, in general the so-called *âme slave* of which Dostoevsky seemed to be representative was treated with a bit of irony. French critics, in particular, shrugged at Sonia Marmeladov, a saintly prostitute taken alive, as it were, from a French sentimental novel. The victorious march of Dostoevsky's works through Western countries in the first decades of the twentieth century is directly connected with the discovery of a new dimension in man, the subconscious, and with the cult of Dionysiac elemental forces merging Eros with Thanatos. Nevertheless, the resistance to the growing impact of the Russian writer, presented by such writers as Middleton Murry and D. H. Lawrence, deserves attention. According to D. H. Lawrence, "the amazing perspicacity is mixed in [Dostoevsky] with ugly perversity. Nothing is pure. His wild love of Jesus is mixed with perverse and poisonous hate of Jesus: his moral hostility to the devil is mixed with secret worship of the devil."

These voices of objection soon were superseded by general admiration, and the fame of Dostoevsky grew parallel with that of Sigmund Freud. It is true that Freud, who for obvious reasons considered a novel on parricide, *The Brothers Karamazov*, the greatest novel ever written, based his paper on the causes of Dostoevsky's epilepsy upon incorrect factual data. As subsequently proved by Professor Joseph Frank in his biography of the writer, Dostoevsky's epileptic attacks began in Siberia and not in his tender age, as Freud believed. For several decades Freudianism powerfully influenced research on Dostoevsky, constituting a period of criticism which we may well call "psychological." A phase which was relatively short and difficult to delineate was that in which Existentialism colored the analyses of Dostoevskian scholars. Next, they abandoned tracking down the author's thought as voiced by his characters and concentrated on the artistic structure of Dostoevsky's extraordinary novels. Indeed, these novels are so extraordinary that the question justifiably arises whether they do not signify the end of the novel as a literary genre.

My students proved to be very receptive when I dealt with the psychology of his characters or when I tried to show how much of the author's intention is revealed by the method of structural analysis.

They learned with amusement, as young people usually do in such cases, of the discrepancies between the *oeuvre* and its smelly kitchen; namely, the personality of this man of genius. However, their comprehension came to an end when they encountered certain facts. For instance, they had difficulty understanding why Dostoevsky loved the autocratic czarist government, and not just after his return from Siberia, when he became a conservative both in his journalism and in his fiction. Sentenced to death together with his twenty-one colleagues, put before a firing squad, which was a comedy devised by the czar, spared at the last moment, he writes three patriotic odes during his enforced stay in Siberia. In one of these, written in 1854 during the Crimean War, he directs threats at France and England; in the second, written after the death of Nicholas I, the czar who allowed him to experience what presumably were his final moments before the firing squad, he compares the emperor to the sun and humbly confesses that he is not worthy to pronounce the emperor's name; the third, written on the occasion of Alexander II's coronation, is a eulogy of the new czar. The poems are very bad, and the desire to better his fate cannot be excluded as a motive, but they agree with what we know from other sources about the views of the author.

This biographical detail, and others of similar nature, belong to an area in which the road of the majority of Dostoevsky scholars ceases to be my road; that is, our attention turns to different things. For me, Dostoevsky is most interesting as a man who in his life had only one serious affair, with Russia, and who chose Russia as the true heroine of his works. It may seem that the psychology of his characters and his discoveries in the domain of the structure of the novel make him a truly international writer, while his nationalism, his worship of the throne and of the altar, his chauvinistic hatred of Catholics and Jews, his jeering at Poles and Frenchmen enclose him within the boundaries of one country only. In my opinion, this is not the case; on the contrary, the more Russian Dostoevsky is, the more he succumbs to his phobias and obsessions out of his love for Russia, the greater his role is as a witness for the whole intellectual history of the last two centuries. Why two centuries? He himself said: "Everything depends upon the next century"—and we cannot deny his gift of prophecy.

In the Dostoevsky family, one of the basic readings was *The History of the Russian State* by Karamzin, and the future writer was familiar with it from childhood. This work sees the source and the pledge of

Russia's greatness in the unlimited, autocratic rule of the monarchs. During his imprisonment in the Petropavlovsk fortress, Dostoevsky wrote a deposition in which he presented his views on the monarchy, and he sounds so sincere that the mere desire to save his skin could not have dictated such words. According to him, revolution was necessary in France, while in Russia no one in his right mind would think of a republican form of government. The history of the Novgorodian republic alone—inglorious in Dostoevsky's eyes—should be warning enough. As for Muscovy, it found itself under the Tatar yoke when the authority of its princes had weakened, and it was saved when that authority was strengthened again—just as, later on, Russia was given strength by "the great pilot," Peter the Great.

How could a socialist, a Fourierist, write in this manner? We may invoke a duality typical of Dostoevskianism, yet we would probably be closer to the truth if we assumed that these two tendencies, socialist and autocratic, always coexisted in Dostoevsky, and it was only the emphasis that changed. His colleague from the Petrashevsky circle, Nikolai Danilevsky, underwent a similar evolution. However, even though he glorified czardom and proclaimed the victorious march of the Slavs in his work *Russia and Europe*, Danilevsky did not renounce the socialist dreams of his youth; he simply made them part of his totalitarian doctrine.

Dostoevsky reasoned like a statesman. In his conversations with his fellow prisoners in the penal colony of Omsk, he considered the conquest of Constantinople the most important task facing Russia. The *oeuvre* of his mature age, beginning with his first trip to Western Europe in 1862, differs from his previous works in that, whereas, before, he was an artist, now the artist and the statesman in him work together. His books describe the spiritual situation of the Russian intelligentsia, and form a chronicle of its spiritual transformations from decade to decade, and even almost from year to year. And they pose an essential question: What do those transformations mean for the future of Russia, how are they a threat to her existence and vocation? Without fear of exaggerating, we may say that these books are a kind of police investigation conducted by a very intelligent public prosecutor who knows what he is looking for, as he himself is simultaneously the investigator and the subject.

The Russian intelligentsia in Dostoevsky's novels discuss the basic problems of human existence, which were by no means alien to characters in the Western novel, either in its eighteenth-century version or in its Romantic version, as, for instance, in George Sand. Nowhere else, however, do the participants in the discussion present the matter in such a sharp light and draw such radical conclusions. They live through in dramatic fashion what Friedrich Nietzsche, a contemporary of Raskolnikov, called "the death of God." Yet in Russia atheism is by no means a private affair of the individual; it is of the highest concern to the authorities, for an atheist, as a rule, becomes a revolutionary, thus confirming the road taken by that forerunner of the Russian intelligentsia's generations, Vissarion Belinsky. In *Crime and Punishment*, the crime of Raskolnikov is, in fact, a kind of substitution. In reality, he dreams of a great revolutionary deed, to which history would provide the justification. In his views and aspirations, he is completely alone: on one side, he is opposed by the authorities, represented by a police officer, Porfiry; on the other side, by the Russian people. When he is in Siberia, his fellow prisoners, simple peasants, want to kill him, as they guess him to be an atheist. Thus, in *Crime and Punishment*, we discover a formula valid for all the mature work of Dostoevsky: the rampart and the foundation of Russia are the authorities of the state and the devoutly religious—as Dostoevsky believed—Russian people, while the intelligentsia constitutes a threat. *What* sort of threat is demonstrated in the novel *The Possessed*. Among the amazingly perspicacious diagnoses in this novel, perhaps the profoundest is expressed by an old military man, who, while listening to a conversation on the nonexistence of God, exclaims: "If there is no God, what sort of captain am I?" That man grasped a link between religion and the sources of authority. Let us not forget that the Russian intelligentsia nourished itself on Voltaire's philosophy and on memories of the French Revolution. The beheading of Louis XVI today seems only one of many sensational events throughout history, neither more nor less important than any other. In reality, it signaled the end of an order based on the conviction that the king rules because he is divinely ordained, while those below him rule by his dispensation. But now other sources of authority were to be looked for—for instance, in a conspiracy directed by one man, Piotr Verkhovensky, in *The Possessed*. The novel that the author intended to be the crowning work of his *oeuvre*, *The Brothers Karamazov*, has for its subject the rebellion of the sons against the father, and a parricide. The question arises whether the weakness and immorality of the father do not annul his authority. Ivan Karamazov answers yes to this question—and chooses his answer as the basis for his rebellion against both his father and God the Father. *The Brothers Karamazov* is, in essence, a treatise on the Russian intelligentsia's act of abolishing the authority of God, of the czar, and of the father of a family at the same time.

Western intellectuals, when writing on Dostoevsky, constantly wonder at a strange disparity; namely, that a man who penetrated so deeply into the psyche of his characters could have such reactionary views. They try to eliminate those views from their field of vision, in which they are helped by the hypothesis of the "polyphonic" structure of his novels. Yet they are unaware of the differences separating them from the Russian novelist. Not one of them, either in his theoretical writings or in his novels, places the interests of the state at the center of his concerns. On the contrary, they are emotionally on the side of those characters who want to abolish the existing order. For Dostoevsky, however, Russia as a state did not mean only a territory inhabited by the Russians. The future of the world depended on Russia, on whether she would become contaminated by the ideas of atheism and socialism imported from the West, just as her intelligentsia had become contaminated, or would be saved by the czardom and the pious Russian people and thus fulfill her vocation of rescuing all humanity. Aliosha Karamazov, in subsequent volumes of the unfinished novel, was to represent a new type of activist working in harmony with the faith of the people.

In his Slavophile idealization of the Russian people, Dostoevsky was mistaken. Yet he could not find any other reason for hope, and so, clearly, there was a dilemma: if "Holy Russia" proves unable to present an effective resistance, the intelligentsia would do to her what the heroes of *The Possessed* started to accomplish on the scale of one provincial town. In the long history of Dostoevsky's critical reception in various countries, the highest place, as far as the understanding of his intentions is concerned, should be assigned to a group of Russian philosophers active at the beginning of the twentieth century, particularly to their pronouncements in a volume of essays, *Vekhi* [*Landmarks*, 1908], and *Iz glubiny* [*De Profundis*, 1918]. According to them, the prophecies of Dostoevsky were already being fulfilled. Perhaps this should not surprise us, as these philosophers were unsympathetic toward the Revolution. However, the opinion that the Revolution fulfilled Dostoevsky's prophecies was also widespread among the revolutionaries of 1917. One of the greatest admirers of Dostoevsky was the first Commissar of Education after the October

Revolution, Lunacharsky. As late as 1920, *The Possessed* was extolled in the official press as a novel which had become reality.

"It is impossible not to see in Dostoevsky a prophet of the Russian Revolution," wrote Nikolai Berdyaev in 1918. "The Russian Revolution is imbued with those principles which were foreseen by Dostoevsky and which received in his works the sharp definition of genius. It was given to Dostoevsky to penetrate the dialectics of Russian revolutionary thought and to draw extreme conclusions from it. He did not remain on the surface of social and political ideas and constructs; he plunged into the depths and revealed that the Russian Revolution is a metaphysical and religious phenomenon, not a political and social phenomenon. Thus, through religion, he grasped the nature of Russian socialism."

The Russians understood Dostoevsky's political worries, for they, just as he himself, thought in terms of statesmanship; i.e., they attached importance to the consequences of a given idea for the existence of the state, whether counterrevolutionary or revolutionary. Their Western colleagues were concerned with the individual, not with France, England, or America. It is true, though, that during the twentieth century an idea has taken root among them according to which a self-respecting man treats the existing, capitalist system as something transitory and quietly waits for its end. An astonishing similarity between the attitudes of the Russian intelligentsia, as described by Dostoevsky, and the attitudes of Western intellectuals a hundred years later leads us to conclude that his anxiety about the future of Russia enabled him to describe a phenomenon of immense dimensions, both in space and in time.

The term "Western intellectuals" is undoubtedly too general, and by using it we risk misunderstandings. Yet if we choose a figure who focuses the traits that we usually associate with this term, we will place ourselves on firmer ground. Such a figure exists: it is Jean-Paul Sartre, sometimes called the Voltaire of the twentieth century. What is striking in him is his extraordinary *intensity* in discussing ideas, an intensity similar to that of his Russian predecessors. The European intellectual upheaval which began in the sixteenth century reached Russia after a considerable delay, and educated Russians had to assimilate in a few decades ideas that, in Western Europe, had matured gradually during several centuries. Hence, perhaps, the exceptional force and virulence with which these ideas were taken up in Russia. Moreover, they were not confronted there by a well-developed, diversified social organism. For reasons which deserve a more thorough analysis than I can give here, a peculiar vacuum appeared, in turn, in the countries of the West in the twentieth century, a kind of nowhere inhabited by the intellectual, who thus, for decades, has been spinning out his concepts beyond any control by ordinary bread-eaters, just as, in Dostoevsky, Raskolnikov and Ivan Karamazov live alone with their reasoning. It is not only his intensity, but also the *abstractness* of his thought, that brings Jean-Paul Sartre close to these characters.

Is it not strange that in freethinking France, in a country which has seen much and has been inclined to shrug at quarrels over principles, suddenly "the death of God" becomes a crucial question, such as it once was, long ago, for young Russians talking about principles over vodka? Undoubtedly, for French Existentialism, and above all for Sartre, it was a fundamental premise—and starting from it (again an analogy with Russia), one progressed to the obligation to be active in order to transform the world, as man, by dethroning God, himself becomes a god and must demonstrate his responsibility through action.

A chapter on Sartre as a Dostoevskian character would undoubtedly open interesting vistas. In such a chapter, it would also be possible to touch upon certain similarities between Sartre's philosophy and that of Dostoevsky. I have in mind here, first of all, Sartre's famous dictum: "Hell is others"; that is, the problem of the relations between a subject and other people, who are also subjects. The individual aspires to wield power over others and to change them into objects, but since he perceives, in the eyes of others, the same desire to change him into an object, the others become his hell. This is precisely the problem of pride-humiliation in Dostoevsky. At the time Sartre was writing his *Being and Nothingness*, a book published in 1943, he could not have known of the book by Bakhtin on Dostoevsky's poetics, in which that matter is thoroughly investigated. And yet the "existential psychoanalysis" in Sartre's book agrees with the conclusions of Bakhtin, though Sartre seems to be unaware of such a kinship between himself and the Russian novelist.

Certain features of Russian life in the nineteenth century may contribute to a difficulty we encounter anytime we try to view the problems which preoccupied the Russian intelligentsia as still valid for our time. And yet Sartre, in his search for freedom, follows in the footsteps of Dostoevsky's Underground Man, a character who inaugurated a series of great philosophical monologists. In addition, Hegel's philosophy (introduced into France in the nineteen-thirties by Alexandre Kojève, i.e. Kozhevnikov) proved to be decisive for Sartre's intellectual development. Likewise, it can already be distinguished in the background of Raskolnikov's article on great men who are exonerated by history if they have committed crimes while acting in its service. Raskolnikov, a latent revolutionary, in his walks about St. Petersburg deliberately avoided the square where the unsuccessful rebellion of December 1825 took place. Certainly, he would have done better to give himself to the cause of revolution rather than senselessly murder a pawnbroker, but in the 1860s, when the action of the novel occurs, the time is not ripe for political acts, and we must wait until the 1870s for the character of Nechaev—Piotr Verkhovensky, from *The Possessed*. Ivan Karamazov, in turn, engages in the most fundamental quarrel with God's immorality in the name of the Promethean obligations of man, and this is precisely the core of Sartre's thought and his attempts to act.

What is to be done? While the title of Chernyshevsky's novel indicates the preoccupations of the Russian intelligentsia of the nineteenth century, it could serve, as well, as the motto for the whole, indefatigable activity of Sartre. He was constantly looking for *une cause* to which he could offer his abilities. All these causes were connected with the hope of abolishing the existing political system and replacing it with another, but with what sort—on this point Sartre continually changed his mind. He pinned his hopes on a succession of countries, and his disappointments were comic and pathetic at the same time. First the Soviet Union, then Yugoslavia, next Cuba, and, finally, China were, for him, the lands of the future, but he ended his career distributing leaflets in the street, together with young Maoist leftists. In his need to provide ever-new answers to the question *What is to be done?* Sartre was by no means an exception. On the contrary, he exemplified a similar anxiety in thousands of intellectuals and semi-intellectuals.

Such a longing for causes engendered by actuality may merely indicate an inner void which must be filled with something meaningful, with a disinterested striving toward a noble goal. Similarly, Dostoevsky's characters are torn from the fabric of everyday life, which secures that internal peace of limited concerns and limited achievements for their not-so-bright fellowmen. Dostoevsky's characters are bound neither by religion nor by the liturgical calendar, and they reject traditional morality. They also regard the accumulation of wealth as loathsome; after all, money can be gotten through crime, mere chance, inheritance, a game of roulette, usury, but never by work. Rural Russia is subject to a certain rhythm of customary activities, while a member of the intelligentsia is enclosed in the magic circle of his mind and daydreams about his exceptional role as a potential savior of mankind. He suffers from a lack of reasons to live, and Dostoevsky tries to define this *taedium vitae*, particularly by creating strong characters who are summoned to a commitment but who are unable to commit themselves because of excessive introspection, such as Svidrigailov and Stavrogin.

This illness, which has acquired vast scope in our century proportional to the progress of literacy, has perhaps not received, heretofore, a precise diagnosis. Possibly, its origin can be traced to a weakening in the perception of *being*, or to a perception of being as something absurd. Behind the nightmares visiting Svidrigailov and Stavrogin, we could perhaps see *Nausea*, as Sartre entitled his novel written prior to his revolutionary commitments. *L'Etre-en-Soi*, or the whole world outside of man, does not provoke in Sartre any feelings of piety or amazement, as it did long ago, for instance, in Goethe; on the contrary, it presses upon him with its lack of meaning and forces him to escape into the realm of human action. Thus, it is a metaphysical question. Many Christians would be surprised to hear that the Voltaire of the twentieth century was representative not only of intellectuals unsympathetic toward religion but also of many clerics and believers as well. For if the Church has for some time been seeking noble social causes to embrace, it is perhaps because there is a feeling abroad that the metaphysical side of Christianity has evaporated, leaving behind only a set of moral precepts about how people should live with one another.

In Dostoevsky, the representatives of the intelligentsia either live in the underground or openly oppose society. Raskolnikov does not consider himself guilty because he killed the pawnbroker and her sister, but because he is weak and defeated by society. After the first, sentimental phase of his work, when his heroes are "poor folk," Dostoevsky introduces a distinction between those who are aware and others who are on a lower level of awareness, and he is fascinated by the former alone. To his horror, this fascination leads him almost to identify with Ivan Karamazov and his parable of the Grand Inquisitor. It should be noted that such a distinction, of the initiated and the rest, is quite typical of those who, in our time, follow the example of the Russian intelligentsia. Perhaps it was unwise of Simone de Beauvoir, Sartre's companion, to call her novel about their milieu *The Mandarins*. To belong to the chosen is comforting, and the chosen are those who grasp the secret of the historical process, so that they know the future. Then they are united not by a common faith but by their shared knowledge. It is a peculiar gnosis which authorizes them to pronounce judgments deduced from presumably unshakable premises, without paying attention to tangible but too down-to-earth reality.

What is the meaning of this transmutation of Dostoevsky's characters, whose traits are recognizable in a different society and a different era? If the Russian intelligentsia became a forerunner of the European and American intelligentsia, according to what rule did it happen? Why did the import—for everything which nourished educated Russia, including the literary models for Dostoevsky, was an import from Germany, France, or England—why did the import result in the construction of such a mirror? We are accustomed to believing that societies, if they resemble each other in their economic, political, and social structures, also find similar means of expression in their philosophy, literature, and art. This assumption seems to belong to that part of the Marxist heritage that has become common property. But in what could czarist Russia, with its division of the population into castes officially registered by the state, with its extreme centralization of power, and with its immense illiterate peasant mass, resemble the developed countries of the West in the second half of the twentieth century? But is it indeed true, as I have hinted, that up to the present time the West has had no intelligentsia, i.e., a specific social layer separated from the common bread-earners, suffering because of that separation and assigning to itself a Promethean role? Or should we simply recognize that ideas lead an autonomous life and that they are more important than economic or political differences? Assuming this, it is possible to maintain that, though the metaphysical foundation of both ethics and authority crumbled in the West owing to what Nietzsche called "the death of God," the very complex praxis of economic growth obscured such problems. At a certain time, they appeared on the surface, and this coincided with the crisis of the parliamentary systems.

The activity of terrorist groups in the sixties and seventies of our century, such as the Weathermen or the Symbionese Liberation Army in the United States or the Red Brigades in Italy, etc., means—as in *The Possessed*—that the legitimacy of the authorities has been called into question. In Russia, the Nechaev group, whose trial provided Dostoevsky with material for the novel, rejected the legitimacy of the monarchic authority and of the whole system founded upon the sacred. In the West, it is the turn of the authority founded upon elections. Of course, the revolutionaries know what makes the "true" will of the people, as distinguished from the apparent one, unaware of itself, and they act in the name of that "true" will.

Modern novelists, with the possible exception of V. S. Naipaul, do not explore the fascinating kinship between the motivations of these groups in the West and the motivations that we find in *The Possessed*—or the considerable differences, in view of the role of the mass media today. This proves, perhaps, that the novel as a genre no longer reacts to events in public life, plunging instead into subjectivity. There is, however, another explanation for this lack of interest on the part of literature in events of, after all, great importance. Dostoevsky reflected on the future of Russia and on the changes threatening her; his thought was that of a defender of the existing order, for instance a district attorney. Upon its appearance, *The Possessed* enraged the progressive intelligentsia, who took it as a libel on the whole revolutionary movement. The sympathies of enlightened public opinion turned toward young rebels of various orientations, who were surrounded by a halo of heroism and martyrdom and whose trials put the authorities themselves on trial. A novelist who dared, today, to choose as his subject the hostile analysis of a terrorist group's way of thought and behavior would expose himself to the reproach of being a defender of the existing order, which is considered an unforgivable offense by people of a certain intellectual level. It should be kept in mind that terrorist activity has drawn its justification from the writings of philosophers, Jean-Paul Sartre, Herbert Marcuse, and others—both terrorist activity on a small scale, practiced by underground networks, and that on a large scale, such as the genocide introduced into Cambodia by former students of the Sorbonne. Since so many people of the intellect openly or tacitly sympathize with terror, it would be difficult to expect from them its portrayal, multilayered but negative, such as in *The Possessed* by Dostoevsky. Moreover, Dostoevsky, in his own time, had to free himself from the literary canons which were binding for the intelligentsia. We would look in vain for similar cross sections from the pen of writers of the

Chernyshevsky type. Thus, it would be proper to reject the widely held opinion that genius took hold of Dostoevsky in spite of his reactionary views. A quite opposite affirmation seems valid: he was a great writer because he was endowed with the gift of clairvoyance, and he owed this gift to his being a reactionary.

Nikolai Berdyaev, whom I have already quoted, noticed in Dostoevsky a capacity for understanding processes that go deeper than social conditions and politics. "Dostoevsky was a great master in unveiling *ontological* consequences of false ideas," he says. "Dostoevsky foresaw that a revolution in Russia would be joyless, cruel, and murky; that it would not bring any rebirth of the people. He knew that a considerable role would be played by Fedka the criminal and that victory would belong to Shigalov." Of course, we cannot but ask ourselves today whether Dostoevsky's diagnosis, conceived out of his fears for the fate of Russia, is also not rich in predictions for the fate of the West. It is easy to accept the premise—prepared, moreover, by evolutionism, which is taught at school and in the university—that there exist immutable laws of historical development. The similarities between the attitudes of the Russian intelligentsia and those of the intelligentsia in the West today may, in fact, be a confirmation of those laws, which led, over there, to the fall of czardom, and which will lead, here, to the fall of a system based on free elections. In the pronouncements of Dostoevsky's characters there was no place for democracy. Raskolnikov believed in the dictatorial rule of great, exceptional individuals; Shigalov, logical in his defense of universal slavery, becomes a theoretician of a revolutionary group in *The Possessed*; while a powerful philosophical mind, Ivan Karamazov, chooses the Grand Inquisitor to be the guardian of people who do not merit anything better, for they are arrogant children and, left to themselves, would not know how to govern themselves. "*La volonté générale*" of Rousseau remains beyond the mental horizons of these dreamers. In their loathing of democracy, which for them is synonymous with bourgeois mediocrity, they embody the views of Dostoevsky himself. In *The Possessed*, he identified the suicide of Stavrogin with the Swiss canton of Uri, and, in *Crime and Punishment*, makes a voyage to America a metaphor for the suicide of Svidrigailov.

The nineteenth century in the West swore allegiance to a new idea, that of the people as the source of authority, for, after the beheading of Louis XVI, that other source of authority, divine investiture, was lacking. Anti-monarchism became a part of libertarian rhetoric. In the United States, which emerged from a rebellion against the authority of the King of England, a contemporary of Dostoevsky, Walt Whitman, wrote poetry such as never existed before, a poetry of the citizen, equal among equals. What is astounding is the speed with which this current swelled and then subsided, and was followed, in the next century, by venomous mockeries directed at free elections and legislative chambers, as well as at the independent judiciary. By choosing Jean-Paul Sartre as a model, we may trace the passage to another kind of rhetoric, that of revolution. Such a rhetoric completely bypasses the question of the sources of authority, which in practice leads to a dictatorship of a few "knowledgeable" leaders presumably acting in the name of the people, and deprives people of the protection provided by the independent judiciary.

Thus, democracy has been abandoned by its most representative intellectuals, just as czardom was once abandoned by the Russian intelligentsia. It is tempting to draw conclusions as to the future, but we may easily fall victim to illusory analogies. The Russian intelligentsia was isolated in the midst of the illiterate peasant masses, which drove it to despair as a force of inertia incarnate. A certain misadventure which occurred in the milieu known to Dostoevsky in his youth has more than merely anecdotal significance. Petrashevsky, the founder of a famous political circle which counted Dostoevsky among its members, somewhat earlier founded a model phalanstery for his peasants, according to Fourier's recipe. The peasants promptly burned down the buildings.

The isolation of the intellectual in the twentieth century is of a different nature. Jean-Paul Sartre's review *Les Temps modernes* encountered a public able but unwilling to read it, as it preferred illustrated magazines, comics, and TV. The universal rush to consumption, the progress of medicine, and the permissiveness of society introduced completely new factors into the equation by creating a kind of soft social tissue, a target for intellectuals' pens and terrorists' bombs. Possible analogies notwithstanding, the differences between Dostoevsky's Russia and the contemporary West are, indeed, too serious to be neglected. Also, the historical past was different in different geographical areas, and we know that the past is always present behind the scene, shaping everyday life. In Russia, the function of the written word as a medium for expressing ideas has been different from what it has been in the West. The complexity of the Western social organism enables it to absorb and resorb various poisons; that complexity still exists in the West and takes on new forms which are less and less ideological.

The revival, in the twentieth century, of the "accursed problems" which once tormented the characters of a novelist from backward Russia mocks everything we know about the "laws" of history. Thus, in looking for signs of the future in such an unexpected phenomenon, we would be multiplying a paradox by a paradox. Nevertheless, there is nowhere else to be found a more faithful description of the tensions and conflicts proper to the twentieth century than in the legend of Dostoevsky's Grand Inquisitor. Russian admirers of the writer very early recognized in this text a strength matched only in the Gospels and the Revelation of St. John, and predicted that it would never lose significance, as it reached to the core of the human condition. Yet its apocalyptic features could shock only in the century in which it was written, a century not only nonapocalyptic but imbued with faith in progress. What to its first readers might have seemed only a terrifying and unclear fantasy, for us has acquired the distinctness of tangible things. For the Grand Inquisitor in this parable appears as someone who knows that man does not know how to be free, that he is a worshipper of gods, and that, if he has no gods, he bows to idols, in whose name he is capable of the worst cruelties. Man wants to feel an authority above him and is afraid of free choice: "He is weak and base. What does it matter if he does rebel against our authority everywhere now and is proud of his rebellion? It is the pride of a child and of a schoolboy. They are little children rioting in class and driving out their teacher. But an end will come to the transports of the children, too. They will pay dearly for it. They will tear down the temples and drench the earth with blood. But they will realize at last, the foolish children, that although they are rebels, they are impotent rebels who are unable to keep up with their rebellion."

This formulation is so full of content that the text resists almost all attempts to unravel it completely. The Dostoevsky who was a partisan of the autocratic power of the czar and an enemy of the revolutionaries imperceptibly changes into the Dostoevsky who bears a grudge against Christ for His failure to bring about the Kingdom of God on earth. In its crucial conclusion, the legend affirms that men are too weak to rise above the laws of nature. Since nature—in other words, reality—

is under the control of the devil, whosoever would rule effectively over men must make the same decision as the Grand Inquisitor: to collaborate with the "terrible and wise spirit of Non-being."

(January–February 1983)
Translated by the author

Maciej Bronski

FOXES, HEDGEHOGS,
AND LEMMINGS

Sɪʀ Isᴀɪᴀʜ Bᴇʀʟɪɴ—an English philosopher and intellectual historian of Russian–Jewish descent, born in 1909, presently a fellow at
All Souls College in Oxford—belongs to the thinkers one knows exist
and are important, yet whose work is known mostly secondhand, as
their writings are scattered in journals not readily available and in
abstruse periodicals. Fortunately, the publication of Berlin's collected
works was undertaken in England a few years ago. The first among
these, the one I will discuss here, is entitled *Russian Thinkers* and
consists of ten essays devoted to nineteenth-century Russian writers
from Belinsky to Tolstoy. Despite the apparent dullness of the subject,
the book is fascinating, and not merely because of the quality of its
intellectual analyses and their presentation (through the filter of an
interesting sensibility, everything becomes interesting), or because
these essays, written over a thirty-year span, provide an astonishingly
unified and consistent picture of pre-revolutionary Russia's mental
life, but for another reason as well; namely, that history, as Berlin
conceives it, is not a mere catalogue of past facts but rather a process
of crystallization. Berlin examines works of the past as if they were
constructs of axes and planes where facts, desires, and ideas of later

157

epochs subsequently settle, creating recurrent paradigms. Put more simply, Berlin discovers in the Russia of the past century modes of thinking and attitudes toward the world that have persisted until today. It is mainly on these that I want to focus here, but will add my own *quamquam* as well.

Longest and perhaps most interesting in the book is the essay devoted to Tolstoy, or rather to his odd conception of history, as illustrated by his novel *War and Peace*. The essay's title, "The Hedgehog and the Fox," is an allusion to an extant fragment of a Greek poet, Archilochus: *"Poll'oid alopex, all' echinos en mega,"* which may be translated as: "The fox knows many things, but the hedgehog knows one big thing." There are numerous interpretations of this line, but probably the poet wished to suggest that while the fox is quite cunning and the hedgehog has only one defense, this single defense is foolproof. Berlin's interpretation is broader: what the fox represents for him is a mind-set, versatile and intrigued by abundance and variety in the world, whereas the hedgehog is focused on an idea, on abstractions, types, and generalities. Dante is a hedgehog; Shakespeare is a fox.

Berlin applies this simple typology to Tolstoy to explain a striking paradox: *War and Peace*, a novel designed to illustrate the author's conception of history as an almighty river in the face of which human endeavor and achievement are ludicrous buffoonery, owes its fame and endurance to its "inessential" descriptive layer, and most readers skip over in irritation the historico-philosophical passages. Flaubert's cry of disgust upon reading the first fragments translated into French: *"Il se répète et il philosophise!"* has faithfully accompanied them ever since, as has the admiration for the "foxy" vividness of the story itself. What explains the "Tolstoy puzzle" for Berlin is that the self-proclaimed prophet from Yasnaya Polyana was a fox by nature and had tried all his life to convince himself that he was a hedgehog; his nature, according to Berlin, mitigated this misunderstanding: what compensates, unwittingly as it were, for the conceptual thinness of Tolstoy's work is the vividness of description and the characters. Before returning to Berlin's interpretation and proposing a certain typological correction (a lemming in lieu of a hedgehog), I would like to summarily sketch a picture of nineteenth-century Russian thought, as Berlin sees it in his book. The fox–hedgehog dichotomy will prove to be useful here as well.

Russia's greatest contribution to the glossary of modern sociological terms is for the author of *Russian Thinkers* the concept of intelligentsia, a social group whose value system is based primarily on such notions as education, intellectual capaciousness, and originality of thought, rather than the particulars of wealth, power, or family connections. This group did not develop in Russia, according to Berlin, until the nineteenth century. The older, foreign-educated managerial oligarchy associated with Peter the Great and his successors was solely a bureaucratic stratum, ever so alive to the "particulars" mentioned above. The break with mundaneness did not take place until the post-Napoleonic period. Russia's involvement in European affairs made the educated elite aware of the gap separating their motherland from those areas of the world considered at that time to be the most developed. During the same period, young Russians sent to study in Germany were becoming infected by what was then the dominant intellectual current there—Romanticism, with all its implications: contempt for average day-to-day existence, admiration for things "lofty and pure," and the conviction that the world is a moldering mass which must be set on a new course. Romanticism was in essence what we would today call a countercultural movement, touching in one way or another upon the whole of society. A romantic—to use today's terminology again—was *"l'homme engagé."* The idea of commitment was a main catalyst of the intelligentsia, and when, in the wake of the unsuccessful 1825 Decembrist rebellion, Russian censorship made direct communication even more difficult than before, discussion about social issues *nolens volens* moved into the realm of literature. The writer became the personification of all collective virtues, the conscience of the land, leader and lawmaker, or at least this was what the other members of the intelligentsia expected. The strongly totalitarian features of this situation are apparent. Social pressure bore down in one direction only: becoming a "hedgehog." No wonder that the majority of nineteenth-century Russian writers are hedgehogs. Belinsky, a sort of Russian Voltaire *à rebours*, promulgator of the gospel of commitment, politicization, and earnestness (*sereznost*). Bakunin, Chernyshevsky, Dostoevsky, and scores of others are all writers with a hard-hitting "mission," however vague its objectives, as in the case of most Slavophiles; however embarrassing its superficiality, as in the case of the "Westernizers." Although Berlin is a conscientious and nonmalicious expositor (unqualified is only Bakunin's characterization as a cynic and a fascist), he clearly sympathizes only with those writers who were able to liberate themselves from "hedgehog" schematism: Herzen, Turgenev, and Tolstoy. He values Herzen for his liberalism, the intuition that ideological abstractions inevitably lead to tyranny, and for the recognition that freedom is the cardinal value. He regards Herzen's observation that "to sacrifice freedom for any other end is to sacrifice human beings" to lie at the foundation of his political philosophy, which makes him "the most interesting nineteenth-century Russian political writer." Turgenev, the author of the celebrated *Fathers and Sons* (1862), whose hero, Bazarov, the archetypal intellectual nihilist meriting not so much the denomination of "the superfluous man" as that of the (later) *gryadushchii Kham* ("the boor whose time is coming"), epitomizes in Berlin's eyes the dilemma facing the wise and sensitive man in a polarized society. After the storm in Russia caused by the publication of his novel, Turgenev, a mild and accommodating man in everyday life, refused to succumb to social pressure and published another "committed" novel, *Smoke*, where both progressives and reactionaries are depicted as uncouth barbarians incapable of grasping life's real complexity. It can be said that Berlin sees Turgenev as a valiant fox who does not relinquish his nature despite the collective assault of the hedgehogs. The figure is justified, as after this novel's appearance the attacks of Russian critics upon him became so barbed (Dostoevsky called him a renegade) that Turgenev was in effect forced to go abroad, where he remained until his death.

While I share Berlin's opinion about Herzen and Turgenev as well as his sympathy for them, I am not in full agreement with his assessment of Tolstoy. I regard Tolstoy without question as an extraordinarily important Russian thinker, but for me his importance has different grounds: I regard him as a writer who typifies the intellectual atmosphere of Russia at the turn of the century, foreshadowing in a sense what was to happen there in the twentieth century. This requires a rather elaborate justification, but I think the matter is important and not solely an academic one. I believe that Tolstoy, unlike Berlin, has more of the hedgehog than the fox in him, and, to be more exact, he is a lemming who uses the technique of a fox to strengthen the persuasive power of his programmatic arguments.

What is a lemming? According to the encyclopedia, lemmings are "small rodents of the Lemmus genus, inhabiting the tundras of northern Eurasia and Northern America, who periodically undertake mass migrations in the course of which the majority of them perish from exhaustion." Scores of readers remember from childhood the harrowing description of lemmings in Selma Lagerlöf's *The Wonderful Adventures of Nils*: thousands upon thousands of animals march inexorably ahead, and when they finally reach the sea, they tread on without hesitation and drown. It is likely that this was the description which cast upon them the symbolic meaning of creatures who for unknown reasons are overwhelmed by a sudden passion to self-destruct. Zoologists suppose that the cause for the wanderings of lemmings is the recurrent overpopulation of their habitat: the animals then embark on a search for new territory, but because they stay in a herd, the "promised land" vanishes like a phantom, and all that remains is the compulsion to journey toward nothingness until death. I am no zoologist, but this explanation strikes me as most plausible, and I propose to apply it to certain human behavior and intellectual postures, which share misanthropy as a common denominator. Misanthropy's most fertile breeding ground is a closed society.

A closed society is like a train compartment where every fellow human being is an intruder. The only virtue expected and demanded of him is that he make himself as scarce as possible: that he not sing, not sneeze, not shove. The less there is of him, the "better" he is. The more he fidgets, the harsher the scowls he will elicit, the greater the ill will he will arouse. Indeed, it would be best if he were not to exist at all. But, as he does, he is expected to demonstrate meekness, for only when he realizes that he is nobody will he be sure to conduct himself properly, and perhaps even move to another compartment.

The feeling of being "closed" in human society has little to do with the size of an area inhabited by a given group and almost everything with the individual's freedom to choose his own path through life. This is in essence a problem of freedom within the confines of one's own group, a freedom which depends on a group's internal organization. One can live in a land flowing with milk and honey and yet belong to a group that for one reason or another—religious, traditional, or "philosophical"—strictly controls the consumption of milk and honey in such a way that an individual from the very threshold of his life knows that he is eligible to receive only so much and no more. The symbolic "milk" can stand for a broader range of goods: nourishment, the freedom from unnecessary suffering, the freedom from unnecessary control, access to information, sense of dignity, influence on decisions affecting large groups of people, and so on.

Little historical knowledge is needed to realize that Russia, despite its size, has always been, at least since its conquest by the Mongols, a closed society. Individual life there was almost always circumscribed by the "estate" into which one was born. The opportunities for improving one's lot were scant, while the threat of falling still lower was enormous. The single guarantee against downward mobility—as a result of falling into disfavor with the czar, for example—was maintenance of the status quo: immobility, conformity, servility. Two solutions are possible in such a situation: either changing the organization of society (in a revolutionary or evolutionary way) or, alternatively, improving the conditions of life internally, without upsetting the social structure. In effect, this second solution is an attempt to influence fellow prisoners, as in the situation of a crowded train compartment sketched above. "Be humble and meek of hearts!"—and we shall all reap the rewards . . . Such I suppose is the psychological basis underlying the polarization of the Russian intelligentsia into the Westernizers (*zapadniki*), those striving to remake Russia in the image of the West and thereby to improve it, and the Slavophiles, those pseudo-Christian proselytizers of meekness and "goodness" symbolized by the myth of the ancient peasant commune, the *mir*.

Tolstoy was, of course, a Slavophile, something trumpeted not only by his famous coarse-wool drawers and his *rubashki* (*nota bene*, his "peasant" shirts were silken and scented with rose petals by his servants, as the count favored this particular aroma) but also by what he wrote and chose to write about. His message never wavered: Man is the lowliest of creatures; the endeavor to understand the world and to direct its and one's own fate is nothing other than *hubris*—the sinful pride of a worm forgetful of his true nature. "Wisdom" for Tolstoy is acceptance of one's own nullity, submission to the nature of things, and resignation (*The Death of Ivan Ilyich*); the search for one's own path to happiness, besides being sinful, leads to well-deserved punishment (*Anna Karenina*); seemingly innocent pleasures are self-indulgent and as such deserve chastisement (*Kreutzer Sonata*); all other attempts to acquire wisdom are nothing but drivel and foolishness. *War and Peace* is a lecture, illustrated with examples, expounding this assertion. Napoleon and Alexander, generals raised on "German drivel," are morons who have failed to acknowledge their own nullity and that nothing whatsoever is in their power; the only one to understand this is Kutuzov—simple, meek, and almost as righteous a man as Ivan Ilyich. Besides him, only Pierre achieves, toward the end of the novel, a glimmering of this "truth."

In my judgment, this novel's sole aim is propagandistic; and this is manifest even in its evolution away from its original conception: Eichenbaum and other commentators have demonstrated that in successive drafts Tolstoy departs more and more drastically from the historical record (Kutuzov was in reality an arrogant, lazy airhead) in order to flesh out more cogently his predetermined thesis about the fundamental worthlessness of the individual. It might be said that this novel provides the most detailed exposition of that disturbing Russian term *lishnii chelovek*—"the superfluous man." His deepest conviction, so deep perhaps that he himself was not fully aware of it, is that people are superfluous in the world. It would be best if they were to "migrate" out of it, like lemmings.

How to reconcile such a supposition with his celebrated "goodness," religiosity, love of the simple folk, and pacifism? I think there is nothing here to be reconciled, so long as it is perceived that what lies at the foundation of these lofty ideals is misanthropy. If man is perenially "unworthy," nothing remains to be done except to be penitent, to withdraw, to resign oneself, and to study one's own vileness. I suspect that one of the motives behind all forms of religious proselytizing is the desire to diminish one's fellowman; once brought to acknowledge one or another "higher being" (in dire times, even flying saucers or mysterious forces that cause teaspoons to vanish will suffice), one becomes less self-absorbed and thus humbler. In Tolstoy's times it was not yet necessary to draw on parapsychology: available were the dim Orthodox God, Slavophile mythology, and the Ruthless March of History, suspiciously similar in terms of its aims to the Marxist Historical Process. And here we come upon some current concerns.

I suspect and fear that Tolstoyan ideology, modernized but un-changed in content, is still ruling Russia and continues to threaten the world. So much has been written about communism that an additional gloss may indeed seem only like so much drivel. Never-theless, it seems to me that its propelling force has yet to be adequately understood. Communism is routinely perceived as a sort of historical misunderstanding: noble idealists meant well, but then thugs took over and ruined the show. What such an account leaves unexplained is why the show has gone on for so long, while steadily winning new fans (hardly idealistic ones) and getting bigger and bigger. The matter becomes less puzzling once we acknowledge that communism has a set objective, and although it does not aim to make people happy in any conventional sense, it does have broad appeal. Its objective, as I see it, is to make people palpably aware of their utter insignificance.

Once this objective is understood, it becomes possible to account for many of the seeming inconsistencies of the communist system. One might wonder, for instance, why a nation able to send spaceships to the moon is unable to provide for its citizens the minimum required for a bearable existence. In terms of the "lemming ideology" sketched above, such a question misses the point. A "Tolstoyan" government of a country that sends spaceships to the moon (and thus itself is a kind of "higher being") has no interest whatsoever in the provision of "frills" for its citizens; on the contrary, whenever able, it will lower the minimum even further. From this point of view, the developments in Poland after the war become understandable and logical, although perhaps not all the country's "leaders" were fully cognizant of what these goals and intentions were. The mysticism of the Communist Party is not without real bases: the Party, the mafia of the mediocre, united by a shared lemming ideology, is indeed a superior force which delegates to certain individuals the task of fulfilling its set objective—which, to reiterate, is to make people palpably aware of their utter insignificance—and keeps them installed in power for as long as they successfully continue to realize this objective and then removes them. It is no accident that all communist leaders leave office in disgrace and that communism has actually no history: apart from the present moment, it is the domain of nonbeing, an Orwellian memory blot. Nonbeing is also the final goal of this system. As such, it is only an "ideal goal," but as life luckily corrects most ideals, it may be hoped that we will not all end like the lemmings in Selma Lagerlöf's story. Nevertheless, such a possibility cannot be ruled out. In Cambodia, "lemming ideology" became forty percent effective within three years.

The above reflections on the margins of Berlin's book are an attempt to grasp literary and political events, not in order to "sling mud" on Tolstoy or even on communism (I am not a believer in the efficacy of incantation), but in order to better understand some matters that concern us all. To understand something is always useful—personally, for instance, it was only in the course of preparing this article that I fully understood the reasons for the instinctive aversion I have always felt toward Tolstoy.

(January–February 1984)
Translated by Michael Kott

Mikhail Heller

HOMO SOVIETICUS

You are like a draft of ozone
for the soul. Hail, zone!
—Valentin Sokolov

*T*HE *YAWNING HEIGHTS* had such great impact on its Russian and foreign readers because Aleksandr Zinoviev was the first to suggest a new insight into the Soviet system. Rejecting comparative methods of analysis, he gave up studying the Soviet society by making analogies with prerevolutionary Russia or the contemporary Western world. Unlike his former colleagues, Zinoviev employs Soviet terminology and Marxist categories not to demonstrate the achievements of the communist system but to document its failings. Here is how Anton Zimin, the author's alter ego in *The Yawning Heights*, describes this methodology: "I am prepared to grant my opponents advantage and to agree to anything they want. You believe that the revolution was a blessing for Russia? Agreed! Unity of the party and the nation? Agreed! From each according to his abilities? Agreed! To each according to his needs? Agreed!"

In *The Yawning Heights* Zinoviev depicted the New (Soviet) World, its rules, and the people living in it. In later books, which today add up to a small library, he further developed his description of the world he so intimately knows. Their principal characters never change—clerks on the "ideological front" who, sometimes with zeal but often less than willingly, with an ironic smile on their lips, do what they are told.

According to Zinoviev, these hangers-on of Soviet ideology represent the core of Soviet intelligentsia; like Roman *auguri*, they share laughs among themselves while continuing to oppress the unordained. The role of the system's critic is usually played by a wise, talented, and perceptive member of the caste who had been defeated in his struggle for an elevated station on the ladder of hierarchy (a loss in the election for a corresponding member of the Academy of Sciences frequently serves as a mark of such defeat) because the caste has no use for brains and talent. "What do you really want?" is a question put to one of the characters in *The Yellow House*. His reply is a summation of desires of Zinoviev's principal heroes: "I would like to enjoy privileges and to score successes, but as a reward for my innate ability, my work, and my fortitude." The impossibility of fulfillment of the deepest human desires in the Soviet system forms the theme of all his books. Implacably, inexorably, the system grinds the individual down, transforming him into *homo sovieticus*, or *homosos*, in Zinoviev's idiosyncratic conflation.

A logician by training, profession, and vocation, Aleksandr Zinoviev subjects the Soviet system to logical analysis and discovers its laws. The system dealt with its explorer without mercy: it forced him into exile in another world, the West, and thereby gave him a priceless opportunity to test whether the laws discovered by him were true.

In 1980, Aleksandr Zinoviev announced the result of this test in a theoretical essay entitled *The Reality of Communism*. In 1982, he returned to the genre that earned him his fame; namely, the genre of *The Yawning Heights, A Radiant Future, At the Gates to Paradise,* and *The Yellow House*. Various reviewers have failed to come to agreement on how to name it. It seems best to call it "Zinoviade." The debate about the genre appears necessary, for it is the particular nature of "Zinoviade" which determines its forcefulness. All those who wrote about Zinoviev were unanimous in noting, correctly, that his books represent a melding of all existing literary styles and genres— philosophical discourse and couplets, logical analyses, and jokes. But the force and sharpness of Zinoviev's books do not derive from the multitude of combined styles and genres, or even from the brilliance and depth of their analyses. The special nature of "Zinoviade" is based on the fact that its author made himself the subject of scientific analysis. With enviable consistency, Zinoviev puts himself on the operating table, and his scalpel opens up the view for microscopic examination. The purpose of this surgery is to reveal the secrets of the system and of the creature it gave birth to. The history of medicine counts examples of heroic doctors who injected themselves with deadly diseases in order to observe their course and find a cure. Realizing that he is infected like all other citizens of the U.S.S.R., Zinoviev proceeded to observe the symptoms and to search for a *panaceum*.

Homo Sovieticus, published in 1982, is in my view Zinoviev's most important book since *The Yawning Heights*. Books written after *The Yawning Heights* built on the discovery made in its pages; they completed the picture of the Soviet world and embellished it with various fates of people ground down by the turning gears of real communism. The significance of *Homo Sovieticus* stems from its depiction of the confrontation between the individual brought up in the Soviet system and an entirely different world. So long as the Soviet man stays home, so long as his flaws and virtues are not measured by the standards of another world, he will remain a "thing in itself." Aleksandr Zinoviev takes *homo sovieticus* out among people. This book could have been titled *Our People Abroad*.

A book with this very title exists. It was written in 1890 by N. Leikin. The full title is *Our People Abroad: A Humorous Account of the Journey by Nikolai Ivanovich and Glafira Semionovna Ivanov to Paris and Back*. The words "and back" sound ironic today. But it never crossed the minds of Leikin or his readers that this could be taken as an allusion or as irony. The matter was perfectly normal: a young merchant wished to travel together with his wife to Paris to see the World Exhibition. They boarded the train, went, saw everything, and came back. Russian readers laughed themselves to tears over the adventures of the young couple because life abroad was different. Restaurants served minuscule portions, forcing Nikolai Ivanovich to order a lot of dishes; hotels did not supply samovars in the guest rooms; some things were more expensive than in Russia while others were cheaper—all in all, things were very strange. Unexpected events, small disasters, and misunderstandings make this resemble the adventures of Mark Twain's "innocents abroad," which inspired Leikin.

In Paris, Nikolai Ivanovich and Glafira Semionovna were mere foreigners. The characters in *Homo Sovieticus* exist abroad as if they were creatures from another planet. They are unlike the natives in their looks and, especially, in their view of the world, in their attitude to other people, their religion, morality, culture, and politics.

Aleksandr Zinoviev had foreseen this while still in Moscow. He wrote that if "the social conditions in the Soviet Union differ from social conditions in the West as much as the deserts or the Arctic differ from the ecosystems of America or Western Europe," then only an individual who possesses the special characteristics needed in Soviet society could survive and accomplish something in the U.S.S.R. In *A Radiant Future*, written in Russia, this new incarnation of *homo sapiens* was still called *Sovetskii chelovek* (Soviet Man), abbreviated to *sochlek*. Having seen *sochlek* in the West, Zinoviev renamed him *homo sovieticus*; i.e., *homosos*. The way these two abbreviations sound to the ear illustrates tellingly the evolution of the writer's attitude toward his subject. Thrown into an alien environment, *sochlek* became transformed into *homosos*: all his qualities and peculiarities were revealed as the protective cover vanished. "I stand before you as if I were naked," a character in the book could say. But he says: "I stand before you completely naked."

"Zinoviade" is a dangerous genre. Dangerous to the writer. Readers have a tendency to identify the author with his characters; they would stand in judgment over Dostoevsky for the rape committed by Stavrogin. In his previous books Zinoviev allowed many different characters to speak; some of them expressed his thoughts. In *Homo Sovieticus* the narration is in the first person singular. In the introduction the author says, "I myself am a *homosos*." Never before had he looked so deeply into himself during his studies of the nature of the Soviet system. George Orwell said "good novels are written by courageous people." Zinoviev's courage stems from his attempt to say everything about himself and others. It is the courage that reminds one of challenge and provocation—a feeling of irritation evoked when one looks into a mirror and sees the reflection of one's own, repulsive visage. Gustaw Herling-Grudzinski, a knowledgeable and understanding student of Russian literature, points out the resemblance of the hero in *Homo Sovieticus* to Golyadkin in *The Double*. In Dostoevsky's story, Mr. Golyadkin looked in the mirror and saw . . . Mr. Golyadkin. The younger Golyadkin, the one in the mirror, was—as Dostoevsky explains—the older Golyadkin's shame, his horror, his nightmare. He represented—we are told—another Golyadkin, but an identical one, a faithful reflection . . .

The nightmarish encounter between the two Golyadkins is almost literally repeated in Zinoviev's preface to *Homo Sovieticus*: "My attitude toward this individual is ambivalent. I love him and I hate him, I respect him and I see through him, I am full of admiration and horror." Zinoviev talks about himself and his reflection. This is why he is "cruel and without mercy" in his depiction of *homosos*.

The hero of *Homo Sovieticus*, "I," is an émigré who lives with other émigrés in a boardinghouse in a West European city. "I" left Ibansk but took his world with him. The subject matter of *Homo Sovieticus* is the same as that of previous books by Zinoviev: endeavors to get a state job at the Institute, construction of an edifice the purpose of which is revealed only at the end. It is immaterial that in Ibansk the job at the Institute (i.e., the Academy of Sciences) depended on the KGB, while in that unnamed West European city it depends on foreign secret services. It also makes no difference that in previous books what was being built was the Privy, the Slogan, and the Monument, and here it was the Bank. What is important is the fact that "I" has not changed; that is, he changed his residence but brought with him the cage he had always occupied.

Stanislaw Lem once wrote a short story which takes place on a remote planet inhabited by creatures astonishingly similar to humans. The system which reigned on that planet, however, forced everyone to live underwater. The inhabitants could communicate among themselves only by gurgling. The planet's propaganda does its best to convince them that life underwater is superior, and that breathing air is politically incorrect, even if everyone must occasionally do it. The ultimate goal is to adopt the life-style of the fish. Zinoviev's *homososes* get so used to the Soviet style of life that in the West they try to breathe underwater, just as before. The boardinghouse in *Homo Sovieticus* is like a raft on which former Soviet citizens, wrenched out of their natural environment, persist in gurgling. On the raft one can see everything, all of *homosos*'s characteristics; his vices and virtues are in plain view. Here the *homosos* becomes multidimensional.

Aleksandr Zinoviev, the discoverer of social laws which determine the nature of *homosos*—a social species best adapted to life in the Soviet system—had predecessors. In *Fatal Eggs*, Mikhail Bulgakov described a situation which seems as if it were literally taken out of "Zinoviade." Under the influence of red rays discovered by Professor Persikov, amoebas begin to struggle fiercely among themselves. "Newly born threw themselves at each other with fury, they tore each other to pieces, which they then swallowed . . . The better and stronger ones won. The better ones were terrible. They were twice as big as the regular ones and exhibited unusual mobility and viciousness." Professor Savitch, author of a book called *Bases of Human Behavior*, which became very popular in the late 1920s, saw revolution as a process of disintegration and destruction of everything given to man by culture. The leaders of the Soviet cultural revolution called this process a "primary accumulation of socialist emotions."

In the 1920s, one could already envision the direction of this development, although few actually did predict it. Zinoviev depicts the consequences—mature *homososes* in the era of developed socialism.

Externally, *homosos* barely differs from a human being. He is a *homo*. But the suffix "sos" is a hyperbole which illustrates certain of his features, eliminates others, and introduces new ones. Shocking self-assurance and unbounded contempt for others, above all for the West, are among *homosos*'s most striking characteristics. This phenomenon has obvious psychological causes, but there are also ideological ones. *Homosos* has sucked with his mother's milk the words of the poet: "Look down on the bourgeois," and the words of the Leader: "Any Soviet citizen stands a head taller than each and every bourgeois paper pusher." According to Zinoviev, sociological causes, i.e., social conditions, explain *homosos*'s implacable enmity toward and pathological envy of others. The socialist system, states one of his laws, is a kingdom of mediocrities who strangle every expression of talent. This is why in all his books it is Zinoviev's favorite characters—the brilliant and the talented—who suffer most. "I" is worst off, spat out by the Soviet system, lost and displaced in his new surroundings. He suffers more than others because he is a genius who knows that "his name could have been an illustrious one in the history of science." Alas, "society is uninterested in those great discoveries due to which your name would be recorded in the history of science," although "perhaps this is the way in which I am destined to be so recorded." But such declarations, in which belief in one's own greatness borders on megalomania, also betray a certain lack of confidence. In such moments, "I" tries to prove his superiority by denouncing all who might threaten his greatness and unique genius. *The Yawning Heights* features among its characters a writer whom the inhabitants of Ibansk call Veracitus. About him, Zinoviev wrote: "Whatever the situation, Veracitus strikes at the most sensitive spot in Ibanskian society. The most important place. Its very nerve." In *A Radiant Future*, Anton

Zimin calls the Gulag "art's genius child." *Homosos* "I" never ceases to comment with irony about "the writer of the Russian soil" and "the great Soviet dissident." The *homososes* in the boardinghouse are of one mind only once, when they debate the issue of "the great Soviet dissident" who went on a hunger strike for what appears to them a ridiculous, pitiful reason—to help one's fellowman!

The stunning self-assurance, astonishing narrow-mindedness, pathological presumptuousness of *homosos* are all perfectly illustrated by the boarders' attitude toward Western culture. *Homo Sovieticus* mentions not a single name of a Western writer, painter, or actor. *Homososes* do not visit museums; their knowledge of Western culture is reduced to "empty-headed films on TV," which they do not understand anyway because they don't speak the language. Nevertheless, they never cease to pronounce judgments on "empty, inferior, stupefying" Western culture. Their notion of culture never expands beyond the limits defined by *Literaturnaya Gazeta*, whose role in the homosovietization of people deserves separate analysis.

"I" is head and shoulders above other *homososes*, primarily because he knows that he is a *homosos*, a special kind, a representative of a higher human species (despite a couple of shortcomings) to whom belongs the future. He is also superior because the impulse which drives all *homososes* is particularly strong in him. The impulse of fear.

The hero of A. Afinogenov's play *Fear*, Professor Borodin, director of the Institute of Physical Stimulators, declared in 1930 from the stages of three hundred Soviet theaters: "We live in the era of Great Fear. A milk woman fears that her cow will be confiscated, a peasant fears collectivization, a worker fears constant purges, a party official fears a charge of deviation, a scientist a charge of idealism, a technician a charge of sabotage." Professor Borodin (Professor Savitch was his prototype) sums up: "Fear follows everyone. Man becomes distrustful, reserved, undependable, slovenly, and immoral." In 1930, Professor Borodin could only see the beginning of the era of Great Fear. More than half a century has passed since then, and fear changed its wrapping, but it has remained the principal, deciding factor shaping the consciousness of Soviet *homososes*. As Zinoviev is fond of saying, the climate of fear in which all his characters live determines the authenticity and adequacy of *Homo sovieticus*. It would be difficult to find another book in world literature which would strike one with equally intense horror: *homososes* are still scared of everything they were scared of in Russia and they are afraid of everything they see in exile. Aleksandr Zinoviev might just as well add to the title of his book: *Homo Sovieticus*—The Man Who Is Scared.

"I," who ridicules the fear of other *homososes*, is himself even more scared. He is even more scared because he is more intelligent. Among "I's" many wise observations, pointed turns of phrase, and apt comments, one merits special attention: "The characteristics of mature *homosos* have so far developed most fully among Soviet people with a relatively high level of culture and education, and also in socially active milieus, particularly in government circles, science, propaganda, culture, and education." This seems to me indisputable, and so is the cause: Soviet people "on a relatively high level," in "socially active milieus," are the ones most afraid. They are afraid of the same things all citizens of the U.S.S.R. are afraid of, only more so. Besides a healthy physical fear, they also feel a pathological, metaphysical fear. Such fear is the child of mature *homosos*'s upbringing. Having overcome Marxism, having understood its essence, "I," the mature *homosos*, will nevertheless carry its stigma for centuries to come. For, first of all, he is a determinist who knows that history does not stand still. Nor does he entertain any doubts about its direction. "I's" dream is "to unite my thoughts and my will, if only for a short while, with some stream of Grand History. At least once in my life." Such a desire, or need "to become one with the mass" as Mayakovsky put it, is the very source of this fear. Y. Pyatakov, expelled from the Party in 1928, expressed this very terror when he said, "Did you ever think that in the great transformation of the world in which our party plays the decisive role, I could be outside its ranks?" Here is how in 1938 Bukharin echoed Pyatakov: "Our life is hard . . . We are only saved by our faith in steady progress. It is like a stream tugging at its banks. If you leave the stream, the waves will throw you aside." Zinovievian *homosos* does not mention the Party, he doesn't even use the term "progress," but he still trembles that the stream of history will pass him by. As Louis Armstrong sang: "Oh, when the saints go marching in . . . Oh, I want to be in that number . . ."

Homosos's determinism is the other side of his conviction that humanity's development is ruled by its own strict laws, which admit no exceptions. *Homosos* has rejected the Marxist formulation of these laws, but he retained faith in the existence of a universal key which opens all secrets. Equally important is *homosos*'s unshaken belief that it is he who holds this universal key in hand, that he is the master of the Secret.

The belief that the Secret exists, that it has been uncovered but is carefully guarded and accessible only to a chosen few, forms the basis of Marxism as the highest of sciences. Soviet citizens took from the Marxists the belief that they are the Grail's watchmen safeguarding the secret of history's progress. The cult of secrecy in the Soviet Union, where everything is secret/confidential, is the main Marxist feature of real socialism: the secret terrifies and attracts. Every Soviet individual knows that he knows. Hence *homosos*'s contempt for people of different species, especially foreigners. Hence his belief that he can understand everything if he wishes. "I" declares: give me the Institute and I will discover the Secret.

The existence of the Secret necessarily requires Guardians of the Secret. Every *homosos* may regard himself as the Grail's spiritual guardian, but physical guardians are necessary as well: The Organs, in Soviet citizenry's graceful designation. In today's complicated and difficult conditions, the KGB is necessary.

Aleksandr Zinoviev does not occupy himself with detective stories; he is uninterested (say, not very interested) in the KGB's small-fry— low-level clerks, interrogators, and hangmen. He is interested in the KGB's higher spheres, those who decide the fate of the earth and the course of history. In his previous books, Zinoviev devoted a lot of space to the KGB; it is impossible to write about Soviet society and ignore one of its constitutive elements. In *Homo Sovieticus*, the KGB ceased to be the organization which controlled and watched Soviet citizens. It flooded the country and the people, it became society. For "I," the phrase "KGB agent" seems too narrow; it is merely a "definition of departmental identity." "I" prefers the neutral socio-logical concept of "Soviet agent" or "agent of the Soviet Union"; in short, *as*. "I" is absolutely right—if the KGB is the Soviet Union, *as* is the most appropriate term. "I" functions as an *as*; the KGB sent him to the West. Through the entire book he reminisces and thinks about guidance received from the Inspirer, his Teacher in life and work. "I" is a puppet in the Inspirer's hands, he is a pawn in the clever global game of the KGB. It is this that gives meaning and happiness to his life.

In a happy coincidence, *Le Montage* [The Setup], a book by the French writer Vladimir Volkoff, was published at the same time as *Homo Sovieticus*. Zinoviev's book is a sociological analysis disguised as a novel. Volkoff's novel contains several excellent sociological obser-vations. Like Zinoviev, Volkoff describes KGB manipulations, to which he applies the French term *montage*. In Volkoff, as in Zinoviev, the sky above the Soviet world is brightly lit by the KGB. The fundamental difference between the Russian writer-in-exile and the French writer of Russian origin who has lived all his life in the West lies in the fact that, for Volkoff, the KGB is the incarnation of the devil (but God also exists), while, for Zinoviev, the KGB is the only deity in the Soviet sky, and soon, perhaps, in the whole world.

The chapter "The Essence of Things," where the Inspirer, following the example of the Great Inquisitor in *The Brothers Karamazov*, spins out a vision of the future, reveals the metaphysical meaning of the KGB's actions. Having understood the objective trends of history, the KGB can "crawl over the entire planet, creep into all its crevices." The KGB should do today what "Marx, Lenin, and Stalin did in their time."

This elevated goal calls for a genius, but "the intellectual functions of historical genius," explains the Inspirer, "can be performed only by a secret agent such as you, or by a midlevel bureaucrat in the Organs, such as I."

The vision of the world is clear. Its fate is in the hands of the Organs. A poet would say, "One God have we—a KGB comrade." Those who pay tribute to the new deity perform the function of clairvoyant geniuses. "I understand everything," says "I," "for many centuries to come." The new idolaters proclaim the *homososes'* Magna Carta: Whatever you do, you will do on the KGB's orders, even if you think your actions are directed against the KGB. The KGB's gigantic plan has foreseen everything; in it there is a place for everyone: the agents, the dissidents, the West, the East. Struggle and resistance lose their purpose—*homosos's* fate is revealed as the best possible human condition. If the KGB is the omniscient, all-powerful God who knows "the objective course of history," to fight him is laughable. And so the main hero of *Homo Sovieticus*, *homosos* exemplary, never stops his sinister, sneering, condescending laughter.

Two books mark twentieth-century history. In 1920, Yevgeny Zamiatin described the future *homosos* in an astounding prophecy. His novel *We*, a diary of the first *homosos*, ends on a confident note: ". . . I am certain we shall win. For Reason must prevail." About thirty years later George Orwell described this victory of reason. *Nineteen Eighty-Four* ends with *homosos* Winston Smith's victory: "He had won the victory over himself. He loved Big Brother!" Another thirty years have passed. The prophecies are fulfilled, the fantastic visions of Zamiatin and Orwell became reality. Reality has now acquired fantastic features; it has become Soviet: *homosos* walks the earth. Like the books of his predecessors, Zinoviev's book ends on a note of confidence: "In the competition between *homosos* and machine, the future belongs to *homosos*."

The victorious *homosos*, stepping forward under the KGB's leadership, sweeps everything away from his objectively correct historic path because one characteristic makes him invincible. However, the same feature determines his frailty. *Homosos* cannot be alone. Among the horrors tugging at him is the fear of freedom, of the necessity of choice, of finding oneself outside the human multitude. Nostalgia used to be defined as a longing for the motherland. Zinoviev's *homososes*, especially "I," desperately long for a healthy Soviet collective. Like no one else, Zinoviev depicted in his books the hell of the Soviet collective. It was easy to see its monstrosity when one sat in its snug lap. Having lost the collective, *homosos* begins to despair—he does not know where to go, how to live. "I" remembers Stalin with regret. Under Stalin, one could "fuse with history." "I" longs for clear connections with the KGB. He longs for the collective: "Since I lost the collective, I cannot find peace, day or night." "I" is a *homosos*-intellectual, a scientist. His longing rests on a scientific theory which revealed the Soviet secret, the secret of the Soviet system: *homosos* does not collaborate with the authorities, he shares in their power. Nostalgia for the collective, longing for the zone, are really longings for power. Zamiatin understood this at the dawn of Soviet power when *homosos* was only being born: "Here we have our scale: on the one side a gram, on the other a ton. On one side 'I,' on the other 'we,' the United State. Hence the natural distribution: tons—rights, grams—duties. And the natural road from nothingness to greatness is to forget that you are but a gram and to feel like a millionth of a ton!"

Many years after Zamiatin's *We*, Valentin Zeka (Valentin Sokolov), the eternal Soviet prisoner and a great poet, wrote: "You are like a draft of ozone for the soul. Hail, zone . . ."

(January–February 1983)
Translated by Jerzy B. Warman

III
What We Write

Bohdan Korzeniewski

THE KNOLL

Lɪꜰᴇ, ᴡʜɪᴄʜ I ceaselessly observe with undiminished wonder and curiosity, has not stinted in providing me with experiences. Both the good and the bad. Most of them, especially the good, have value only for me. Of what possible use for anyone else is the fact that every spring I am struck dumb with rapture at the birch tree sending forth its first leaves and basking in the warm breeze in an almost human way? Or that I am still amazed at how much beauty there is in a woman's smile as she nods her head in assent or only with the hint of promise?

As a rule, people take little interest in the joys of others. They much more readily enter into others' sufferings. Adversity has true social value. For that reason, it seems, I have derived more benefit from what I have learned about human nature in conditions typical of collective life. The special characteristics of this life are revealed by the sole fact that it ran its normal course in an extermination camp, in Auschwitz. This puts the picture into sharper focus, but in no way falsifies it.

Only rarely have I gone back to my memories of my stay in the camp. For a while, during the first weeks after my release from the camp, I was besieged by persistent nightmares. In my dreams I kept running in panic toward the dense osier bushes on the banks of the Sola and tried to hide there, although I knew the attempt was futile since enormous German wolfhounds were used in pursuit. I would wake up with a start, my heart thumping loudly, just as the dogs were encircling me. After falling asleep again with much difficulty, I would resume my dream where it left off. I would be down on my knees holding my hands over my head, trying to ward off the blow of a raised stick, while a Kapo or an SS man standing behind me would say in a calm, almost caressing tone of voice: "*Aber Hände ab, Hände nieder, Mensch!*"

But soon the real and incredibly exciting dangers of my Underground activities totally freed me from these nightmares. I used to sleep greedily, as if saving my energy for more important things than inner disorders. After the war was over, I felt no need to divulge the degrading experiences that result from slavery in any of its forms. I would talk about what happened in a disconnected fashion to those closest to me. Without actually knowing why. Perhaps to prove that I trusted them.

For all these reasons, my reminiscences of camp life have been preserved in my memory with such vividness, as though they occurred only yesterday, not decades ago. I can call up from memory with the utmost precision the barrenness of the sparse, parched grass, on which we were allowed to sit in two rows, after the frantic run from the trains to the camp amid the barking of the dogs, the shouts of the SS, and the blows of their sticks. Today I am astonished by what I failed to notice then—that in that infernal din no sound at all came from the prisoners. Neither their moans, nor their gasping for breath. They ran in silence. It was the first sign of that obedient silence in which tortures and death would be suffered by the people in the camp, where only the bellowing of the guards could be heard.

I can still see that ironic half-smile on the face of a prisoner from an earlier transport, now a functionary, who grabbed the untouched loaves of bread out of our hands. We had been given them just before the doors of the freight cars were bolted at Warsaw's Zachodnia Station, and brought them with us to our destination clutched to our breasts. Still more astonishing, we didn't drop them when at daybreak the doors of the train were suddenly wrenched open on both sides to let in a band of SS men, crazed and excited by alcohol, showering blows with their sticks on our heads and hands as we tried to shield ourselves, and dispensing kicks skillfully aimed at our stomachs. To the accompaniment of their insane howls: *"Loos, loos, nieder! Du Schweinehund!"* we jumped down from the cars directly under the blows of their sticks and in the midst of the dogs jumping at our throats. All prisoners, or *Zugänge*, arriving at the camp would be received with the same welcoming ceremony. It was one of the tried and proven methods of enforcing obedience. It had been used for centuries with excellent results by cattle ranchers when they drove their huge herds into the pens. The human herd, crazed by fear, differed little from the animal herd. Thrown out of the cars, the men huddled together, pushed and shoved, squeezed into a quivering mass, and almost trampled one another as they tried to get back as far as possible from the outer edge, which was most exposed to the constantly raised sticks and the barking dogs straining at their leashes.

When this swirling mob buffeted back and forth between the rows of soldiers finally swept into the roll-call square and the last of the beaten herd went through the gate flanked by guards with ironic smiles on their faces, the SS men suddenly became silent, efficiently formed ranks of four, and marched off, chanting their joyous: *"Hola-li, hola-la!"* Only then did one notice to one's astonishment that the entire unit consisted of no more than thirty men and six dogs.

In the courtyard, some distance from the gate, there stood a group of SS officers, clad in tight-fitting uniforms, stiff black-rimmed caps, shiny boots, and brown gloves. They all had whiplashes with a leather loop at the end, which they either held under their arms or played with, smacking them on their high boots. In the course of subsequent camp life we learned what great significance casual movements of those whips could have for our fates. But this time the camp's dignitaries did not make use of them. After a perfunctory inspection of the panting crowd of prisoners, they reached a mutual understanding by a slight nod of the head and walked off, nonchalantly continuing their conversation, which probably had nothing to do with the latest transport from Warsaw. The commander of the unit which had driven us behind the barbed wire had undoubtedly already reported that the number of prisoners, if those who died during the trip were counted, was exactly the same as set forth in the accompanying document.

After the officers left, several prisoners in white-and-blue-striped outfits and similarly striped berets came over to our crowd paralyzed in anticipation. Some of them were holding sticks. They formed us into two columns by pushing us rather than telling us what to do, and led us off to a side of the square where the trees were still green, and allowed us to sit down. A moment later they passed along the columns in twos, holding a blanket by its corners to collect the loaves of bread that had been given us for the trip. They did it with a contemptuous smile, which we could not understand at this point. They looked at the untouched round loaves, as though they could not believe their eyes. One of those functionaries, a German Silesian (to judge by his accent), could not keep from expressing his contempt to us directly. "You stupid fool," he muttered, taking a loaf of bread out of someone's hand, "you'd better kiss its round ass goodbye, you'll be dreaming about it for many nights to come."

For the whole first day in the camp we were in the power of the men in striped outfits. Only shortly before dusk, during the evening roll call, did we have the honor of standing before the true authorities in steel-gray uniforms and stiff caps. By then we had already learned to keep in step in march time barefoot, and to raise our right hands in unison to our shaven heads at the order: *"Mütze ab!"* We also underwent many other initiations that instantly made us aware that our lives had changed drastically. After these initial experiences, we learned little that was new during the rest of our stay.

There were at least three reasons why I acquired a new profession and became a gardener in Auschwitz during my first day. The first was the game the Kapos played with the newly arrived prisoners, with the permission of the camp authorities. The second was my natural curiosity about other people, so lively that at times it threatened my instinct for self-preservation. The third, and perhaps the most important reason, was my destiny, always smiling mockingly but favorably, which so far has enabled me to escape unscathed from seemingly hopeless situations.

The first of these reasons deserves to be considered separately. Many errors made by people from a refined milieu arise from a faulty understanding of loutishness. The consequences of this misapprehension are highly dangerous. It warps our knowledge of the world, in which changes are occurring that in no way correspond to our received ideas. These notions have been shaped by the illusions and beliefs of the last century, which are of little use nowadays. The greatest difference between our era and previous ages is that, in huge areas of the earth, almost unlimited power can be seized and exercised by total louts. Nazism was almost an ideal manifestation of this type of regime. For that reason, its most loathsome traits can be found in all systems where coercion serves as the chief method of ruling. In this context, the words "ruler" and "ruling" acquire a fullness of meaning that they have not had for ages. Those who swear by force, starting with the meanest flunkies, have had restored to them the power of inflicting pain and death, perhaps the greatest authority that one human can have over another. The error in understanding loutishness concerns the ways of utilizing this vast, unlimited power. It has usually been assumed that the lout is satisfied with his physical superiority, which is an all too evident proof of his power. Thus, the vast, murky regions of a lout's soul are all too easily overlooked. This soul is begotten by nature but formed by the system. And this system has its own set of values, different from ours, but no less highly developed. It took many centuries for human civilization to develop not only the notion of giving orders but also the need for such feelings as revulsion in face of oppression of the weak, and the desire to defend the persecuted. So far, history has not presented us with many opportunities to express "higher emotions" such as goodness, compassion, sacrifice, self-denial. On the contrary, in our times it has unleashed other, primeval forces hidden under the well-scrubbed skin, the freshly ironed uniform, the newly washed underwear. Are they really primeval? Don't we actually see in such a formulation the total blindness of the heirs of the old civilization? After all, today's barbarism, so haughty and victorious, has its own system of values, although vastly different from ours. Where we, for example, place freedom, it puts obedience; where we display pity, it applies cruelty; where we show compassion, it flaunts loud and brutal sneering. In a word, whether we like it or not, it is yet another variant of human organization with a system of laws and customs appropriate to it. It also encompasses a different understanding of man, providing cognitive pleasures different from our own. We were about to become acquainted with one such experiment.

In the meantime, we were taken to the baths. There, after being stripped of our civilian clothes and having them placed in numbered bags, after having all the hair on our bodies shaved off, after being driven through cold showers, after being smeared with zinc ointment to prevent the mange, we were now transformed into prisoners in the concentration camp at Auschwitz. The whole thing was done very efficiently, since we got only a pair of badly worn pants and a striped jacket with a large black number sewn on the back and a red triangle on the front, with a number and the letter P below it. The number on the jacket corresponded to that on the bag with our civilian clothes and, from now on, was to take the place of everything that we had once been in our previous lives: name, surname, profession, and entire past, brief or long, since the transport included people past their prime as well as adolescent boys. But the majority were men at the height of their powers, about thirty years old, like myself—the most dangerous of all. By pure chance the striped outfit I received was more or less my size, a fact of no small significance, since it didn't incite the guards to cruel mistreatment. Those less fortunate, who had one pant leg which would not cover the knee or another which fell in folds over the foot, instantly attracted the attention of all the guards, both the ones in stripes and the ones in uniforms. For fully grown men, they displayed an amazing ingenuity in devising cruel games to prey on human awkwardness and unsightliness. This was part of their permanent repertory of jokes and a source of a deep satisfaction since it confirmed them in their feelings of superiority.

My number was 4880. This number, which had to be said in German at all times, *achtundvierzig achtzig*, I can still say loud and clear, even when aroused from a deep sleep in the middle of the night. The same applies to the two other sentences which I learned several hours later. They more than sufficed as a means of communication with our superiors throughout the entire time in the camp. These were: *"Jawohl, Herr Kapo!"* and *"Häftling Nummer achtundvierzig achtzig meldet sich an der Stelle."*

Among the many things that somehow failed to enter my consciousness then, and which I am now discovering to my great surprise, is the fact that I felt neither hunger during the entire trip in the sealed cargo car nor, later, cold during the first day in the camp. Yet fall had come early, and the days were chilly. And I was exposed to the cold as never before in my entire life. I should have reacted to the cold very strongly. I was barefoot, with a bare head freshly shaved, and I was almost naked, since the striped outfit made of cheap, washed-out fabric could not even serve as pajamas. So, from this contact with the harshness of nature, I did not retain any bad memories, although I had spent the entire day until dusk walking barefoot on the gravel paths, carrying armfuls of roof tiles to the Industriehof, and then down on my knees I had cleaned off the moss grown over them for years, by rubbing one tile against the other. On the other hand, everything that happened prior to my first job as slave laborer, when we all came out of the baths after having been transformed into prisoners, became sharply imprinted in my memory. I still can see before my eyes the image of a huge crowd of people who looked more like beggars than prisoners. Most of them wore striped outfits that didn't fit their bodies in the least, with pants of varying lengths and jackets which either hung down to the knees or did not reach the stomach. Some wore old military uniforms of various colors, with a huge square patch sewn on the back. A few stood out, having the red circles painted in oil paint on their backs and fronts. Later we found out from the prisoners from the earlier transports that only the Polizeihäftlings destined for a quick death by shooting were marked like that, while the majority of us were only Schutzhäftlings, entitled to live a few months longer. The second transport from Warsaw brought about six hundred people. And now they stood helplessly in a corner of the square not far from the baths, and looked at one another in painful stupefaction. We did not know how to behave, since from the moment we changed into the striped outfits the first and probably the most menacing of prison laws went into effect: we all understood clearly that nothing depended on us anymore.

For some time, we were left alone. Nothing was going on either in the broad courtyard surrounded by neat buildings or on the roll-call square, which soon was to become all too familiar to us. At the entrance gate crowned with the slogan in big wooden lettering *"Arbeit macht frei,"* by the guard box there stood two elegant SS officers looking at us while nonchalantly smoking cigarettes. A moment later they disappeared behind the barrier. Only then did we notice that the entire square was encircled by motionless prisoners in striped outfits like ours, but of a better cut, and worn with a touch of military elegance. They not only had new shoes on their feet and berets on their heads but even had colored scarves around their necks. Most of them wore their berets and scarves with a certain flair, almost as in a parachutists' unit. Clearly, they were waiting for someone. After some time, a very tall prisoner emerged from the guard box, walked to the center of the square and came to a stop, put his arms behind his back, and stared at us for a long time, shaking his head all the time, as though he could scarcely believe that in such a model camp such a disgusting band of tattered wretches could be found. At last he started to move in our direction, stopping a few steps short of the first row. Again he fixed us with the calm and penetrating gaze of a cattle trader appraising a newly corraled herd. As his glance shifted from one prisoner to the next, it was as though he were pulling out the most desirable specimens. A glimmer of increasingly studied amusement appeared in his eyes. It could have been taken for benevolent interest, if it weren't for a flicker of singular curiosity whenever his eye fell on a prisoner whose looks indicated he was one of the intelligentsia.

"Do any of you," he asked in correct German with a harsh Berlin accent, "know the German language well enough to faithfully render what I am going to tell you?"

Someone in the crowd raised his hand.

"Step forward and stand next to me," he ordered.

Glimmers of amusement again appeared in his eyes as he watched the approaching prisoner. The volunteer was a model of all the ineptness characteristic of intellectuals. He had immediately put on whatever had been thrown to him, without even trying to make a trade with those standing next to him. His pants, with uneven legs, reached only halfway down his calves, while his jacket, with a big patch on the back, hung down below the knees. Soon we became convinced that people who looked like that had only a few days to live. And then only under the most propitious circumstances, if the Kapo came across someone in his unit who was even more amusing in the grip of the terror that precedes death.

Our Kapo was watching the timorous and unsteady gait of the newly designated volunteer-interpreter with such tension that his whole body slanted forward. His attitude was shared by all the Kapos standing around the courtyard. They had become equally alert and slanted their bodies forward as well. Obviously, they were expecting something that would arouse their admiration, but what, we could not possibly know at that time. It was several days later that I found out what kind of display of virtuosity we were spared that day. This very tall, slim, sinewy man, who seemed to be all hard muscle beneath tense skin, had, only a few years before, apparently belonged to the elite of Berlin's criminal world. He was a notorious car thief, successful in eluding the police for many years. Finally captured, he quickly attained an eminent position in a succession of concentration camps. He had so distinguished himself as a Kapo that in Auschwitz he attained the highest position a prisoner could hold. He became the prisoner in command of the camp, the Lagerältester, the chief prison trusty, with the same unlimited powers as the official administration.

Many a time later I had an opportunity to witness how good he was in fulfilling his duties.

He would appear quite unexpectedly during the short breaks for the midday meal when the prisoners waited in line by the well to clean their soup bowls, or simply milled about the square trying to find anyone willing to swap a few bread crumbs for a cigarette butt. At the sight of his tall figure towering above the crowd, the square would become empty in no time at all. Everybody would get out of his way, using the Schnellschritt, which was the compulsory way of walking in the camp. Only invalids and old people could not get away fast enough. What happened then was what we were spared on our first encounter with him. The Lagerältester, without altering his elastic rhythmic gait of a gymnast, would pass by the sluggish prisoner's left side and, as he went by, hit him beneath the nose with the edge of his open hand. This seemingly slight, almost casual touch had the impact of a pistol shot right in the face at close range. Once the victim was struck, his legs would not even twitch when he fell to the ground. There was a saying in the camp that it was easier to commit suicide by getting in the way of the Kapo's hand than by running against the electrified barbed-wire fence.

This time, however, no such demonstration took place. The Kapo allowed the volunteer-interpreter to stop at arm's length from him, and with a few well-aimed punches pressed the prisoner's arms to his sides, pushed in his belly, prodded his head up, and ordered him to look him straight in the eye.

"You'll translate slowly and distinctly"—again, with an almost imperceptible punch, he knocked in the prisoner's belly, and with another straightened his back—"so that everyone in this wretched crew understands what I'm going to say."

He spoke smoothly, in well-turned phrases, clearly savoring his own performance. First he informed us that he would not deal with matters that we would learn about from the Herr Camp Commandant himself at the evening roll call. The one thing he advised us was not to forget the single most important sentence in his speech. Which went like this: The slogan over the gate, "Work makes man free," was no lie, since it was possible to be released from the camp, but only through the chimney.

With our eyes we all followed the movement of his hand pointing to the tall red chimney. The chimney was working. A thin streak of dark smoke came puffing out of it.

"But before you're transformed into such a streak of smoke," he continued, "you'll have the opportunity to learn a few things which will make you into different people. These things will allow you to understand real life, quite unlike the life you've been leading and have gotten used to. Now I'll start with myself. Take a good look at me."

He stepped back a few paces, straightened up, and effortlessly turned first to one side, then to the other, like a model at a fashion show.

"Not bad, eh?" he asked after returning to his previous spot. "Do you suppose you're in the presence of an ordinary prisoner? Is that what you think? Don't anyone be fooled by my striped outfit. I wouldn't advise it. I'm the Lagerältester, your highest superior within the camp, the deputy to the Commandant; in other words, someone who decides whether you live or die. You don't understand, do you? All right, I'll explain it to you."

From his explanations, delivered in the calm, even tone of an army commander preparing to take his troops to the front, we learned that he had reached his high position because the concentration camp was governed by the most democratic laws that mankind had so far discovered. Namely, that the prisoners were ruled by their fellow prisoners. This system of self-rule allowed for a wide margin of freedom, as the SS overlords intervened in the camp's internal affairs only if they noticed any departures from the rules in force, or if they introduced new rules. In actual fact, the daily life of the camp was run by SS-appointed prisoners of proven worth who had had at least several years of experience. He himself could boast of six years spent in various camps, starting with the protective-custody camps and ending with the penal camps, from which one usually came out only through that exit—again he pointed to the chimney still emitting a thin streak of smoke—but he came out through the gate. True, the gate did not lead to freedom, but it opened up the possibility that after the final victory, which lay in the not too distant future, he'd be able to gain that freedom. For that reason, for his part he'd try to do everything in his power to see that that date was not put off. And he didn't need to explain what that meant.

He glanced over the motionless crowd with an expression that took one's breath away. He was quite sure of the effect he was producing, and a smile of satisfaction spread over his face.

Furthermore, he wouldn't keep it a secret—his calm voice was counterpointed by the interpreter's, so terrified that it almost sounded like a prolonged scream—that he'd execute what was expected of him by the authorities with total ruthlessness. "Those men over there, the Kapos"—another gesture, pointing to the men lined up in the distance—"will perform their task faithfully. Nothing that you were used to in your former lives, protected by various legal paragraphs, will stop them from fulfilling their duty. And their duty is the enforcement of obedience, total and unconditional, by any means they see fit. To put it simply, every Kapo is entitled to punish every instance of insubordination—and he alone determines the extent of the infraction—and punish it by death if he so chooses. There's no need for beating around the bush. But that doesn't mean"—he was clearly enjoying his reasoning—"that the Kapos can act absolutely arbitrarily. Punishment must be harsh, but just." He'd like to be properly understood. We could not judge the justness of a punishment by the method of inflicting it. The inflicting of punishment could be a source of pleasure for the person doing the punishing; there was nothing that specifically forbade deriving satisfaction from inflicting death, as in any job that's done efficiently. On the other hand, it was forbidden to kill solely for the sake of satisfying a craving for cruelty; such an act would be considered ordinary murder.

"Having heard these explanations, you'll know"—at this point his manner of speech was even more precise—"how to work once you are taken to work. But before that happens, you should know that Herr Commandant has bestowed a special privilege on you today. Usually a prisoner is not asked to choose his own Kapo, just as a soldier is not asked to choose his own corporal. This time, however, to commemorate your first day in Auschwitz, a day you should remember for the rest of your lives, Herr Commandant permits you to choose, absolutely voluntarily, not under any duress, your own superior and guardian. You have the right to point to the Kapo of your choice, and from that moment until evening roll call you'll be under his tutelage. Your chosen Kapo will be your teacher and your supreme judge as well for the remaining hours. So choose well. Remember, you'll never have another chance like this. Look carefully at the Kapos standing over there, make your choice, and stand by the one you've chosen as your commander for today. You've got three minutes to decide."

He took a stopwatch out of his pocket, placed it on the palm of his hand, waited the prescribed three minutes, and yelled, the way it's done at sport stadiums: *"Hopla! Schnell! Noch schneller! Leute!"*

We started to run toward the center of the square, spreading out in a broad line. The Kapos stood at attention, but the style of execution left something to be desired. Some kept their berets on their heads; others held them in their hands, pressed to their thighs. One could admire their well-groomed but closely trimmed hair. This attention to appearance was also reflected in their elegant, freshly ironed striped outfits and shiny military boots. In the very center, attracting the attention of all, stood, as if on a display, two exceptionally handsome men, whose good looks, however, were Spanish rather than German. Slim, tall, perfectly built, with expressive, almost histrionic, dark-complexioned faces, they could have served as a model for SS men, for how an officer in the best army in the world should look, if the ideal of that elite had not been the blond warrior. One of them especially, slightly younger, had beautiful chestnut-colored eyes, set in a swarthy face, that inspired special confidence. The delicate mist of a reverie or a dream suffused his features. He seemed not to see the hundreds of anxious but hopeful eyes fixed on him. He appeared to be immersed in his own world, far removed from this spacious square surrounded on two sides by one-story buildings, formerly barracks, and closed off by a low barracks housing the camp's kitchen.

At the command barked from behind: "Choose! Fast!" at least half of the prisoners raced to the dark-complexioned man who looked so kind. The other half clustered around his companion, who showed his teeth in a wide grin, and around a few other Kapos who did not arouse instant fear.

For a brief moment, I stood alone. From the very beginning of the Lagerältester's performance, I had been watching with tense, almost painful concentration a Kapo who was standing on the right flank. Something about his behavior seemed to indicate that he was not taking part in the experiment with the newly arrived prisoners. With his head bent down slightly, he was using his thick stick to draw zigzags at his feet, as if patiently waiting for the show to end. Clearly he did not want to take part in it and did not hesitate to show it. Perhaps he could afford such a display of independence on account of his exceptionally revolting, even frightful appearance. His round head was covered with wiry white hair almost indistinguishable from a pig's bristle. His bushy eyebrows were the same color, as were the totally white eyelashes over his small, pale eyes. To complete the picture, his nose was flattened, probably from a blow of someone's fist, his mouth very wide, and his arms and hands, constantly toying with the stick, were so long that they almost hung down to his knees.

So as not to leave myself any time for reflection, I ran over as fast as I could and stood next to him. No one came along with me. He waited for a moment to see if anyone else would follow my lead, then looked me over carefully, his watery eyes peering out from under the bristle of his eyelashes, not concealing the fact that I had won his acceptance.

"What's your profession?" he asked.

"I'm a professor," I answered.

"In a high school?"

"No, at an institute."

"What do you teach?"

"Theater history."

He sighed deeply, either out of compassion or out of amazement and, without altering his friendly attitude, punched me in the jaw. Undoubtedly he intended it as a friendly blow, but I saw stars.

"Nun gut," he said, "but from now on you're not a professor but a gardener, understand?"

"I understand," I immediately agreed.

"Repeat."

"Ich bin Gärtner," I eagerly assented.

"Wrong!" he corrected me angrily.

"I don't understand."

Again, but this time without mercy, he hit me in the jaw with the edge of his open hand. *"Scheiss und Tausend Jahre als Grossvater blutige Scheiss,* you've got to repeat it right: *Ich bin Gärtner, Herr Kapo!"*

"Jawohl, ich bin Gärtner, Herr Kapo!" I assented with total conviction.

He nudged me with his shoulder in a comradely fashion, which was an unusual distinction, although I didn't realize it then. Especially in that it gave rise to a conversation which I in no way deserved, other than through my reckless behavior.

"I see that you understand German," he began, looking over at the square, where the Kapos were drawing up their units of sixty to seventy men each in rows of five.

"Yes, Herr Kapo, I understand, Herr Kapo."

"Then listen and mark every word I say. Repeat."

"I'll listen and mark every word you say, Herr Kapo."

"Good. I've been a prisoner for six years now. I've been through many camps. And I'm still alive. Know why?"

I was silent.

"You're smart not to say anything. Because you don't have any idea. But I tell you why. Because I was lucky enough to meet the right people, who taught me the most important law of camp life. And what does this most important law say? It says that in the camp one must avoid work. Whoever works dies, understand?"

"I understand, Herr Kapo."

"*Scheiss,* you still don't understand, but you will in a couple of days, if you survive that long. You'll find out right away, starting today, that you'll be given only as much chow as is needed to keep you alive for four weeks of hard labor, twelve hours a day, out in the cold. That's all the time any of you have before you're dead and cremated, twenty-eight days, got that?"

"Got it, Herr Kapo."

"So every effort you prisoners make brings you one step closer to a freely chosen death, of your own free will, a kind of suicide, and you probably don't want to die, right?"

"Right, Herr Kapo."

"Got a family?"

"A wife and a daughter, Herr Kapo, but that isn't why . . ."

"Shut your trap. How do you know I won't run to the Schreibstube and squeal on you? But I won't squeal. I want to live, too, for similar reasons. That's why I'm telling you that in the camp one mustn't work, right?"

"Right, Herr Kapo."

"Now mark my words carefully. You mustn't work, but even more important, you mustn't make it obvious that you're not working. If you're not careful and make it obvious, you die even faster than the ones who work, understand?"

I kept silent.

"You're keeping quiet? That's smart. No point pretending you understand, when you don't. You still don't know that anyone who is unwilling to work and fails to conceal it dies a painful death. I'll kill him myself. I'll have to kill him to survive myself. You don't believe I know how to kill? I know how to kill. You'll see."

A group of several score prisoners led by the young Kapo whose movements were so graceful that it seemed he was floating through the air was coming in our direction in disarray. It consisted mainly of people who could already be called goners. There was an air of resignation about them which indicated they would not stand up against their fate. Evidently, in herding them together, the Kapos had already made the first selection.

"So you've got your Kommando, Horst," shouted the Kapo with a broad smile but stopped to let the sluggish crowd go by. "The cream of the crop. You haven't had anything like that for a long time. Have fun."

He held between his teeth the thin stick with which he had been driving the tottering squad like a flock of geese. Clearly he was having a wonderful time. With the springy step of a sportsman getting ready for a warm-up, he ran over to his squad formed in rows of five. By now his Kommando resembled a geometric figure. As did all the Kommandos marching about the square in various directions. The slim Kapo with the dreamy eyes was walking alongside his smartly marching Kommando. He would accelerate the pace, or slow it down, scrutinizing the rows of fives marching past him, as if he wanted to get to know the men who had flocked to him in such a hurry. His face was fixed in an expression of almost unbearable expectation.

My Kapo pointed at him with his stick. "Why didn't you choose him, like all the rest?"

"I was scared."

"Scared of what?"

"Of him."

"You may have a chance of surviving after all," he said, smiling for the first time, and his amusement revealed an intelligence that made one forget his physical ugliness. Despite that, the newly arrived prisoners looked at him with gloomy apprehension.

"Tell those friends of yours what I have told you. And warn them that I'll kill on the spot anyone who squeals, and you in the bargain. I have to defend myself, understand?"

"Yes, I understand, Herr Kapo."

"And as for that handsome Kapo, you'll find out a thing or two about him soon enough."

I did indeed learn a thing or two soon after returning from work. The news spread like lightning. The beautiful, daydreaming Kapo had killed seven prisoners in his Kommando.

He did it with a calm, keen curiosity, typical of true researchers who in their laboratories try to discover the secrets of life. Perhaps he was driven by a desire to discover an even greater secret, the secret of death. In his investigations he functioned in a skillful and purposeful way, obviously acquired through long practice. He would ask a clumsy prisoner in a quiet and gentle voice to lie on the ground and spread his arms wide. He would even speed up the process by prodding the victim with the toe of his shiny boot. Then, his legs astride, he would plant his feet firmly on the outstretched arms of his victim, and place the sharply pointed end of the cane, which he had been playing with all the time, on the prisoner's Adam's apple. Then he would feel the windpipe with light touches of his cane, and either press on the larynx so violently that the throat burst immediately, or do it gradually, diminishing time and again the pressure when the victim's pupils began to disappear under his eyelids. During the entire execution, he would look intently at the victim's face, and into his eyes first begging for mercy, then bulging from terror, and finally filmed over by the mist of approaching death. His body bent forward, the Kapo would not look behind him. He certainly knew by heart what was taking place behind his legs spread wide. He knew very well the moment when the body stiffens in a bow, its heels sunk firmly in the grass, and when it struggles, contracting and kicking the ground as if the dying man is still trying to escape.

After having inflicted the punishment, when the body had already gone limp, the Kapo would shake off his absorption in his work and begin to notice the people in his squad. He would look at them as they stood petrified with terror, his eyes expressing astonishment.

"*Das ist schrecklich, Leute, nicht war?*" he would ask, as though he himself was surprised by what he had done. "*Natürlich, Leute, das ist schrecklich, aber das ist ganz warscheinlich und ganz notwendig, nicht war, Leute, verstehen sie, Leute?*"

On the way back from work, as the Kommandos in columns of five entered the square, the lanky Kapo walked with a light, almost dancing step at the head of his squad. The bodies of those who had been killed were carried in the rear, then piled in a heap at the end of the column, so that the number of those present would come out right during the report. Only then could we see that a similar thing had happened in other Kommandos, although not on such a scale. The other of the two handsome Kapos, the one with the dazzling smile that showed his magnificent white teeth, had killed three prisoners with a blow of his open hand aimed below the nose, while the Kapo with the genial looks of a farmhand had killed only one.

And apparently it was the victim's own fault for not jumping aside in time, when the Kapo charged menacingly at him with flailing fists, intending only to frighten him.

Our Kapo did not as much as poke a single man with his stick, although he brandished it over our bent backs so vigorously that passing SS men would pat him on the shoulders in approval. The way he was able to get away with it deserves a separate description. I spent six days under his care—the word "care" is in this case the right word—my first six days in the camp. During those six days our Kommando of forty men performed work considered murderous even in Auschwitz. Our task consisted of transporting from the concrete works to the opposite end of the camp enormous poles, known as "pipes," weighing half a ton each, which to this day support the barbed wire surrounding the entire camp. At that time they still carried electric current. Here our frightful commander constantly displayed abilities which should be put to use whenever work arouses anger and hatred. In order to sink the poles in the ground, we had to dig pits one meter in diameter and one and a half meters deep. To give but one example, not until we had dug those pits half a meter deep were we allowed to stretch our bodies, and we shoveled the dirt with such force that it seemed we had struck an underground spring. The Kapo circled around with his stick upraised, and whenever he spotted someone from the upper echelon, he would burst out yelling with a vehemence that very few could match. He would insult us as "pig dogs," "putrid cows," "stinking rotten corpses," "stupid, lazy brutes," whom he would teach to work properly. He even knew how to strike a digger on the back with his stick so that it caused no pain but made a loud crack. But once the pits were dug deep enough so we could hide in them, he ordered us to crouch down in the ground, keep close to one another so as not to lose body heat, and sit still, keeping our shovels filled with dirt just in case. At the first sight of an officer's uniform in the distance, our Kapo would resume his frenzied dance around the pits, and we would shovel out the prepared supply of dirt with such zeal that it was dangerous for anyone to be in the area. Thanks to such shows of industriousness, the constant control over us lessened considerably, and we could sit undisturbed for long stretches, our backs against the warm dirt. Sometimes we gained as much as one or two extra hours of life.

But after six days, in our capacity as the Gartenkommando, we were given an assignment that was even more dangerous. We were ordered to remove intact a small knoll located in the garden behind the villa which before the war had served as the living quarters for the commander of the regiment, and now was occupied by Herr Commandant Hoess himself. Because of the knoll, Herr Commandant Hoess did not have a good view from his bedroom window of the SS barracks where he went every morning to carry out his official duties. Likewise, from the barracks, he could not see without obstruction his house, which as an exemplary husband and father he wanted to keep under a watchful eye. It goes without saying that, in carrying out this work, we could not alter in any way either the shape of the knoll or the placement of the bushes and the perennial flowers. The execution of this job might serve as a model, no longer achievable nowadays, for the preservation of park monuments. Because of the great importance of the assignment, our Kommando was joined by two other Kommandos, and three new Kapos were added to supervise the job. We were also supplied with the appropriate tools. First we brought to the site wheelbarrows, shovels, crowbars, as well as long, wide planks. These planks served as a roadway. Along them, always running, we had to roll wheelbarrows full of dirt, or, what was worse, whole bushes freshly dug out, with the soil attached. For the men using such a makeshift passageway for the first time in their lives, the planks were a sort of circus wire along which one had to run fast, high above the arena. Derailing one's wheelbarrow was every bit as dangerous as a fall in the circus. One of the Kapos would immediately spring at the miserable wretch and, dispensing blows with his stick, help him scramble up again on the track with his load, so as not to slow down the others coming by on the run. In the case of a more serious accident resulting in damage to the plants being transported, the guilty party would be surrounded by several guards, and if their "help" in lifting up the overturned barrow was ineffective, the Kommandoältester supervising the entire operation would personally inflict the punishment. It was known as the "seesaw," since what it consisted of was this: the Kapo would place the handle of a shovel across the throat of the man lying on the ground, then stand astride the handle and with a few powerful back-and-forth motions choke the victim to death. But it was not a frequent occurrence. By the time the job was completed, in five days, we counted two or three men killed that way. Our own Kapo, constantly brandishing his stick, did not have a single victim on his conscience.

After morning roll call, we were assembled to make our report about the completion of the task. Dawn was barely breaking. An early killing frost, to use the gardeners' expression, had blanketed the grass with hoarfrost, and the asphalt road on which we were beating march time with our bare feet seared like white-hot tin. Every shard of gravel cut sharply into our soles, causing excruciating pain. The Kapo formed us into ranks of two before the Commandant's villa. He gave our squad a look which told us that this time the stakes were very high, teetering between an extra portion of soup and the gallows. *"Ruhe, meine Knechte,"* he said, "if any of you as much as clears your throat . . ." And with a glance he indicated the wheelbarrows neatly lined up to the rear. From each of these protruded the handles of two shovels, creating a perfectly even fence. From the experience of the previous days we knew very well what the handles of those shovels could be used for. We did not even dare move our legs, which were going numb. Clouds of white fog seeped slowly from behind the dense thickets covering the banks of the Sola, which could barely be seen in the distance. The mist brought with it a penetrating morning chill.

After a few minutes, one of the villa's side doors half-opened and a big, strapping girl with ample breasts in a tight-fitting apron came out onto the steps. She yawned with gusto, as she plaited her thick braid, and then came down a few steps to have a better look at the immobile group of prisoners. Her broad, rosy-cheeked face broke into a grin of malicious, triumphant mockery. By that grin she demonstrated that she belonged to the master race. Then she wagged a finger at our Kapo, who, after a look at the front windows, sent her a kiss, making a discreet smacking noise. When she set his mind at rest with a yawn that served as a sign that they were still asleep in the house, the Kapo ran over to her stealthily. They disappeared behind the villa, and only the girl's excited squeals and a loud thumping noise indicated that our guard was still very much a man. But evidently something had stirred within the house, and the maid reached the door in a few heavy bounds and our Kapo ran back to the column and stood at attention on the right flank.

Yet the house betrayed no activity. Not even a shadow could be glimpsed behind the billowy white curtains. Nonetheless, we went on standing at attention, with our arms pressed tight to our thighs. We stood like that for a long time. The fog from over the river had meantime drifted through the barbed-wire fence, its frayed ribbons of mist rising slowly higher and higher. Soon the fog obliterated the guard standing in the watchtower with his machine gun aimed in our direction. He immediately started singing something in a low, throaty voice, no doubt to let us know that he was on the alert.

All of a sudden the door was flung wide open, as though someone inside had pushed it hard. *"Hab Acht!"* croaked our Kapo, his voice stuck in his throat. We fixed our eyes on the door; we had been standing at attention for quite some time. But it wasn't Herr Commandant Hoess who appeared in the doorway. Out came a little boy, perhaps five years old, wearing short Tyrolean pants, barely visible from under a tight-fitting green military jacket with the SS lightning on its black collar. He wasn't wearing the cap with the silver death's-head; he was bareheaded and his flaxen hair was cut in the style fashionable among upper-echelon officers and party officials. It had been introduced by Marshal Hindenburg years before and was now favored by Reichsführer Himmler. Following the example of the adored conqueror of the Masurian Lakes, the lad had his temples shaved almost to the skin, but a short brush of hair stood up on the top of his head. He held a small Mauser rifle in his hand, probably especially manufactured for the children of dignitaries, since the weapon did not look at all like a toy. We exchanged anxious looks, unsure whether the boy was going to use us as a target. The boy, however, did not grace us with a single glance. Apparently, he had far more interesting things to do. He planted himself on the threshold, legs spread wide, the rifle at his right foot, held out at arm's length. His pose suggested that of Frederick the Great's grenadiers standing guard by his study. Then he started to go through the drill exercises, stomping his feet and striking the porch's cement floor with the rifle butt. *"Ein, zwei, und drei,"* he repeated in a high-pitched childish voice, completely absorbed in what he was doing.

His movements were well executed. *"Sehen Sie, Scheiss,"* said our Kapo admiringly. *"Wunderbar, Scheiss, nicht wahr?"* He suddenly interrupted himself and wheezed out: *"Achtung! Mütze ab!"* Again we fixed our eyes on the open door.

But the Commandant did not appear this time either. An eight- or nine-year-old boy came out of the villa with a springy step, his highly polished boots shining brightly. He wore a full SS uniform, with the insignia of a Rottenführer or Oberrottenführer. A small sword was fastened to his belt, and he was holding a riding crop in his hand, the unmistakable mark of a camp officer. The riding crop has been invested with great power, much greater than the king's scepter ever had. A casual gesture with it meant being condemned to death, or granted life. Its power was to grow to unheard of dimensions, when countless numbers of old men, women, and children were led to the gas chambers straight from the trains.

The boy in SS uniform now used it to inflict punishment. He leapt out onto the porch, his riding crop upraised, shrieking in a high-pitched, cracking voice. In his other hand he held a black-rimmed cap. The word *"Scheisse,"* in its many camp variants, *Scheissedreck, Scheisseschweinerei, Scheissefresse, Scheissewagen,* pervaded that terrifying shriek. He shoved the cap he was carrying on the smaller boy's head and secured it more firmly by a blow to the head with his riding crop. *"Hab' Acht!"* he squeaked, his face red with anger. The younger boy did not even lift his hand to the painful spot. Apparently, he had experienced similar treatment before. He sprang to attention. Displaying the hot temper of a drill corporal, the older boy demonstrated the proper execution of the command "Present arms!" He put the riding crop under his arm and kept slapping the younger boy's face mercilessly, without regard for his subordinate's success in the execution of a given command. The younger boy's head swung from side to side, tears streamed down his battered face, but not a single complaint was heard from him. On the contrary, something like a flash of pride appeared in his eyes, the pride of taking part in such a demanding game.

Herr Commandant Hoess appeared in the doorway quite unexpectedly. With his back to us, he was straightening the holster of a heavy pistol attached to his belt. Our Kapo noticed him first. *"Hab' Acht!"* he croaked ecstatically, although we had been standing at attention with our eyes fixed on the door all the time. The Kapo's shriek interrupted the older boy's educational zeal. He jumped away from his brother, and stood with his legs astride, his left arm resting on his hip, his right raised in the air. With a flick of his riding crop he ordered his brother to pay attention, and, by means of several commands given in a squeaky voice, placed him in the position "Present arms." Then he goose-stepped over to his father and saluted with his small sword, clicked his heels, and, imitating the barking favored by the SS, spewed out a report. Herr Commandant received it at attention. He even raised his hand to the rim of his cap. "Give the order 'At ease,'" he said solemnly and, once the boys had executed the command, gave vent to his bottled-up joy. Bursting out time and again in peals of happy laughter, he patted the older boy on both cheeks, lifted the younger one up, kissed his face still red from repeated slapping, glistening with tears, but beaming with pride, and clasped them both to his legs. Finally he gently pushed the boys toward the door. "Go to your Mutti," he said. "I must go now." The word "mommy" had the softness of an angel's wings, an angel who had by chance strayed here at daybreak and then flown away, terrified.

With a heavy, soldierly step he came down the stairs toward us. In his behavior there was no trace of his former manner. Obviously, he knew how to separate his private life from his official duties. In his life as a functionary there was evidently no place at all for a personal relationship with the people in his power, a power so vast that, to find something comparable, one would have to go to the chieftains of barbarian tribes, or the kings of cities like Assyria or Babylon where cruelty was the law of the land. He was more than the proverbial lord of life and death. He was solely the lord of death. It did not register in his psyche or call forth in him a lurking desire to dominate; he simply did not realize what power the state had given him. In principle, the death of five million people does not differ from the death of one person, as long as it is invested with the majesty of the law. Death was the concern of a governmental institution under his jurisdiction which he tried to direct as any self-respecting bureaucrat would. After all, he was not the one who made the decisions as to when and how it was to be inflicted; such matters were decided on orders from above. Orders would be delivered in envelopes appropriately stamped "Strictly confidential," "For office use only," "Destroy after reading." Who would dare disobey them? His conscience was absolutely clean; he had only to take care that the utility in his charge operated efficiently and brought in the expected profits for the state. Moreover, it seems unlikely that back then, in the autumn of 1940, he had any inkling of what an enormous task he would soon have to face. He could not grasp imaginatively, if he ever used his imagination, the thousands of people, the inhabitants of entire towns walking days on end in a huge procession to the low, rectangular buildings beneath the red chimneys. For the time being, his camp had scarcely eight thousand inmates, and it only differed from scores of similar camps in that a special experiment was being conducted here. The object of the experiment was to arrive at a solution: the best possible way—without resorting to mass murder—of doing away with young, healthy, able-bodied men, within four weeks. Among the various methods commonly employed by louts, such as starvation, fear, and work beyond human endurance, there were others that one would hardly think louts capable of devising. They testify to a quite penetrating knowledge of man, whose annihilation is the goal. And certainly deserve to be recognized as an art of destruction. We were soon to learn about one of these techniques.

Nothing yet announced the coming danger. Herr Commandant Hoess did not in the least instill the fear which later on became associated with his name, as one of the most notorious in the history of genocide. There was nothing in him of Himmler, the degenerate with gentle manners and a receding jaw, or of Goebbels, the lame devil of that religion of fools endowed with a keen and cruel intelligence. Hoess did not differ in the slightest from the countless thousands of tall, well-fed, stylishly uniformed men who at that time goose-stepped through the conquered capitals of Europe. He was ordinary in every sense of the word. In civilian clothes, wearing his Sunday best, he could be taken for a prosperous artisan, perhaps even the head of his guild, and would enjoy an irreproachable reputation among his neighbors as a reliable master craftsman and an exemplary father of a family. In his military uniform he did not show any desire to stand out either. He dressed more modestly than many of his subordinates, who far from the front lines shone as elegant officers and, in the face of death, others' death, maintained a tough, soldierly bearing. Hoess did not adopt any pose. Undoubtedly, such a frivolous idea never entered his mind. He wore a military uniform of greenish-colored woolen cloth known as *feldgrau*, whose shagginess and bulkiness aroused despairing envy in us. We could almost feel the warmth he must have known in such a uniform, under several layers of soft underwear, in heavy boots with woolen socks, wearing a warm cap that protected his head from the drafts of frosty dampness which penetrated to our very marrow.

Something in our appearance must have displeased him, as a shadow of irritation flashed across his broad, meaty face. He wagged a finger at our Kapo, who immediately ran over and stood at attention, his cap pressed to his side, three steps from the Commandant, as required by the regulations. With a casual flip of his hand the Commandant pushed the Kapo out of his way and came over to our Kommando. *"Mütze ab!"* croaked our Kapo, as if someone had seized him by the throat. We raised one hand to our shaven heads and pressed the other, holding nonexistent caps, to our side.

"Caps not received yet?"

"No, Herr Commandant, the caps haven't been received yet," the Kapo acknowledged fearfully, as though he were personally responsible for our failure to execute the order in conformity with the regulations.

The Commandant took a look at our bare, soiled feet, the color of dirty snow, and made a face again. Undoubtedly, he would grimace the same way if someone displaced a ruler on his desk.

"No shoes either?"

"No, Herr Commandant, the shoes haven't been received either."

"What about socks?"

"The warehouse, sir, won't give out the socks before the shoes are distributed."

"The war, *Scheisse*," Hoess murmured, sighing softly as if apologizing to someone unseen but ever present. Apparently, in his mind, imbued from childhood with reverence for order, even the prisoners destined to die from hunger and overexertion in four weeks' time were entitled to receive the "basic allotment of clothing." Only the mass transports to the gas chambers in the years to come and the repulsive sight of the *Muselmänner* crawling behind the barbed wire brought about a change in his way of thinking. We may assume that he had to overcome some moral scruples in the process.

But the sight of our column glued to the ground in expectation, and the wheelbarrows lined up behind it with shovel handles protruding from them, must have reminded him of the order he had given a week before.

"Report!" said the Commandant, his voice registering clear aversion.

The Kapo, obviously scared by the tone, obediently informed Herr Commandant that his order to transfer the knoll 256 meters to the northwest of its original site had been carried out yesterday. The garden Kommando present here had strictly followed instructions. The knoll in its new location had retained exactly the same form as previously. It had not lost a single of its former qualities. The grass turf, cut and moved by numbered strips, had been placed on a layer of fertile soil thirty centimeters deep, and the bushes and the bulbs of perennial flowers had been transplanted exactly as they grew before. Great care had been taken with regard to their natural requirements and exposure to the sun, so as to eliminate the shock of adaptation to new conditions. Would Herr Commandant be kind enough to take a look at the work done and check to see if any errors had occurred despite all efforts to the contrary. Should any errors be found, the guilty would be punished accordingly, having deserved it by their negligence.

Hoess did not even turn his head in the direction of the knoll that now rose up on the left side of the villa. Undoubtedly, this kind of behavior was no less predictable in a system of persecution that led to genocide.

"The knoll looked better in its original location," he said indifferently. "Move it back."

It is not difficult to imagine how the work went now—we flung ourselves into it, with a loud rattle made by the wheelbarrows on the frozen ground. The howl of the Kapos, the flashing of their sticks, and the grating sound of prisoners breathing floated over our Kommando. Wheelbarrows kept rolling off the tracks, strips of grass turf broke whenever there was a spill, and shovels were more frequently used for the "seesaw" than for shoveling dirt. When finally, one week later, our Kommandoführer was able to report to the Lagerältester that the work had been completed, at least one-third of the prisoners, out of a total of four Kommandos, had lost their lives.

It is fair to assume that this kind of torture was originally devised by Germans for Germans. In effect, a society as committed to obedience as it was to hard work must have been deeply pained by a way of doing things in which obedience was made to further useless work. Our experience showed that this principle had much broader implications. The idea of destruction through senseless work was aimed at that basic human need which has been a motive force of civilization and which has become an almost inborn trait—the habit of constructive action. This habit asserted itself with an almost irrational power. After all, we had done the work on the orders of a man who for us was the incarnation of pitiless force. In terms of common sense, it should have aroused in the prisoners—not so long ago free men and now transformed into the most wretched slaves—passionate hatred. And, in addition, this work was intended to satisfy the whim of a despot, and was thus devoid of any rational justification. And yet it was not just fear of punishment that made us perform the job well. It was contagious, just as the desire to overtake a rival or an enemy brigantine would certainly have spread to the galley slave chained to the bench below the deck. After having expended all his strength in the competition, he might even have smiled once the race was over and his ship victorious. But he would have been plunged into the deepest despair, and let an overseer kill him on the spot without any resistance, had he seen through the small opening for his oar that there was no battle or race, that he had been forced to make a murderous effort the sole object of which was the murderous effort.

Now I can finally disclose the reason that has led me to return to these deeply humiliating memories. My reluctance to do so has once again been vanquished by my deep attachment to the nation to which I belong not only by the fatalism of my birth but also by conscious choice. Since 1945 I have had many opportunities to leave the country, which once more has fallen into slavery and been subjected to a series of inexplicable and undeserved humiliations. I have resisted this temptation because, to my mind, emigration would amount to running away. Once before in my life I experienced the deep shame caused by running away and I do not wish to repeat it.

It also happened in Auschwitz. A high ransom paid by my family to an officer from Aleja Szucha brought about my deliverance; my name was included on the list of eight prisoners to be released from the camp. It came about at the last possible moment, since at the time I weighed only thirty-four kilos and my face was swollen from hunger and scorched by the winds. I was, in fact, close to the state where one gives up all effort to preserve one's life.

After changing into our old civilian clothes—nothing was missing, not even a handkerchief—and after signing a document at the Schreibstube committing us not to disclose what we had witnessed in the camp, we were taken to the railway station, accompanied by a slim and elegant SS officer. On that particular day the camp was enveloped in thick fog, and the prisoners were not sent off to work. They would have had too many opportunities to escape. In rows of five they ran around and around roll-call square, prodded by the Kapos armed with sticks. The Kapos raced furiously around inside the circle. On the outside stood a solid line of SS guards clutching automatic rifles, their fingers on the trigger.

On our way from the Schreibstube to the gates of the camp, we almost had to brush against that human ring circling the square and making a noise so typical of the camp. Above the mass of running men there rose up the grating and whistling sound of breathing that

indicates pneumonia. At that time, only a few were granted the
privilege of dying in the camp clinic. Their death was speeded up by
especially hard labor. Our departure lasted long enough for many
in that crowd of seven thousand men running at a heavy gallop to
notice that we were leaving in our own clothes, with our hats in our
hands. We could see their faces turning one after the other in our
direction. The majority had an expression of such bitter and heart-
rending jealousy written on their faces that it literally made us choke.
But far more disturbing than such jealousy were those friendly smiles
that appeared on some of the faces, frequently accompanied by tears
welling up, and by lightly sketched signs of the cross intended as a
farewell to us, miraculously saved. Those signs indicated the kindliness
that man shows his fellowman only very rarely, possibly only in
circumstances like those I have been describing. Seeing those fingers
tracing the symbol of a blessing given by the dying to the living, it
was very difficult not to break away from that line of civilians following
the SS man, to keep from joining the men running in rows of five
around the square. The fact that we did not do so is still, I think,
felt by all eight of us—if all of us have been granted enough time to
settle our accounts in peace—as a singularly repulsive act of cowardice.
And this feeling was not in the least lessened by the thought, which
we shared soon afterward in the train compartment, that such
voluntary self-condemnation to death by elaborate torture would
have cost us much more than life itself. It would have meant
abandoning the hope that, once we were released, we would be able
to realize the goal—constantly returning in our feverish dreams—of
one day feeling against our cheek the smooth butt of an ordinary
"kbk," the rifle of the Polish infantry. I see no reason to be ashamed
of frankness or to avoid pushing it to the most frightful extremes. I
still dream such dreams often. And nowadays they return with brutal
urgency.

This confession explains, I hope, why one is sometimes justified in
returning to memories which are otherwise destined to be forgotten,
like everything else that hurts the ordinary human pride everyone is
entitled to. A nation that has gone through such experiences certainly
deserves a modest change for the better; at least it shouldn't, some
forty years later, be forced to move knolls. History takes no notice
of merit and is influenced even less by compassion. We know that all
too well. But we also know that it conceals from people the secrets

of the future which no one can predict or foresee. And yet it allows us to retain hope, even if it has to be called heroic hope.

(January–February 1985)
Translated by Jadwiga Kosicka

Wlodzimierz Odojewski

THE JOURNEY

FIRST THERE WAS DUSK. It shrouded his body like fumes, like smoke, so how could he have had a premonition of anything? Even when he would briefly wake up or only lift his eyelids ever so slightly, not enough to be fully awake but only to hear—the ringing of the telephone in the entrance hall, footsteps, incomprehensible moving about in his room, words whose meanings he did not grasp: "the judge, Uncle August, something or other in Krzyztopol . . . Aleksy . . . *Durchlassenschein*"—or to discern his mother's figure or the perplexed face of one of his aunts stooped over him in the mire of light which grew abruptly intense. Suddenly the obscurity cracked in two when Roza the chambermaid brought in a tray with breakfast, stooped over his bed, and stood there gazing at him with fear-filled eyes as his arms rowed helplessly on the pillow as if he were still unable to tear himself from sleep. And through the door which had been left open again barged in the sounds of nervous rushing about in all the other parts of the house. The sounds were louder and more persistent than before, even though nothing could have happened to explain them (not that he was trying to understand anything—why the girl was standing there like that, silently, or why she appeared to have no intention of leaving his room, perhaps because he was still asleep, struggling to endure her attentive gaze), until at last, from among all the other sounds, his ears isolated Katarzyna's footsteps.

So it was probably only at that moment that he had a premonition. Or actually a few seconds later. When Katarzyna appeared in the doorway and entered his room, despite the fact that she had never done it before and, knowing her, he knew that she should not have done it at all. Or, actually, later still. When he became aware that the sound made by her steps was different, and when he saw Roza flee as if she were blown away by a draft. He really felt it then. Before he heard the first of the two sentences spoken by Katarzyna, her voice perturbed and restrained: "You will not be able to help Aleksy like this at all, he doesn't need it, and you may end up not coming back yourselves!"—after which they stared at each other in amazement, as if they had only just noticed one another: she, him in bed, in his unbuttoned pajamas which revealed his chest, his hand still holding the glass which had no milk left in it; he, her standing in the back of his bachelor's bedroom for the first time since she had come to live in the Glebowiecki household three years before. And then she uttered the second sentence: "Anyway, do what you want, it's your family's business," but in a new resigned, reconciled, almost submissive voice, and then she turned away slowly and her hand touched her forehead in one of those unconscious gestures that mean nothing but which one remembers forever.

Even before she left, he thought the second sentence was unnecessary. Didn't she know that he could figure out what it was that the whole family wanted from him, except she, Katarzyna, she who perhaps more than anyone else should care about what he must do for his brother. But the door had already closed behind her. And immediately, as he dozed off again, he took that awareness of the premonition with him into the darkness of sleep, and he dreamed on as the sounds continued to reach him, movements throughout the house, telephone calls, conversations—"Uncle August is in Krzyztopol . . . a *Durchlassenschein* . . . Aleksy, some papers from the *Ortskommendantur* . . ." and everything would be ready soon—until he was awakened for real, brutally torn out of the warm darkness of slumber. And everything would be ready because everything really was ready: his suitcase and his suit for the trip lying on the chair next to his bed, and the documents needed for the trip east, and the permit issued by the Germans to travel through the zone adjacent to the front. And soon he, too, was ready. In the chaise which took him to the railroad station in Krzyztopol, sitting with his mother, uncle, and Aunt Felicja, he listened to the two women's instructions in a stupor, to that multiplicity of words which could be of no use to him, words that people usually tell each other before they part, without really understanding them. Later, as he looked out his compartment window, he managed to catch a bleak smile in his mother's face and a nondescript gesture of his aunt's hand. His mother's smile failed, for by the time he guessed what it was supposed to be, it had dissipated into a sad grimace on her lips. And he did not understand the movement of his aunt's hand at all.

And he thought: "Of course, it had to be like this. Fate willed it. That I meet with Aleksy right now and not some other time. The least appropriate time. After I've taken his wife away from him." And later still, on the platform which was slipping away behind the train, the two women remained motionless, frozen, immobilized by his last glance. He heard the shout *"Transportführer!"* behind him, as it penetrated the multilingual din. When he turned back from the window, he saw a minuscule ginger-haired man leap out of the mass of workers wrapped in the smoke of home-grown tobacco, and a moment later this whole Polish–Ruthenian–Bessarabian collection of people, who were likely traveling to do forced labor in the depths of the Ostland, reluctantly gathered together their wretched bundles and slowly rolled over to the next car, leaving behind them the reek of grease, of unwashed skin which had been on the road for a long time, of bread and bean soup. And into their place marched Hungarian soldiers of some auxiliary service who had been standing in the corridor. He sat down in the corner by the window, crawled inside his jacket, closed his eyes, and pretended to be asleep, though he was no longer sleepy. He heard Uncle August speaking German, and the voices of the Hungarians in their language so unlike any other European language, and the persistent uproar in the hallway where the *Bahnschutze* were searching luggage and checking documents. And every time he opened his eyes he would see the hairy greenish faces of the pauper-peddlers traveling with their bundles, which were probably loaded with mediocre food, faces out of which peered extinguished eyes outlined in red and which would suddenly disappear from view as if someone had chased them away. Then the *Bahnschutze* disappeared, too, and the Hungarians, who had already settled in nicely, unpacked their knapsacks, sliced their bread and their rationed *Gummiwurst*, and began eating gloomily. In an effort to distance himself from this time and place as quickly as possible, he repeated to himself: "This is how it was bound to be. Even though this is the least appropriate time for me to go there"—until at last he felt the rush of the accelerating train as it cooled down the compartment, even though it was not wind but merely movement of air, which forced into the car the sap-filled, rustling, green breeze of pines. And perhaps it was this rush that made everything which he preferred not to think about right now (the confirmation of the crime committed against his brother, what he had done to his brother's wife, where he had led her) roll further and further away from him to the rhythm of the clanging wheels. And even though he still heard Katarzyna's voice, as she emerged out of the mist under his eyelids: "You wanted it. And you wanted him to die. Yes, you did" (no, he had *never* wanted it), her face, made hideous by irony, quickly dissolved into the darkness, and then all he could see was a tall crane of a woman, her hair parted in a white line and joined at the nape, smooth and heavy like liquid brass in which the individual strands were indistinguishable, leaving an incredible impression of a flowing substance with a shimmering, metallic surface. Then the head disappeared, too, and he heard: "Don't leave me. I am incapable of being alone," a voice coming from those vast depths of darkness, and he thought about that day at dawn when Katarzyna was really close to him (no, not in his sleep, as at this moment, or many times before, when her face also came close in the darkness that swallowed her up together with her head, arms, body) and said: "Don't leave me alone." Already then he had predicted that the warm spring would be gone irretrievably, a long summer would set in, rains and cold would come, before she would again repeat with the same unforced honesty: "Don't leave me. I am incapable of being alone."

He woke up as the train was again leaving a station. They must have traveled quite a long way, as the compartment was bathed in twilight. Uncle August sat across from him with his eyes closed, rocking lethargically, softly, to the rhythm of the car's movements, leaning on his flabby hands. Only when he, Pawel, heaved himself up and his handkerchief fell out of his pocket did his uncle jump and reach out to pick it up from the floor (it was Katarzyna's handkerchief, and it even had her monogram embroidered in one corner) and handed it back to him. He eyed him the same way he had once before, at dawn, when he saw Pawel running out of that other bedroom, his tragic look still full of surprise, when he asked: "So it had to happen? Now?" in a stifled but inquisitive voice. And Pawel answered: "No. No. Certainly not," feeling his uncle's hand on his hand and hearing again: "Tell me the truth. Maybe I would have done the same if I had to keep a woman. But now? Just now? Tell me the truth," and then he tore himself away from his uncle in the direction of the window and barked so sharply, "Leave me alone! Damn it, leave me alone! It had nothing to do with Aleksy," that the Hungarians who had been talking in low voices fell silent and looked them over full of wonder.

Afterwards he stood with his back to the compartment, leaning his elbows on the rim of the lowered window. In front of him there was only a moving, passing misty depth. Though he opened his eyes as wide as he could, he saw absolutely nothing. Only some time later, after he stopped straining his eyes and the wave of blood flowed down from his head, the mist began to lift, and slowly a forest emerged, together with dots of shrubs and dogwoods on its edge, looking like nuns walking single-file in the opposite direction to the train's. The shadow from the trees grew deeper and darker, and when at last he turned back, he could barely see the compartment. Only the glowing red point of a cigarette lit up again and again, marking Uncle August. He said to him, calmly this time: "We will pass Baranowicze in four or five hours." He waited for a while, but no, his uncle did not say a word; his cigarette soon died out.

He again heard his uncle's voice sometime in the middle of the night. An explosion burst on their ears together with the crunching of crushed metal, preceding by a split second the fierce rattle of a machine gun. Suitcases and trunks were tumbling down from racks. His uncle's voice was controlled, cold, different from before. He was comforting a fellow passenger, saying that that was only on a sidetrack from Ostrog, that they were approaching Krzemieniec, and that everything had ended happily—for them, at least. Then the train again picked up speed, the glow was left behind, and people came away from the windows. He overheard their frightened comments, but no longer his uncle's voice, and he thought: "If he asked me now . . . And if I didn't have to watch that bewildered, condemning look . . . Maybe now I would tell him why I did it. And maybe he would understand." Then for a long time, or so it seemed, there was dead silence. And when he opened his eyes again, they were at a larger station. Faint little lights of railway workers' lamps flickered rapidly;

locomotives huffed and puffed on the sidetracks. He heard the shouting of commands, in Ukrainian, then in German, and somewhere in a distant compartment the melodiously broad, Ruthenian-accented voice of a man who seemed to be talking to himself (although he was talking to Uncle August, because his cigarette glowed again, outlining his profile in the dark), an extremely tired old voice, thoroughly resigned. He heard him saying that "together with Poland, sir, the question of freedom for us Ukrainians has also been defeated for a long time to come. Actually, for the Byelorussians, Lithuanians, Letts, and Estonians, too. Poland's fall, sir, is Moscow's greatest success. History will call it Europe's most cruel defeat. And nothing can be done about it now. Because whatever my compatriots are still doing consists only of mad spurts. And most of the time they are primitive and dishonorable spurts, my sir. Only Soviet Moscow will take advantage of them. She will swallow us up sooner or later. And maybe you Poles, too. Even though you have such ancient traditions of statehood. We did not, sir, neither you nor we, see our real enemy." And the rumbling of wheels ground up the rest of his monologue. Later Pawel must have shifted, because his uncle turned in his direction: "Aren't you asleep?" He livened up, thinking that his uncle would again ask him about that other thing and that he would be able to reply truthfully. But the next question was indifferent: "Would you like to eat something?" And so he replied that no, he wanted to sleep, and the speed and the rushing air and the sound of the wheels really did put him to sleep.

Then it was broad daylight. On the bench across from him, a fat civilian was lying on his back, asleep, breathing through his open mouth, while one of the Hungarians was reading a newspaper and the other passengers stood in the corridor watching the landscape. Standing in the compartment's doorway with Uncle August was a man in the sackcloth robe of an Orthodox priest, who was carrying on about the nothingness of being and the misery of wandering on this earth, and Uncle August nodded in agreement but without much enthusiasm. Outside, the plain was giving way to a forest. Clearings and bunkers began to appear along the tracks, and here and there one could see shattered train cars which had been thrown down the embankment, and from time to time steel-blue Storches flew low over the burning earth through the burning sky. The train had gone well past the prewar Polish–Soviet border. Pawel remembered the thought with which, it seemed to him, he had fallen asleep: "Now this, too, is in store for me. My brother's body," and he heaved himself up.

He did not feel well and had a headache. He pulled out of his suitcase food his mother had prepared for him. He ate his breakfast. After a few sips of coffee from his flask, he felt keenly sober and regretted having eaten. He could not chase away an illusion of profound cold. He pretended to be sleeping when the passenger across from him woke up. He shivered slowly, violently, evenly, feeling in his innards the ham sandwich he had just eaten, still warm from the coffee and packed into a hard mush, which was being subjected to the slow, incessant quaking of the train, as if his stomach, weighed down and filled to the brim, were an independent, foreign object in his body. He thought: "Knowing Mother, I should have guessed earlier that she would find no peace until her first-born son rested in his own, consecrated soil. But, these days, what soil can be called truly one's own? And even if it is one's own now, how much longer will it be that?!" And then he thought that soon he would have to look at Aleksy's abused, worm-eaten body, into those forever empty eye sockets of his. He would have to look at the body which had not yet completed its earthly wanderings despite the fact that he, Pawel, had long wanted to take for himself—and now really had— what had been perhaps dearest to his brother's body. And as he looked at it, he would have to ask himself yet again, something he had done so many times already, whether he had acted properly. He really knew that now nothing would stand in the way of their meeting. But the headache dulled his thinking. His sense of only superficial observation, sharpened to the limits of endurance (no doubt, an effect of the coffee), for a few seconds at a time would freeze in his consciousness this monotonously unchanging landscape which rolled outside the window, forests, fields ripe for harvest alternating with fallow ground, here and there ruins of villages with intact homesteads lost here and there among them, and shabby train stations guarded by soldiers in the uniforms of the Ostlegion or the Byelorussian police. But he did not retain anything of this, or of the faces of the travelers, who came and went. His ears isolated sentences in various languages, often also in Polish, but his mind did not hold more than scraps, and then only briefly: that in Warsaw baking soda cost eleven zlotys, in Minsk fifty Ostmarks, in Smolensk they pay as much as sixty-five for a kilogram; that yeast sells best because everyone knows that it can be used to make bootleg liquor, but sugar is in greatest demand. After a while, Uncle August's face again approached his. His bald red head resembling a pumpkin, with sweat streaming down it, leaned over him. His uncle asked him whether he was not well, and he heard his own voice, surprisingly steady and cool and answering to the point, that it was nothing, that he felt fine, that he was still sleepy. Even though in reality he was not sleepy at all, and again he heard his uncle's voice: "One hour more to Minsk." He watched his uncle sit down with a sigh, pull a large plaid handkerchief out of his pocket, and wipe his face, head, and neck with very slow, imprecise motions, unnaturally stretched out in time, and then fold it in four, seemingly slowing down his motions even more, put it back in his pocket—and then they were in Minsk. The ruins of the station, the Red Cross hut, *"Verpflegung und Betreuungsstelle,"* rusted scrap metal, severed cables, bent and empty gasoline drums, empty cans, coils of barbed wire, partly burned wooden beams strewn everywhere. Farther down were latrines, crowds of peddlers loaded down with huge parcels diving under the cars to escape inspectors. And again his uncle's voice: "It seems that a train will soon be leaving from one of these tracks for Smolensk. Let's look out for it. If we miss this one train for civilians, we will waste the whole day." It reached him with a delay, after the judge had already left the compartment carrying both their suitcases and squeezed through the door. And right away Pawel followed his uncle, ran across the platforms, and stopped in the bright sunshine in front of a long freight-car depot. He could still feel the thumping in his temples and stared blankly at the policemen who were checking documents. He answered their questions, how else but in accordance with what was written in the documents: his name, where he came from, where he was going, why. He was surprised at his voice, so quiet that he could barely hear it himself.

Afterwards he was inside the train. He lay on a bundle of straw between the boards which served as imitation benches, occupied by an international riffraff of nondescript occupations who had been herded in by an armed guard, and he reassured his uncle that he really was all right, that there was nothing wrong with him, that he had lain down only because there was nowhere to sit, although in fact he had been there before all the seats were taken. And the humid heat which heralded a storm and the hot stink of the car tightened around his neck like a girdle.

The train cut across vast expanses of pastures and forests, floodplains and swamps: tufts of wicker surrounded by swamp, dwarf pines, alder, clumps of heather surrounded by blue blotches of bog bilberries, a thick grid of lazily winding creeks, and the black eyes of still, black waters. The names Smolensk, Katyn, and Kosogory came up more and more frequently in the conversations of his fellow passengers. But he continued to push away what awaited him there, at their destination. It only happened later. At one of the little stations where they stopped a while longer because the tracks were being cleared after a recent bombardment. He jumped out of the car and ran to find a well, but instead found a winding stream in a marshy birch wood. After drinking from it, he took off his suit jacket and washed himself, and then, standing there with a wet face and wet hands, listened to the sounds of the station. It happened right then. He felt an incomprehensible, almost metaphysical fear of something sharp which might soon strike violently, and unexpectedly. Until that time the names of those places had been distant concepts, very far away in space and therefore unreal, and now their reality felt the same as when, before, someone said Gleby, Czuprynia, Krzyztopol, or Lwow, Warsaw, Cracow.

The banging of crowbars against metal and people's shouts carried far from the tracks; there was no more roaring of airplanes high overhead, but only the cries of young hawks. And for a long time he listened tensely to the shouting of those two names, Smolensk and Katyn, inside his head. At first he did not notice the flock of children, little savages in rags, who had approached him and were looking him up and down with frightened curiosity. The bravest one touched his jacket, which hung on a branch. He noticed them then. As he examined them closely, the shouting inside his head, the anxiety, the metaphysical fear of an abrupt and sharp something that would soon strike, all disappeared. He accepted it. All of a sudden he was reconciled to everything that would befall him, and in his thoughts he said to himself: "They are poor, too. They, too, have been driven to the bottom of this pit." He took a few Ostmarks out of his pocket and held them out to the children in his hand, but they shrank back distrustfully, and only after he placed the money on the ground and stepped back did the oldest boy approach it cautiously and pick it up. As he walked away, he looked back once more. He saw the boy bow deeply after him, from the waist down, in peasant fashion, Russian fashion, in this ancient motion of a slave. And he repeated to himself: "They have been in this pit for centuries."

The bored Germans standing in front of the little station house were amusing themselves by throwing rocks at cooking pots which had been stuck on a picket fence, and the stinging odor of creosote blew from the heated rail bed. A *Feldfebel* sitting on a bench called over to a young girl passing by, carrying raspberries and wearing a worn-out man's linen shirt tied at the waist with a colorful scarf. The soldier pulled her to him and sat her on his lap, and Pawel saw him feeling up the girl's breasts, which were barely defined under the linen; he saw her tearing herself away, weeping quietly. Then the soldier slapped her in the face, and she reeled toward the wall and stood there: gray, pale, her distorted mouth a round black opening framed by rotting teeth, wide open and ready to shout. And he saw the German walk away lazily toward the Russian prisoners who were clearing the tracks, while the Germans playing by the fence and laughing sang after him: "*Lass das sein Otto, du bist ein Schwein, Otto . . .*" But then he was back inside the car, back on his bundle of straw, lying on his back with his eyes open, gazing at the ceiling. The rattling inside his head was gone now, not a shout, not a voice: he was perfectly calm. Some time later the locomotive whistled, the grating of axles carried to the back of the car, the joints rumbled, the steam huffed slowly and deeply, and the train was on the move again. Pawel dozed off. When he woke up, they were in Smolensk.

They were put through the sieve of police control, listening to the voice that floated out of the loudspeakers on the walls: "*Wir geben die Luftlage . . .* enemy airplanes approaching from the northeast are heading south . . ." After being lost for a few moments, they managed to emerge from within the skeleton of the railway station. The city presented itself to them as rows of bare walls gaping with emptiness and at the same time brimming with heavy, hollow despair. They walked down a shattered street paved with cobblestones and dotted with bomb craters which had been filled with black slag. Here and there, three-story buildings still standing bore signs reading Haus Liechtenstein, Haus Sachsen, Haus Brandenburg, and still more Hauses, Germania's bridgeheads in the Far East of Europe. Farther down were barracks, and the sign: Feldbauleitung d/Lw Smolensk-S d. Between the barracks stood bunkers made of wooden logs covered with a thick layer of soil. Uncle August and he would stop and in Russian ask the rare passersby, who slipped on by, wearing oddly tailored capes, for the local Touristenheim. They answered reluctantly and in fear. The Germans were almost invisible. They only noticed a handful of German soldiers, at the end of the street, coming toward the casino, the impressive quarters of the former *Dom Krasnoy Armii*, as the sign which had not yet been obliterated announced. Curfew was approaching, and fewer and fewer pedestrians could be seen. They walked through a completely devastated part of town, following their instincts, until his uncle said: "I just hope they won't smash us here." Because somewhere in the distance an air-raid siren howled, artillery blasts shook the air, and the burned-out walls echoed the sound like muffled, almost human voices. But they did encounter a patrol of German gendarmerie, who turned their suitcases inside out but did not treat them too harshly after hearing their explanations and showed them the way to the square in front of the Byzantine cathedral, outlined in the moon's glow like a silver peak over a black canyon, and they found the barracks they were looking for. There were still some brief formalities to go through in the registration office. The German who stamped their documents even smiled with understanding as his uncle told the reason for their trip. And a hefty girl with a broad face, pretty in a coarse way, who sat at the telephone exchange, certainly a Russian and a translator, looked them up and down and said in fairly correct German that a priest from Warsaw was also there, having come for the same reason, and in the morning they could go with him to the place in a special car. When Pawel bowed slightly and said "Thank you" in Russian a little louder than was necessary, she looked at him again. At him, and not at his uncle. He caught an odd movement in her head, and all of a sudden it seemed to him that an expression came into her eyes of remembering something, not consciously, without wanting to, a return to the past which troubled her too, a turning back and at the same time an effort to expunge this remembrance, this evocation, or whatever it might have been, from her mind. He took their key and wanted to walk away with his uncle, but the woman's eyes held him back. But only for a second or two, because then, immediately, her look once again lacked depth, expressed nothing: neither interest nor indifference, neither goodness nor meanness. Nothing whatsoever. Her eyes were simply cold, indifferent, a little sleepy perhaps. Again he thought to himself: "They, too, are in the pit. Maybe they don't even know it. But they have an inkling of it."

Once in their room, he washed, chewed on a piece of bread without much appetite, undressed quickly and without turning on the light, and jumped into bed. Lying on his back, he gazed for a long time through the window, which had not been covered with paper, at the pockmarked, scarred walls across the street, which, sieve-like, revealed the bulging domes of the Smolensk cathedral. And he also looked at the sky, colored by the glow from the German bombardment, and at the moon. He thought about the Russian girl at the reception desk and what he thought he had seen briefly in her eyes, something like a pale reflection of guilt or shame, but he decided that it had been an illusion. Uncle August, who right after their arrival set off to find the priest whom the girl had mentioned, had not come back. The floor creaked in the hallway; someone was rattling a bucket. Through one of the walls he could hear a conversation between two women, low voices swelling with reproaches, and water splashing in a basin. One of his neighbors was speaking German, and the other one mixed Russian words into her German. They were having an argument which soon died down, and he heard the creaking of bedsprings. Somewhere downstairs, nearby, a guard's steps tapped rhythmically on the pavement: there and back, there and back, seemingly the only sounds in the city other than the occasional crack of a shot. As he lit a cigarette in the dark, he thought about Aleksy's closeness, and immediately, probably for the first time since leaving Gleby, about Katarzyna's words that Aleksy did not need *it* at all, what they wanted to do. And he wondered whether she had meant his and his uncle's trip in general or his mother's wish that they bring his brother's body back to Gleby. He found no answer. His fingers which held the cigarette quivered lightly and regularly. When at last he heard the judge's footsteps in the hall, he turned his back to the room. He did not stir when his uncle tried to start a conversation, or when he moved about the room, huffing and puffing from agitation or emotion, trying to attract his attention with noise. For a long time he heard him tossing in bed, unable to sleep. He, too, could not get to sleep. He had stopped thinking about Aleksy's proximity. Now he was thinking about what had happened that time in Gleby between him and Katarzyna, and whether it had had to happen right then, as his uncle had asked. He also thought how waiting too long for a woman ends up burning out everything in your heart, even the sense of fulfillment, and you feel as if nothing had happened. He dozed off as dawn approached. He dreamed about a gray rain, spring floods, and the village informer, Antypko, who drowned puppies in the pond, inside a sack. The bereaved bitch would howl faintly somewhere in the distant open spaces.

When he woke up, he was alone in the room. He got up, washed, and shaved. He was perfectly calm. The same young Russian woman was sitting at the reception desk. He asked her about his uncle, the judge, and received no answer. Her hands snatched the key to his room from him with a sharp, angry movement. So he asked again, this time in Russian, thinking that she had not understood. She replied that the person he was asking about was in the restaurant, and with a movement of the head indicated a side door. The car would be there in a few minutes. And all of a sudden last night's remembrance in her eyes, that flash which had lasted barely seconds and which she had immediately extinguished, came back to him: that memory, that thing, that guilt or shame—he had no name for it— was back in the girl's eyes. He knew that it would be enough if he looked into her eyes, and it was there. And right away he understood what it was: those spring days two years ago, probably rainy and gray days, maybe still blighted by late frosts, those sealed trains packed with thousands of men in Polish uniforms which rolled through the town and then stopped at the next station, just past its most distant outskirts, and *they* herded those men out of the cars and into the small wood to kill them by shooting them in the back of the head. The girl's eyes followed him as he turned slowly toward the restaurant door. Now, unlike last night, he seemed cold and sleepy because in fact, deep down, he was nursing a humiliation which would not disappear but only move aside, only recede slowly as he himself moved away. As he entered the room which had been pointed out to him, no longer able to see the girl, he had the impression that this humiliation of hers had been dragged in from there and was now all around him. But he remained calm.

The man sitting at the table with his uncle was a monk, a Bernardine, a representative of the Warsaw Red Cross. Pawel joined them and, the calm that refused to leave him still there, listened to their conversation, or really to the monk's monologue, to his quiet voice, which seemed to rustle impassively, and at times was drowned out by the din in the room. And as he listened, he tried to make out who were these thousands lost without a trace in the depths of the Soviet Union who had still not been found among the corpses of Katyn that the monk was talking about. And all of a sudden his heart stiffened, his tendons, muscles, and blood all tightened, something, everything in him hardened, and the bright sun shining in through the window seemed to slide down over him, concentrating, thickening, cutting off his breath. He held his breath on purpose, and immediately heard that it was not true, his heart was still pumping, there was banging inside his temples, and it was only outside him that silence had fallen. The monk's voice continued to resound in this silence, but everything else had died down, set, was hanging over him in silence. Then this silence leaned over him, demanding, waiting, calling for a decision. "I must find Aleksy. I must. It makes no difference whether I've hurt him or not. Whether he would have wanted me to do what I did to his wife or not. Now I simply must find him, and that's what matters most." He repeated the word "must" with a gloomy, abated determination, a steadfast, desperate determination. And he found him.

It was an hour or two later. After riding some tens of kilometers in a dilapidated truck driven by a Russian and half full of no longer very young men and women who seemed to have come from very far away (it turned out that they were the relatives of the murdered from Silesia), and after walking a kilometer through fields and woods because the truck took them only as far as Gnezdovo, a hamlet by the train station in the middle of swamps from which, in the words of the Bernardine, they had been herded to their deaths, to the Katyn forest. It may already have been high noon, so distant was the time when Pawel had gone down to the reception desk and talked with the robust Russian girl with the evasive eyes. It may even have been a different day altogether when he finally found him. He found him in the sluggish, lazy, oily heat, in the sandy, hilly clearing, among stooped Russian prisoners of war who shoveled the top layer of soil, with Germans from the Feldpolizei standing over them with mouths and noses covered with wet handkerchiefs, not far from a long table at which sat notaries and near which milled Polish doctors in protective oilskin clothing, soiled with the excrement from the corpses piled as high as their waists or higher, in the sickly sweet, nauseating odor which wafted out of the ditches, permeating the surrounding area, blocking one's breath, convulsing throats and stomachs. He found him even before he saw, through the thick chemical vapors, in the deep ditch, in the entanglement of legs, arms, and heads jutting out of the soggy soil from among the lichen in the rusty water, in the scorching white sunlight, among the bodies which had been thrown about carelessly, some of them tied with leather thongs, others with wire, when once again he repeated, this time aloud: "I must find him." He found him then, although it was not at all Aleksy, his brother, or anyone resembling him, because it was an Aleksy, like all the others, deformed, unidentifiable, duplicated, close and at the same time distant, already immersed in time as in this swamp where they all lay. But he was from the same tribe, body, bones, scraps of flesh and splinters of bone which in him, Pawel, were still alive as he stood over the ditch and no longer repeated "I must find him," but only a short, quiet, faded: "Oh God, oh God, oh God . . ."

And then he heard his uncle's half-whisper: "He is not here. They dug him up a month ago and moved him. They will soon tell us where he is buried." He did not understand. And he turned, shifted, and on shaky legs reached out his arms to his whispering uncle: "What did you say? He is not here? What, he is not here? But he is." And seeing only the festering wound-like ditch in the earth (on legs that refused to do what he wanted even before he moved), he began to descend into this human mass and these fumes of rot, shouting: "But he is here! I found him! I am going to find him!" until one of the men in a white lab coat jumped up from the table and grabbed him, because he would have got stuck at the bottom of it all, would have collapsed into it.

When he slowly regained his balance and turned around, Uncle August was by his side. His uncle's face was martyred. Only then did the words reach him: that Aleksy had already been buried somewhere else. But Pawel still felt that he had not had enough and had to absorb it all for all the rest of his life. He had become firm inside and so strong that he tore himself from his uncle's hands, which wanted to pull him away: "Leave me alone! I'm all right! Leave me alone! Go away!" And he stopped over the ditch, froze in midstep (froze, after having shifted virtually all his weight onto one leg, the other leg almost lifted off the ground), and with the cold-bloodedness of a reporter, or rather of a lab technician who examines, looks through a slab of glass to fix an image, he fixed this image in his memory forever: layers of corpses, several meters deep, dressed in Polish officer's uniforms with well-preserved buttons and decorations, in heavy winter coats, layers of corpses decaying, in the complex process of rotting, and at the same time mummified, probably because of the soil's sandy content. Then out of this mass, this entanglement, he identified the individual faces of those who lay face up, skinless faces, mouth cavities and eye sockets showing through a film of muscle and membrane, skulls with identical exit wounds on their foreheads, matted with hair which had already lost its color, and hands preserved impeccably with untouched skin and nails, their veins visible, until his uncle spoke again: "Come, let's walk over there." Only then did he turn.

His uncle stood before him, his face white as chalk and covered with moisture, his lips bloodless. They linked arms and walked away from the edge of the ditch to the other side of the clearing. The man in the white lab coat came up to them again. He said: "Lieutenant Aleksander Woynowicz, gentlemen, I think, is buried somewhere in one of the front rows. In one of the mass graves over the hill." "Let's go," Pawel said quietly. "Not yet," replied his uncle. His eyes were half-closed. "I will wait for you afterwards," said the man in the white lab coat. "Over there in the forest ranger's cabin." He nodded in the direction of the forest. "In the depot we have all kinds of small objects that were found on the victims. The Germans are allowing people to look at them. This is his number"—and he handed them a slip of paper. He turned away. He was long gone but they still stood in silence, and Pawel soundlessly repeated the four digits written on the piece of paper, which had been torn out of a notepad, fixing them in his memory. He then said them aloud, and his uncle shuddered and said, "Let's go."

They walked slowly back to the edge of the clearing. Their arms were no longer linked; only their shoulders touched. They walked avoiding the long ditches which had been emptied earlier, one of which extended into a gigantic letter L as high as the highest peak. They could still see the few dozen or maybe few hundred bodies which had been exhumed that day and placed next to each other in rows. The sharp, traumatic breeze from over there followed them relentlessly, crushing their chests (it would follow them for a long time to come), and the Russians at work digging up the bodies accompanied them silently with their inquisitive and humiliated eyes. They walked toward the path that led to the higher part of the clearing, but halfway there his uncle stopped, sat down on a felled trunk under the oaks, and, dejected, said: "When I was in jail there . . . in their camp over . . . in the Urals . . . and later in exile . . . And earlier, too . . . In that horrendous transport in −50 degree cold . . . Everywhere there, you know? Over there! I saw a lot of death around me. What am I saying, death! Many deaths. Our Polish deaths. But now . . . Now, no, no . . . This is completely different . . ." And even though Pawel wanted to interrupt him, he could not bring up a sound from inside him. And the judge wiped the sweat off his bald head because the tears that had been on his face (if they really had been tears) had dried up on their own in the sun, and he heaved himself up from the tree trunk. Then Pawel said quietly: "This can't be compared to anything else." His uncle was silent. Again they walked away in the sweetish, nauseating, horrific odor, an odor which even the wind could not blow away. On their way they only passed Russian workers, who in twos were carrying the disintegrating uniformed corpses on wooden stretchers, corpses that were falling apart, deformed by the process of rotting, with moist soil still on them. Later his uncle spoke to him one more time: "You are right. This can't be compared to anything else. It shouldn't be compared to anything else."

The well-trodden path eventually led them to rows of graves some dozen yards in length. They were very close to the forest now. Pawel began to walk faster and, leaving his uncle behind, soon found the place. It had a plate and a number. And nothing else. Similar plates with higher and lower numbers had been fixed into the soil, half a foot apart, to the right and to the left. The whole long grave had shriveled up in the sun; it was pale gray, and its edges were crumbling from the heat of the first summer days. Pawel repeated Aleksy's number over and over in his mind, not quite consciously, as if it were a prayer, and once he even said it aloud, and that was all it was: a number made up of four digits, a dried-up gray mound, a section, a section of this grave a few inches long, the hot sun up there, and underground, down there—five or six feet underground—perhaps also under a layer of lime, was he, Aleksy, his brother.

It was very quiet. No one was there except an old Russian who appeared to be a villager and who had probably been hired from a neighboring village to look after the cemetery. He had brought over on a wheelbarrow some squares of wet turf and was now covering one of the graves with them. But farther away, at the edge of the cemetery, next to a tall cross made of birch branches, they could see a few women. His uncle and he stood there, not talking, not looking at each other, staring at the plate which had been fixed into the soil, at the other plates to the right and to the left and in front of them and behind them. By the thousands. The rustle of leaves which carried from the forest was delicate and monotonous like an unceasing whisper. Later a woman approached them. She said that the Bernardine Father was now burying the bodies which had been exhumed that morning and asked whether they would like to take part in the funeral. Her face was tight and black, immersed in the fierce shadow emanating from her eyes. They followed her in silence. And then they were there. On the highest point on the hill. They saw the cemetery from a bird's-eye view, spread out below them, seven huge graves in the whitish mist of the heat and the dry, diffuse aroma of pines and oaks. They looked all the way to the vast rise of the thick forest which covered half the horizon, and they sensed another forest beyond that rise, a whole mass of pines and oaks which did not rise up, did not shoot up but seemed to peer out, leaning deep over this blood-soaked place.

As they came closer, from far away they heard the litany for the souls of the dead to rest in peace, as it was being intoned by a group of men and women standing around a monk in a liturgical robe. And again they saw Russian prisoners, their heads bare, their faces expressionless. They would carry over the bodies, now covered with tarpaulins, on wooden stretchers, stop by the ditch, and holding on to the tarpaulin they would tip the stretcher, slip the body off into the ditch, and then the next, and the next, and the next . . . Their hands, coarse from work and almost black, moved quickly and efficiently. Then the soil would slide off their shovels into the ditch. It would slide off softly, without the characteristic thud it makes when it lands on a coffin, but loud enough to bring out a hollow echo. And the rustle of the forest accompanied the voices of the praying people, the voices which spoke of matters which were done with but about which no one could be indifferent. Pawel heard his uncle's whisper: "May they rest in peace, and may eternal light shine on them." And it seemed to him that his own whisper and the word "Amen" merged with his uncle's whisper, which was no louder than the rustle of the forest, but then it was no longer his uncle's whisper or his whisper but the monk's, in a voice which was barely audible, monotonous, somehow lost in the open space and diminished by it, by the enormousness of the air and the enormousness of the cloudless sky, as he spoke, whispered: "They have not disappeared but merely moved on to a thousandfold life. Into the memory of their dearest, into the lasting memory of our nation. But also into the memory of the nation which inflicts torment and death on others as easily as on itself. To us, they will forever remain a symbol of martyrdom, to their executioners a source of eternal guilt and a burning stigma of shame on their foreheads. Also to their children and their children's children, until one day they will decide to face this crime of their fathers and decide to throw off this shameful stigma and once and for all abandon the path of barbarity. And this will be the service which those whom we are burying here now will render. Do not weep. They are without life but they have not died. They are not enclosed in this earth but liberated from it. It is not beneath this earth that they are being interred forever: they rise from its black depth to enter and remain in every one of us. They are dispersed in their disintegration but they are present in our temporal life, in our sadness and our joy, in our anger, in our gentleness and our goodness, in our rises and our falls, in our lowliness and our meanness, in our excellence, fairness, nobility, and love, in all our passions and deeds, in our sleep and in our waking. They are also in the countless particles of life that surround us: in the darkness and in light, in the flowers and branches, in the air and in the sun's rays, in the dew and in the rain, in the wind, in the rustling of the night and of oak leaves. In unstopping and unstoppable life, in the course of time, until the end of barbarity and until *true freedom*. They are in everything, indivisible from us the living, and from those who will come after us. Even though they no longer have a heart that can bleed from wounds . . ." And Pawel thought to himself, as if to spite the monk: "He is nearby, he is somewhere so very near us that I can almost feel his breath, but he is here only . . . Only here . . ." as he gripped his moist, cool lump of soil before tossing it into the depth.

Later the ditch was filled in, the soil formed into a rectangle and packed, and all these people who had traveled here from the other end of Poland to participate in the funeral rites dispersed to the graves of their nearest: husbands, sons, brothers. It was almost afternoon when Pawel and the judge came down from the hill and once more immersed themselves in the odor of corpses. The man in the white lab coat who they knew was waiting for them on the path led them through the wood to the forest ranger's cabin. Pawel's uncle asked the man something that Pawel did not hear. But he heard the man's answer. He was saying that they would soon finish the work, it was becoming dangerous here, the forests were full of Soviet partisans and the front line was close by. "The Germans think we should find over ten thousand corpses from the prisoner-of-war camps in Starobielsk and Ostaszkowo. But no . . . So far, gentlemen, we have found only those who were in the Kozielsk camp. They may come to over forty-five hundred. No others. Of course, I mean ours. Foreigners, yes. The woods in this area are full of graves. Wherever you dig, someone is buried there. But those are Russians, Byelorus-

sians, Ukrainians; in general, Soviets. They used it as their place of
execution fifteen years before. The area was fenced off and belonged
to the NKVD." Then the ranger's cabin appeared in a clearing.

The guard let them in without asking for identification, and only
after they were inside did the man in the lab coat explain to one of
the Germans why he had brought them. A moment later they were
in a large, whitewashed room. Around a table stood people examining
documents, photographs, objects. The man in the white lab coat left
the room and came back bearing a long gray envelope marked with
a number, the same number that Pawel now knew by heart. He shook
the contents out on the table, and they saw a page from a Russian
newspaper folded in four, a few one-zloty pieces, a scrap of a military
pass with Aleksy's particulars in faded handwriting, covered with
spots and stains, a uniform button with an eagle on it, and a blackened
and rusted cigarette case. "No letters?" asked his uncle. "No, no
letters. This is it," replied the man in the white lab coat. Pawel
reached out, and because the German standing across the table
nodded in approval, he picked up the cigarette case. He felt the cold
penetrate his hand and thought incredulously that this was what was
left of Aleksy: the silver cigarette case encrusted with ivory which
Aleksy had taken with him to the front in '39. This memento, this
symbolic case with the engraved initials of Great-grandfather Stefan
and the date 1863, which Grandfather had been given after Great-
grandfather, Father after Grandfather, and Aleksy after Father, and
now he, Pawel, held in his hand.

They walked back alone. Next to the Feldpolizei's barracks, in
which a lab had been set up, stood a handful of people waiting for
the truck which had been promised by the Germans. No one spoke
during the ride. None of the women cried. Only their eyes insistently
returned to the forest fleeting into the distance, to the winding line
made by the road which ran back faster and faster, to the horizon
marked by a line dissolving in the redness of the sun. The men
looked into each other's eyes to ask the mute question. Their faces
were all alike, lost in thought, inaccessible, still leaning over the
depths of that earth in which they had left their sons and brothers,
the depths of time in which they lost them. Or perhaps they were
gazing out of that time, out of its depths into an uncertain future,
whose cruel darkness opened up before them like a chasm.

It was only in Smolensk, as they sat in the *Touristenheim*, that his
uncle spoke: "And your mother imagined that they would give us

Aleksy's body and that we would be able to take it with us," and his voice was full of the dread of the Katyn clearing but also of bitter irony. For, indeed, all of them in Gleby, though they supposedly knew what had happened and how, had imagined it differently. And so he replied: "Let it be, Uncle. I know, we couldn't do that." They spoke in odd monosyllables, with long pauses between: "I will pack our cases." "Fine, Uncle." "The train for Minsk leaves in four hours." "Yes, I know, Uncle." "I think there's another one later tonight." "That's good, Uncle." At last their suitcases were ready, the departure formalities taken care of in the office, the documents stamped, and his uncle unscrewed the thermos flask and took a swig of the remains of the stale, cold coffee which had come with them from Gleby. Pawel, lying on his bed, smoked a cigarette and stared at the hole-ridden wall across the street; the outside slowly took on the grayness of shadow, until finally dusk filled the room so that only the windows were outlined on the wall as lighter squares. Curfew was near.

They walked to the train station through an almost deserted city over which hung the stale odor of burning. Terror and stalking death permeated the air; airplanes growled overhead. As soon as the overloaded train started, the Soviets began to bombard the warehouses along the tracks. But soon the flashes from the explosions, which revealed in the dark depths of the car the tossing people huddled in panic, stopped. Their terrified eyes and faces, everything, disappeared; even the voices were silenced. And if it had not been for the vapor from the breaths around them, one might think that those people had stayed behind in Smolensk. Pawel, immersed in the quick, rhythmical rumble of the wheels of the speeding train, reviewed the day that had just ended, for he had known all along that he would not be able to fall asleep before looking at it, and so he looked at it once again from the beginning, hour by hour, minute by minute, forever imprinting all its details in his memory.

They finally arrived in Krzyztopol in the late afternoon of the next day, hired horses, and reached Gleby at dusk. Then what he had not wanted to think about during the entire return journey happened. When he stepped on the porch and heard an aunt calling that they had arrived, he was forced to think about it, and he thought about it the whole long time it took them to come running from all the different rooms into the hallway and stop to fix their eyes on the two of them standing there, suitcases in hand, dusty, dirty, tired, tormented in their crumpled suits with their crumpled faces, all of them in a semicircle a step or two in front of the two of them: Aunts Felicja and Wiktoria, Mother, Katarzyna, and the servants in the back. At that moment what he had wanted to say, what he had imagined he would say, because he had thought it out carefully, sentence by sentence, on the train, suddenly fled. Mutely, he looked from his mother to Katarzyna, who touched her forehead with her hand in that gesture he remembered from before the journey, then only at his mother. After a time he realized that they were waiting for him to say something, anything, and not remain silent. "They do not release the bodies," he said. He could barely endure the women's expectant looks. He knew what they were thinking. "It's all true," he added. Then he stepped back. And again. All he could do was go to his room.

(May 1973)
Translated by Maya Latynski

Slawomir Mrozek

THE NOSE

I<small>N MY SIXTEENTH YEAR</small>, that is, shortly after the end of World War II, a nose suddenly popped up on my face. A big nose, the kind known as aquiline, especially prominent when compared to the rest of my not yet fully formed body. Prior to that, I had an ordinary nose, fairly regular and straight, which did not attract anyone's attention, certainly not mine.

I discovered my new nose one day when, taking advantage of the absence of my elders from the house, I was attempting, with the aid of two mirrors, to weigh the possibilities my looks gave me. As it was, thoughts about the mystery of sex, particularly the opposite sex, had already caused me many worries, so now I was trying to find an answer to the nagging question of whether I had any chance with the girls.

The day was unforgettable, and the discovery quite horrid. One has only to remember how strict were the standards for male beauty at the time. Neither Eugeniusz Bodo, the leading man of Polish prewar cinema, nor Johnny Weissmuller, the first of the Hollywood Tarzans, had such noses. Let alone Errol Flynn.

But a nose like that was a calamity from yet another point of view.

That type of nose can also be referred to, when the need arises, as a Bourbon nose. Apparently, the kings of that famous French dynasty had them. They also can be seen in a smaller and subtler version in some noble profiles of the Polish aristocracy. Frédéric Chopin, for example, had something of the sort, and even the simple Polish mountaineers were equipped with these noses—at least in pictures. That's all well and good, but who's all this talk for, and just who are we trying to fool? The Bourbons, Chopin, we know all those tricks, no one's taken in anymore. My nose was unambiguous: it was Semitic.

So how am I to show myself in front of others? I'll be taken for a Jew, and if things should take a turn for the worse, I won't be able to prove my innocence, no matter how convincing the evidence to the contrary. As we know, especially after the years of the German occupation, the Jews are masters of pretending that they're not Jews, so it follows that the more one denies he's a Jew, the greater the probability that he is. And even if one were able to prove one's innocence, before one cleared one's name unpleasant things could happen. And isn't the very suspicion, and especially the need to prove it's not so, an insult to a Christian?

That's it, the suspicion. Even if nothing bad happens to me, even if no word is said, they'll think it to themselves when they look at my nose. But how am I to prove that what they think is false, if the thought remains unexpressed? No one can be made to admit that he's thinking something, even if he actually is. He could deny it and yet go on think-ing it to himself. "I know what you're thinking to yourself when you look at me, but . . ."—that's much worse than pretending not to have any idea what he's thinking about me, and suffering in silence. Thus I was suddenly seized by fear, a feeling of helplessness, and the bitter-ness of outraged innocence. That damned nose.

In my surroundings, in my family, we knew everything about the Jews that we needed to, but nothing more, nothing less, but somehow it turned out that there weren't any of them in my immediate neighborhood, or in my circle of acquaintances. They simply were not talked about, neither frequently nor rarely, neither with any particular malice nor, of course, approvingly, just in the normal way.

And what was the normal way?

There's something other than anti-Semitism, something harder to define than anti-Semitism and less engaging as a subject of discussion, hence rarely taken into account. An anti-Semite acknowledges the

Jew's existence if only to negate it and to desire his destruction. It follows that the anti-Semite recognizes the Jew as his enemy, and hence as his partner, and becomes attached to him to the point of obsession and fixation, thus making the idea of Jewishness the basis of his own existence. The anti-Semite cannot live without the Jew; he cannot exist, think, or feel. On the other hand, the kind of person I am now talking about can do without the Jew, not as one human being can get along without another who is alien to him but nonetheless a fellow human, but as—and here is the crux of the matter— one does without, say, birds with fish scales, or fish with birds' feathers. Is that better or worse for Jews? It depends on the circumstances. For example, the vascular system is the same in every human being. Therefore, if a person bleeds, he should be helped, and his wound properly dressed. On the other hand, if a Jew happens to bleed, for example, because of the actions of an anti-Semite, it would be just as though a fish with feathers started bleeding. Hence, his bleeding is not human, or even animal; it is Jewish, which means it is nothing. It can certainly be watched, but without any feelings, either of hatred or even of aversion. Only out of curiosity.

In my surroundings, in my family, then, there was no anti-Semitism. But was there something else? I don't wish to sit in judgment, or to overstate the case. Let's say, to put things judiciously, that there was a trace of something of the sort. At any rate, it was never put to the test. During the German occupation, not one single Jew on the run ever came to our house asking for help. Of course, it never would have occurred to anyone to go looking for one of them. Now, if a Jew had made it to our house, I'm certain that he would not have been handed over to the Germans, I'm almost certain that he would have been fed, but what else? To risk one's life because of a Jew? The Germans used to kill with equal savagery the Jew they had caught and the Pole who had helped him. What happened to the Jews during the German occupation was no cause for joy in the circles I belonged to, rather it aroused feelings of horror, but this horror was simply part of the general terror of the war and the occupation. After all, what was going on between the Germans and the Jews was their affair. Not ours, and therefore we shouldn't have anything to do with it. An unpleasant business, even worse than unpleasant, perhaps even frightful if we cared to think about it, but not our affair.

So much for that. And now, at just this precise point, out of absolutely nowhere, came the nose.

From that moment on, whenever I happened to walk through the Planty promenade in Cracow, past the benches on which were sitting the idle toughs who were always ready for action—I tried to cope with the following dilemma: how to walk so as to move exclusively *en face*; in other words, so that my profile could not be seen from any point of view? Geometry teaches us that that is impossible. So does life.

A Difficult Situation

I don't want to overstate the case. At that point I was racked by fears and subject to paranoia; one cannot emerge unscathed from a war and an occupation of such brutality, when one is only fifteen years old, after enduring five years of that kind of thing, embarked on as a nine-year-old child. The problem of my nose was certainly rooted in the social reality that then confronted me, even if somewhat blown out of proportion by my neurotic imagination. At school my nose was not an issue, which cheered me up, since there is nothing more cruel or ruthless in asserting the infallibility of the lowest instincts than a group of male teenagers. (In those days, the upper schools were separate for boys and girls.) At any rate, the horde always left me in peace, sensing that I was an outsider with a special destiny. That does not mean that I felt myself left in peace or that I disregarded the horde. The horde had not noticed my nose, but I knew only too well that I had it.

This became even clearer when finally, during a break between classes, one of them stepped forward and said right to my face, "You, kike."

I remember his name, but I won't disclose it here. He was all muscles and known for his rambunctious aggressiveness. The horde did not join in. This meant that they had concluded it was a private scrap between the two of us, nothing out of the ordinary, and that to provoke me, he had used an exceptionally crude insult, stronger than the ones we were accustomed to, which had ceased to produce any effect anymore. But, in one second of panic, I was certain that my assailant had said what he really thought. And because of this certainty I had failed to strike him, I had not reacted, to my eternal shame according to the horde's code of honor. But is it only according to their code of honor?

Of course, I was afraid of his strength, but that's another matter; fear of that sort can be easily overcome when one acts on impulse. But what kind of impulse would that have been in my case? Evidently a kind I didn't have.

Then, was that horrible insult not only a horrible insult but also—somewhere in my innermost being—a revelation of my shameful secret? But what secret, for God's sake, if I am not a Jew but a Roman Catholic! Or, if I had reacted and hit him—would that have been an admission that he was right, and would I have hit him as a Jew who was called a kike in an insulting tone of voice and therefore obliged to defend his Jewish honor? But how can I admit something when I have nothing on my conscience? Or should I fight as a Slavic cavalryman whose Aryan honor has been offended? Perhaps so, but I'd have to have another nose for that. Whichever way I turned, I was blocked. My situation was further complicated by the fact that my assailant, although not of a dark complexion, had, as they say, characteristic features. So maybe he was . . . ? Could it be that he wanted to avert suspicion . . . from himself? Fortunately, the whole incident was soon publicly a matter of oblivion, but unfortunately I could not forget. Especially since I was burning with shame because of my unmanly behavior. I had chickened out, but what was the real reason? That was the snag—I couldn't make head or tail of it. I had behaved badly, but no matter how I looked at it, I couldn't figure out what my behaving badly consisted of. But it was badly all right. And that "badly" was certainly not without connection to what happened shortly thereafter and to the way I behaved then. "Badly" is seldom without issue.

The Provocateur

There were two Jews in our class. One, whose name I have forgotten, was a Jew who had a certain "leeway" if I can put it that way. Good-looking and affable, he would not deny that he was a Jew if asked, but his admission was somehow nonchalant, elegant I would say, and inconsequential. At any rate, he quickly passed through our school life and disappeared with the same ease with which he had taken part in it. But did he ever really take part? He had been among us, but rather as a traveler who on each of his trips conforms to the native customs politely and deftly, nothing more.

No special issue was made of his Jewishness. Was it because he did not "look" like a Jew? And yet it was common knowledge that he was a Jew, although his nose—a fact which astonished me and which I considered unjust—was entirely "normal," almost like Errol Flynn's.

Or was it because all attention was focused on the other one? The other one was not only a Jew, he was ideally suited to be one. True, his nose was smaller than mine, but everything else about him was exactly what you could once see on the Nazi anti-Semitic posters of the past, and what you can now see on Moscow-made "anti-Zionist" posters.

Of course, that's exaggeration, but there was something unpleasant about his exterior. He was fat, of an unhealthy complexion, with thick lips which Stanislaw Ryszard Dobrowolski would describe as "lewd and slimy," his eyes bulging and myopic; he had a speech defect that made him stammer and sputter saliva, especially when he was overagitated (and he was constantly overagitated, because of his own efforts, and because of all the care taken to make him so), and a bizarrely deformed head with no neck to speak of. I remember his name, but I'll substitute a fictitious one. Let's say: Cwibelsztajn. It sounds every bit as insolently and provocatively Jewish as his own.

This Cwibelsztajn was not only a Jew, not only such a perfect Jew at that, but he was also proud of it.

Had he endured his fate with humility, owned up to his inferiority, apologized for being a Jew, had he scrambled for favors and good graces, things wouldn't have gone so badly for him. Then at least he would have been in his proper place and played his proper role. But he proclaimed his Jewishness loudly and arrogantly, as if it were a value worth at least as much as Polishness. When we were saying our prayers before and after classes (in those days, prayers were still said in schools: "We give thanks to you, O Lord, for the light of learning, may we be enlightened by it," etc.), he would stand with his head held high, proud and defiant, or so it seemed to us, when he should have been, if not frightened by his not belonging, then at least uneasy about it. His absence from religion classes (in those days, religion classes were compulsory) was legal and as natural as his presence would have been unnatural. But for us this naturalness qualified as unnaturalness not because he was absent but because he was excluded from and cast out of the community, while the legality was a legalization of our contemptuous disapproval of the outcast. And at the same time we would silently envy him the right to be absent, since it gave him free time.

If he had run away, avoided us, or at least not looked us straight in the eye, he would have fared much better. But he fought back when attacked, and when he couldn't defend himself, he himself attacked. He was unyielding, ruthless, and aggressive. And who did he think he was? That wheezing milksop, that cringing freak! Such behavior called for a just punishment, and he himself was responsible if he didn't have an easy life.

It was rumored that he belonged to a secret Jewish organization, the Haganah, whose goal was the establishment of the state of Israel. Maybe he did belong to it, if in fact the Haganah had cells in Poland at that time. But they said that to be funny; just imagining Cwibelsztajn with a gun was hilarious. And such subjects were funny in themselves. Once, when during a discussion Cwibelsztajn defended the right of the Jews to their own state, the conclusion was drawn that such a state would have to have its own navy. Jewish sailors! That made everyone roar with laughter.

For the record: one should not think that this brief period (for the day came when Cwibelsztajn failed to show up anymore) was for him a constant pogrom without a moment of respite. There were times of relaxation, camaraderie, or simply attention being diverted elsewhere. Besides being a Jew, he also was our peer and classmate who shared our fortunes at school, and the natural laws of coexistence cannot be limited—such is the nature of coexistence—only to negation and conflict. And the horde, apart from being a horde, consisted of separate and very distinct individuals who did not always act as a horde. And the persecution, even when it got worse, never yet—that is, up to the time of the events I am decribing—reached the stage of fighting. In any case, there are many forms of persecution, especially in the life of a school, or a barracks, or a camp. Only one thing was certain—and here he did not have a moment's respite: he could not be sure of a day, or an hour, or a second.

At no point did I join in the torturing of Cwibelsztajn. Maybe because I simply don't like torture; reading the Marquis de Sade is as exciting for me as reading Marx's *Das Kapital*. Anyway, I could safely not torture Cwibelsztajn, since it was in keeping with my position as an outsider. And I should add for the record that torturing Cwibelsztajn was not compulsory. Whoever wanted to could, whenever he felt like it and as much as he wished.

Cwibelsztajn was an excellent student, and not only because he was exceptionally bright. He studied with an inhuman diligence that was extremely irritating, since to have contempt for top students was considered good form. Not to work at all, but somehow to get by, was the fashion of the day. But, in his case, it wasn't just diligence; he studied against us, to spite us, and despite us. As a challenge. Like everything else he did, or did not do. He was all challenge, and provocation.

So he got excellent grades even in those subjects for which he was less gifted by nature. There was just one thing he couldn't handle: gymnastics, which was what they called physical education. That was the only setback to his willpower, when out of breath, red in the face as if he were about to drop dead (couldn't be funnier), obscenely clumsy, he would try repeatedly to execute the simplest exercises. The sight of him gave physical-education classes an added attraction. The way he would trip over his own feet, lose his balance, fall down, pant, get red in the face, and still not be able to do it. But he would keep trying, over and over again, always with that same dogged but futile determination. Finally, probably out of fear there might be a serious accident for which he would be held responsible, the gymnastics teacher excused him from what was for Cwibelsztajn torture and for us sheer delight—he may have consulted his parents or guardians (we knew nothing about his personal life) or obtained a doctor's certificate of poor health. I won't say an exemption, or medical release, since Cwibelsztajn never wanted to be exempt from anything. Apparently he'd had some heart trouble, or some other kind of trouble, no one knew for certain, since no one really cared. At any rate, he dropped out of gymnastics, but two things about him were remembered long afterwards: his desire to shine in this field, too, and his total lack of physical coordination.

A Free Period

It happened during what was known as a free period, when we were left unsupervised and told not to leave the classroom, but, of course, everyone felt free to do as he wished. It all started with a pair of boxing gloves. I do not recall now who had come up with the idea

of daring Cwibelsztajn. Maybe it was a collective idea and arose all
by itself. Several nonsportsmen joined the sporting element, some
undoubtedly out of a sincere desire, others out of boredom, but also
quite possibly for reasons totally unrelated to Cwibelsztajn but having
to do with settling their own problems. Here I have in mind a short,
pockmarked boy who, although certainly not a Jew, was the laugh-
ingstock of the class. He suffered because of his diminutive size,
pockmarkedness, and God knows what else, since not all the laws
according to which one's place in the herd is established are yet
known. He occupied the lowest rank in the hierarchy. (A Jew is quite
another matter; a Jew is beyond any hierarchy, because a Jew does
not belong to the herd.) At any rate, this little runt got very enthusiastic
about the plan and proved to be the most energetic in its realization.

Half jokingly, Cwibelsztajn was challenged to a brief match—well,
rather, a bit of inconsequential "sparring." The joke rested on the
certainty that Cwibelsztajn would be singularly inept at boxing, but
would not refuse despite that.

Why didn't he refuse? After all, he knew what the story would be.
What was he counting on? There was nothing he could count on.
Then why did he accept the challenge, knowing that he had simply
been dared and had no chance if he accepted their dare? I doubt
whether his courage was a natural trait of his character. I even doubt
whether it was solely courage and nothing more. He was visibly
scared when they put the gloves on his hands; he started sweating
and turned pale; he was scared to death. Probably he overcame his
fear—so well founded in reality and on basic common sense—for the
sake of certain principles, for the sake of defending something that
went beyond his personal and private concerns, something we did
not know about or want to know about, but which for him was of
the greatest importance, far more important than his own fear, pain,
or loss of health.

The little runt kept hitting him and hitting him so effectively—at
will, and at no risk to himself—that almost immediately blood began
to flow from Cwibelsztajn's nose. Now, blood is a serious matter, and
when it's scented by man or animal, the situation becomes radically
different. Then something changes so fundamentally, in both man
and animal, that there's no telling what it can lead to—only one
thing is certain: that this "something" starts to acquire a sort of
autonomy, escapes all control and takes over. And what does that
something do to man? It depends on the kind of man. It did nothing

to me, nothing, in the sense that I did not stir from my observation post, where, at a certain distance (as usual) from the site of action, I was watching everything. I was riveted to the spot from the beginning and remained riveted, I even got more riveted, I became absolutely riveted. And what I remember most clearly is a feeling of the reality of it all, but everything made it seem impossible that it was happening, therefore creating a sense of unreality too, resulting in an overwhelming, irresistible, and totally futile desire for nothing to exist, whether real or unreal, including myself.

Just at that moment one of our classmates entered the room, a classmate whose name I remember and am going to reveal. His name was Leszek Herdegen. He was tall, with blond hair and the looks that the German race theoreticians dreamed of. He had taken part in the Warsaw Uprising, was a prisoner in the German camps, from which he had escaped several times, had a father in the West, and a dog as well as a beautiful fiancée, wore an American surplus military jacket, smoked cigarettes, bicycled, and spoke in an authentic, exceptionally ringing baritone voice which carried far. He was an unwilling and indifferent student, but the teachers somehow forgave him much, although he treated them with a sort of naïve disdain. He was unanimously accepted by the class and enjoyed high prestige and an awesome reputation; he conformed to the rules of the horde perfectly, with the exception of sport, which he despised, and yet in his case that was no drawback. He was "okay," as "okay" as one could possibly be.

Upon seeing what was going on, Leszek turned pale and started to yell. Never at any other point do I recall a similar instance of his yelling that way, although we remained friends for many years afterwards. He showered Cwibelsztajn's torturers with the choicest curses and insults, but what is even more strange, he used words like "infamy," "ignominy," "disgrace," "shame." No one stopped him, opposed him, or even tried to protest. And even if someone had tried, he would not have succeeded in contending with his fury, or with his eyes, which had turned white with rage, or his voice, which caused the windowpanes to rattle and the benches to shake, and which could be heard as far away as Wawel Castle. As if it were he who had been personally insulted and then gone berserk, or at least as if Jews had been beating a Pole, and not vice versa. The torturers disappeared into thin air, and all that was left was a handful of confused teenagers.

But in that confusion there was a sense of great relief. And who knows, perhaps even the short, pockmarked runt was grateful to Leszek for somehow straightening out the situation. As though Leszek had saved not only Cwibelsztajn from something bad, but also the pockmarked little runt himself. Relief, and a feeling of liberation from something.

Leszek is no longer alive, Cwibelsztajn has disappeared from sight for good, my nose has remained with me. But now I even like it. It has caused me much suffering, but if it weren't for the nose, I would understand very little now and feel even less.

(July–August 1984)
Translated by Jadwiga Kosicka

Marek Nowakowski

THE CONVERSATION

H E REACHED THE TOP of the stairs and faced the main entrance.
From here he looked at the outside world, thinking that perhaps
this was the last time, and he wanted to take it all in. All of it. A little
girl, very much like his daughter, was passing by, carrying a satchel
on her back. In front of a store, a line was taking shape, and he also
noticed a large delivery truck with COLD STORAGE written on it. Two
men in overalls were carrying some bags. He looked at the leafless
branches of a nearby tree, dotted with crows, and at the sky.

As soon as he walked in, he was stopped by a buttoned-down guard
who demanded to see the summons and then dialed a two- or three-
digit number, using the phone inside the enclosure, said something
curtly, and told him to wait.

He sat down on a bench in the waiting room and looked at a sign
made of *papier-mâché* and mounted on a large canvas. The sign read:
"Forge thoughts into deeds."

Above the sign he saw the white eagle on a red field. An ashtray
on a stand in the corner was full of butts, one of them still smoldering.
For a few minutes he stared at the rising line of smoke.

He did not have to wait very long.

"Come with me, please," said a young fellow with a thick, bushy mustache, who appeared behind the gate. He was wearing a leather jacket and faded, washed-out jeans.

"The elevator is out of commission," he explained as they walked up the stairs covered with a rust-colored rug.

On the third floor they reached a long corridor and stopped in front of door number 34. The young man politely pointed to a chair, turned, and disappeared.

The place was bustling with movement, doors slamming, people—mostly men—coming and going.

He watched them intently.

It was easy to see who worked here and who didn't. The contrast between the two, in both manner and appearance, was striking, and yet, on the surface, one couldn't tell them apart. But it was in the way they looked around and the way they moved that they differed the most; one couldn't mistake one for the other, without knowing exactly why. He searched for an explanation in vain, and the effort was beginning to exhaust him.

He remembered some of those people; after all, he had dealt with them before, more than once.

He felt drained and his spirits were low. Each time his wife brought up the subject of going abroad for good, he would say no, but in his heart of hearts he really wanted to go.

The atmosphere at the institute was unbearable, his work was restricted, everything seemed petty, sterile, and hopeless. Letters from colleagues who had emigrated made him think of what might have been and also of what was still possible.

He was tormented by his own personal troubles, another result of that memorable night in December. It was during that time, just after the crisis, when he was hiding from the police and kept moving from one place to another, that he met this girl. It wasn't a casual affair, just the opposite, and it was still going on, making his life extremely difficult. After all, he had a wife and a daughter he really adored. Constant tension and a split personality, all because of a very young woman who was more attractive than his wife in every way he could think of.

Nothing about the future seemed promising. He definitely didn't feel like a hero. Would he have enough strength to endure what was coming? The question seemed silly. He started going through all his pockets, couldn't find any cigarettes, and suddenly felt full of life and energy. "Hold tight!" He remembered this expression from his sailing days.

He glanced at his watch and discovered that half an hour had passed. That's how they do things, he thought. They call you and then make you wait. It's anxiety that they're counting on, the questions you'll be asking yourself before they see you. Why am I here? What do they want? How much do they know already? He was overcome by anxiety, just waiting and thinking.

An old man was walking down the hall, looking at all the doors anxiously, trying to find the number written out on the summons which he held clutched in his hands.

A fat man in a quilted coat passed him, walking in the opposite direction. He seemed to know where he was going and why.

How to spot those who had been called but in fact were informers? The old man was probably all right, but how about the quilted coat? One could always recognize informers—their eyes had the alertness of a pickpocket's.

He was disgusted with his obsessive thoughts and felt miserable. His wife was absolutely right. "Let's get out of this sewer," she had said when he told her about the summons.

He sat up straight so suddenly that an employee of this district office of internal affairs who was passing by at that moment almost stopped. Feeling like a thief caught red-handed, he was ashamed of himself.

Door number 34 opened wide and a man in civilian clothes appeared. He recognized him instantly as an old acquaintance, the regular interrogator, his, as it were, own guardian.

The officer invited him warmly into the room. "Sorry to be late," he added. "Something urgent that had to be taken care of. You forgive me, Doctor."

Since their very first meeting, the officer had insisted on using his title. Was it snobbery on his part, some kind of inferiority complex, or sleazy politeness and hypocrisy?

They were facing each other, and, as always, he felt overwhelmed by the officer's towering figure, which made him feel even smaller and more feeble—the contrast between them always irritated him.

The officer pointed to a chair, waited for him to sit down, and only then took his place behind the desk.

"Cigarette?"

He refused, pushing the pack away.

"I took the liberty of interrupting your work at the institute," the officer said and tapped the desk ever so lightly.

His hands were strong and white, nails cut short on long fingers, wrists covered with hair inside clinically clean cuffs. He was quite a dandy. A jacket of brown tweed, a light-blue shirt with slightly darker blue stripes, a brown tie, a button-down collar with slightly rounded tips, as the latest fashion decreed.

He wondered where all this came from. Had to be foreign. Does the officer go abroad himself, or do his colleagues from other departments bring him things? The coats, jackets, a raspberry-red turtleneck sweater which he wore many times that winter were good quality, too. He wondered.

"How are things at the institute?" The officer's voice was warm and pleasant to listen to. "You've had some problems lately, haven't you? Hard-currency budget has been cut, and a few scholarship deals are off, isn't that so?"

The officer never failed to show interest in his work, and he must have had some training in science, because he knew quite a lot about the institute's internal mechanism and who was doing what.

"By the way, those mini-computers for the staff have been delivered, haven't they? They're smart little bastards. You won't have to waste valuable time on routine calculations."

He looked at the officer with awe of sorts. Son of a bitch really knows what's going on. Who is his source? The new lab assistant? Quite likely.

"Are you going to refuse to answer my questions as usual?" The officer laughed, showing his strong white teeth.

The officer was truly handsome. Tall, broad-shouldered, a swarthy oval face with a strong grayish beard, his jet-black hair smoothly combed and parted, his brows black, too, joined over his nose so as to underscore the intense blue of the eyes. Blondes must be crazy about him. Once again, he thought of this Adonis with envy. Unfortunately, women were not exactly running after him.

"I haven't made up my mind yet; I'm immersed in the past," he replied.

He wasn't lying. From the instant he walked into the room he felt he was both there and here. The feeling was growing more intense all the time. Then he started on the first floor and they were taking him to the second. Every day for a month, the same officer would have a chat with him, sometimes twice a day, in the morning and after lunch. It was during that time that he called him his guardian. The click of the key in the keyhole, and the guard would lead him to the corridor, barking, "To the slammer!"

They would walk up in silence. The guardian would be waiting and then would politely show him the chair. The opening questions were always the same and were asked in the same sequence: surname, first name, mother's maiden name, age, occupation. Then the real thing. He never answered any questions. After all, he had been tutored by veterans of many interrogations. The principle was to keep mum.

The officer was asking questions patiently. The time in between questions wasn't wasted—he was given to understand that they knew a lot, that it was childish to refuse to answer questions, because that could only make things worse. Also, the merciful intent behind Article 57 of the Penal Code was explained to him. The officer painted a dreadful picture of many futile and wasted years spent unnecessarily in jail. This prospect seemed truly terrifying; he seemed quite incensed by the danger to his health, talents, nervous system. He seemed overcome by the impending tragedy of having to adjust to solitary life in prison. His voice trembled when he asked, "And what would be the point of taking such risks, Doctor?"

He remained silent, although he had no trouble imagining those days, months, perhaps even years, in jail. His hands were trembling and he had to hide them under the table.

The officer put the papers away and started to talk casually about all kinds of things. The idea was to transform this ordinary, bare interrogation room into a café setting, where two friends have just met for an hour in the late afternoon. As a matter of fact, the officer was about to make some tea. But there was no doubt that the interrogation was under way.

The officer tried to upset him with visions of freedom, with stories about his wonderful weekend trips.

The officer's tan and strong muscles suggested good health and a sense of well-being, as if he'd just come down from a cozy mountain lodge surrounded by snow-capped spruce, where skiers stretch out on deck chairs, enjoying the sun and patting a huge sheepdog that walks slowly among them.

The officer also enjoyed telling him about current plays and films. The implication was that in the evening he liked to go to the movies or see a play with his girlfriend, fiancée, or perhaps wife (most probably a tall, sensuous blonde). His comments on *Raiders of the Lost Ark* were very apt and astute and brought back childhood memories of fascination with distant travel.

One day the officer told him about his own past, about his previous career. He had been an athlete, specializing in water polo, and liked reminiscing about his last goal during an international competition. This, he would say, lowering his voice, was the good life—"good perks, per diems in dollars, you could buy something, bring it back, you know what I mean."

The officer was groping for some kind of connection, wanted to create an impression of intimacy, but to no avail.

Although there were moments of weakness on his part, he would tell himself, "I mustn't give in, my God, I mustn't give in." Most of the time he was appealing to supernatural forces, praying for strength that would allow him to come out of this predicament unscathed. So, during those supposedly off-the-record conversations, he was silent most of the time.

"One can't get a word out of you," the officer complained more than once. "You are terribly suspicious."

"After all, you are still interrogating me, aren't you?"

The officer laughed, but his eyes remained cold. As a matter of fact, his eyes never changed, never relaxed, no matter what the expression on his face.

Switching abruptly from a friendly chatter to stiff bureaucratese, he would sometimes catch him unawares.

"A major change has taken place in the documentation concerning your case," the officer said casually one Monday, put the papers back into his briefcase, and left the room.

The interrogation ceased for several days after that.

On another occasion, the officer banged his fist on the table and the muscles on his cheeks tensed up into hard lumps. "You've gone too far," he said sternly. "We may have to change our approach."

The officer's strong, broad hands were resting neatly on the table. They seemed calm, but there was something menacing about them.

He was thinking at that moment with relief (he had always feared pain) that, after all, they had stopped using physical torture some time ago. He was glad to know that, but . . . Who knows? Perhaps they still do it sometimes?

He glanced again at the officer's lazy, menacing, peaceful hands.

As if the force concentrated in them expected a signal. He felt compelled to keep looking at them but managed to glance at the window covered with a thick curtain.

"You dwell on the past too much," the officer said. "You're too emotional. Prejudices, animosities, what's the point? You don't like me, now be honest!" He laughed heartily, showing a row of brilliant teeth. "But I'm just a professional, nothing but. If I behaved one way and not another, it's because I had to follow orders from my superiors. I had to do what I had to do. But that's in the past. Why contemplate the past? Why should you dissect it? You're a scientist, after all, not a romantic. Times have changed; we're in a new phase. Normalization, I could call it, meeting the demands of the people halfway. I don't think we're that far apart, not really."

"We were really close in jail"—he couldn't resist saying that.

"We're fighting for the same cause, but from different positions," the officer continued calmly, ignoring the nasty dig. "I think I can understand that. Unpleasant experiences, the sentence, all kinds of ailments, the blacklisting, all that leaves permanent marks. Very stressful. But . . . " The officer pushed a pack of cigarettes toward him.

He was concerned about his health and for several months had been trying to give up smoking, so he had no cigarettes on him. But he gave in and lit one.

The smoke was delicious; it filled his lungs to the brim. He felt a sudden surge of energy and interrupted the officer. " 'We're fighting for the same cause . . .' You sound truly patriotic. We're talking like one Pole to another, aren't we? That's the method. A national idyll, let's love each other, united we stand, divided we fall. We resisted the partitioning powers; the Nazis, Stalin couldn't bring us to our knees . . . You work for an institution that everybody fears, but in fact you want the same things as I, others, you're with us all the way!"

The officer nodded mechanically all the time, without really listening to what was being said.

Angry with himself for having launched into this tirade in the first place, he stopped abruptly. There was no point engaging in polemics here; he was brought here for a different purpose. He was angry at his inability to control his temper—common sense and experience told him that he should. For a thirty-five-year-old, he had quite a past in the movement.

A few friends wanted him to go with them to Jasna Gora, to take part in a pilgrimage intended as a demonstration by political prisoners. But he wasn't interested in martyrdom of any kind. Pathetic, futile pose, he thought. He refused and they didn't like that.

The officer leaned forward, put both elbows on the desk, and looked at him intently.

"I'm only thinking my thoughts," he explained, "private ones."

"Oh, yes," the officer agreed and lit a cigarette. "Look, Doctor . . ." he began.

How stylish can we get! Such a pleasant conversation between two equal partners. While he was watching this well-mannered and exceedingly polite gentleman sitting quietly behind his desk, he could see him in that other scene, inside his apartment.

A detachment of them rushed in and started turning his book-shelves, desk, and closets, even his trash can, upside down. The officer, who was obviously in charge, sat on a chair behind the desk and smiled with compassion as he lay in bed.

"Oh, yes, the flu. It's been like bubonic plague this year. It first attacks the throat and then . . . I had to stay in bed a few days myself," he said and glanced at his people as they were going through books and papers. "Make sure you've looked everywhere," he said, and he pointed to another batch close to the radiator.

A small shelf above the bed caught his eye. It was full of books on physics, most of them in foreign languages. It turned out that he could read English quite well. He pulled out a volume of essays about twentieth-century physicists, made sure that nothing was hidden in it, and then stopped at a chapter on Heisenberg. He said something about Heisenberg's behavior during the war. After all, he never left Germany.

Here he was, in agony, about to die from a cold and a cough, shivering and stifling, surrounded by brutes disemboweling his most precious treasure trove, but strong enough to indulge in a long tirade about Heisenberg, Werner von Braun, and other scholars.

The officer listened intently. His comments suggested that he knew what he was talking about.

This went on for quite a while, until the decisive moment came: he was told to get up and get ready to leave the apartment.

"You'll be going with us now," said the officer, and watched him as he started to put on a pair of underpants.

"Just a moment." The officer touched him at that moment and told him to squat. Seeing the surprise on his face, he pressed down his back lightly and approached him from the rear.

"Take off your underpants," the officer barked in a cold, impersonal tone.

As he was emerging naked from this terrifying moment, he felt humiliated beyond endurance. The professional skill with which the officer bent his back and standing behind him, his legs spread wide, broad-shouldered and elegant, as he moved his hands down his spine and scrutinized every inch of his scrawny, protruding ass—all this was more than he could bear, and he knew he would never forget that moment. He pondered this experience many times in prison (he called it "The Problem of the Transition from the Heisenberg Principle to the Ass") and was quite shocked to see that behind the table at his first interrogation sat none else but the officer himself, his old friend.

After a while he got used to seeing the officer there and referred to him casually, in a sort of friendly way.

That scene came back to him as clear as ever and he met the officer's watchful, piercing look with equally cold, implacable eyes.

They were locked in a struggle for a while and then both gave up. The telephone rang and the officer quickly picked up the receiver. "Yes, hello," he said briskly, but then his tone changed instantly, it became warm and soft. "Oh, it's you! Of course not. No need to worry . . . I can do it later . . . Yes, I did get that. Exactly the kind you wanted. Definitely. See you, Granny."

He put down the receiver, glanced at him furtively, even sheepishly, and reached for a cigarette. The man on the other side of the desk showed some interest in the officer's personality, his true nature. What was he like? Affectionate with his granny, his voice caring and capable of warmth. He knew how to comfort her with that voice. Granny! Mother, mother-in-law, or simply grandmother. Grandmother and grandson.

"This conversation is becoming extremely difficult," the officer complained suddenly. "You resist me, Doctor . . ."

"Indeed, your intuition is serving you well, Lieutenant."

"Captain."

"You have been promoted. How nice. Congratulations."

"I keep thinking," said the officer, bowing his head slightly, "about these blocks in our conversations. How can we remove them? How can I convince you? You overestimate the importance of some things."

He leaned on his elbow and looked genuinely troubled. "Your view of us is entirely wrong. The Praetorian Guard, the ruthless cohorts, right? But in fact we only follow orders. Orders, you understand?"

He could understand this explanation. He could even believe it, and he was on the point of nodding. But at the last moment he stopped himself and kept the inscrutable expression on his face, like a tightly sealed container trying to protect itself from the corrosive effects of outside impurities. A thought was taking shape in his head.

All over the country, a large number of people, young and old, work in many departments of internal affairs, hidden in small buildings, within government agencies and other official entities, and in the impressive-looking buildings occupied by the ministry in the capital. What guides their actions and their thoughts? Something they like to call a necessity of a higher order, blind faith, concern for Poland's survival?

What kind of Poland do they have in mind? A dependency, a client state perhaps, one of many territories united under a large umbrella? He and they shared the same language, they were all born here, their past is very similar, even identical, their parents are also from here, their memory . . . They came from the same origins as all of us. Have they lost, then, the ability to think for themselves? Has the official view of reality preempted all others and become a sheer reflex that controls all their thoughts?

Maybe they are the most despicable among us, people without faith and without hope, poisoned by everything in their upbringing, strengthened by their daily work in the conviction that theirs is the only freedom possible in a fettered world. Ennobled by their work in their own minds, in their limited view of themselves, they think themselves superior to the mob, the unruly mob they have been ordered to guard and protect from folly.

Perhaps . . . He did not want to get trapped by his own dogmatic thinking. He wanted to be free and unprejudiced in his analysis. What kind of person is the officer, anyway? Perhaps just a bureaucrat; above all, anxious to please his superiors—somebody who has been doing this kind of work for many years, locked up in a cage of his own making. Perhaps on his own time, in matters that have nothing to do with his job, he is a decent person. Perhaps he thinks and evaluates things the same way as other people. For a moment this optimistic view cheered him up. After all, one day in prison he offered to take a note to his mother and posted it himself.

"I can understand," the officer said. "You don't trust me. But the circumstances are entirely different this time. You're not under any kind of suspicion, I'm not interrogating you, or recording anything you say. You can see, Doctor, I'm taking everything into consideration, the viewpoints of both sides. I do have an imagination, I am not an automaton. I am alive, I can see what's going on, I have my own doubts, I agonize sometimes, I draw my own conclusions. So it seems to me that from time to time an ounce of goodwill from your side would not . . ."

At that moment the telephone rang and the officer picked up the receiver.

"Yes. Of course. Yes." Then he said something else. "Yesterday he began to break down . . . Soon he will break down completely, don't worry." At the other end, somebody laughed with gusto. The officer laughed the same way. That was all.

But for him this laughter was ominous—it brought back memories.

He spent his first night as a prisoner in the basement of the police station. They had come to get him at noon. The officer and somebody else from security. The officer, who was wearing a well-cut loden coat and black boots with thick heels, exuded strength and energy. Disheveled, dirty, and unshaven after a dreadful night on the planks of the basement cell, he felt the contrast between them keenly.

They led him into the courtyard and to the car.

"Your hands, please," said the officer.

Before he could think what that meant, he felt the cool, metallic touch of the handcuffs embracing his wrists. At the same time the officer gave a big yawn, his jaws almost cracking, and looked up at the wintry blue sky. He stomped his foot and the snow cracked. As he was pressing his boot into the snow, he yawned again and said to his companion: "Wonderful conditions. It would be nice to grab a pair of skis and slide down a hill now."

They pushed him into the car and sat down, one on each side.

He was dying for a cigarette. There was a pack on the desk, but he didn't reach for it, just shoved his hands inside the pockets of his jacket.

He had enough of this vague and exhausting conversation. He tensed up in the chair and began: "We're talking about nothing. Our conversation makes no sense whatsoever. To prove this to you, I have to state some obvious facts. I'm sorry, but some elementary things have to be said to clarify matters. To show the fundamental difference which cannot be ignored. What kind of partnership can there be? What do you represent? Security forces. You have done everything you could to show that whatever the democratic opposition attempted to achieve was engineered by traitors, foreign agents. While the security people represent the noble, pure good of the nation, the bedrock of its future, we are just a bunch of troublemakers, hired opportunists, scum. What kind of dialogue can there be between you and me? You, with your official conscience that nothing can disturb, and I! Force is not concerned with such figments as truth, justice, the aspirations of the majority, basic human rights, etc. I don't see what it is that we could discuss here. I see no reason why I should. None at all. You'd locked me up, I was released when the amnesty came. I demand that you tell me why I have been called to report to this office . . ." His mouth felt dry, he was drained. "Besides, I can't waste all this time. I have work to do, you know."

The officer looked at his watch. "I have work to do, too," he said, "but I do it in a different way."

He smoothed his black, shining, neatly combed hair. "Well"—his attitude changed now, he sounded very prim and official—"you have been summoned to be issued a warning. We know that you haven't severed your connections with the political underground. We're watching you guys, we're waiting. This is by the way. This time we are concerned about November 11, the anniversary of independence. We know that celebrations are being planned—a Mass in the cathedral, a march to the monument, meetings, speeches. It was all announced in your own little publication, wasn't it? I strongly suggest that you stay away from all that. Particularly since the amnesty from which you benefited a few months ago was conditional. Con-di-tion-al!"

Blood rushed to his head. He tightened his fists, straightened out his thin body with its concave chest, and bristled; he really looked like a rooster, small but all set for a fight. "I am a free man," he declared. "At least, despite your allegations, that's how I feel, and I'll do what I think is right."

The officer was still smiling pleasantly, but his eyes remained glassy and cold. Only the tightening of his fingers on a Ronson lighter showed that he was angry.

"If it were up to me"—he was playing with the lighter—"I would drown you guys in a ditch filled with quicklime. Like newborn kittens. But don't worry, Doctor. I don't allow emotions to control my behavior." He smiled broadly, his teeth glistened like a toothpaste ad in a color magazine. "I'm a disciplined member of my department. On the other hand, if I were told to proceed . . ." The officer paused and looked at him intently. He could not stand the intensity of this look and lowered his head.

He could easily imagine being grabbed by the officer's powerful hands, could hear the rattle of the metal bracelet on his wrist. He could imagine being thrown into the abyss filled with the deadly whiteness of quicklime. The last image in his memory would be this engaging, handsome macho face with its fleshy mouth, square jaw, large nose, and black eyebrows joined above a pair of glassy eyes.

"That's it for today," the officer said. "I warned you about the possible consequences of your actions, and let me say this again: Don't provoke incidents in the city with your presence. Let me add, confidentially, that the best idea would be to get away for the weekend. November 11 falls on a Sunday this year. You could take a little trip to the mountains . . ."

"Can I go now?" he asked.

The officer nodded and got up. "If you want, I can give you a lift to the institute," he said, straightening his tie and brushing a speck off his sleeve. "I'm going in the same direction."

He didn't say no, and the officer assumed that he had accepted the invitation. As they walked down the hall, they passed quite a few young, handsome men, who greeted the officer warmly but cast quick, careful glances at him.

They all had cold, impenetrable eyes with which they observed everything that crossed their path.

At the gate, the officer mumbled a few words to the guard, who let them through.

They got into a parked car and the officer turned the steering wheel nonchalantly with one hand. He drove fast, full of confidence. A Mercedes with foreign plates in the next lane caught his eye.

"What a wonderful machine!" he exclaimed. "Super! I love cars, don't you?"

Oblivious to the question, he was completely submerged in his chaotic, racing thoughts.

He felt surrounded by thick, impenetrable darkness.

Slouched in a comfortable seat, he was being driven in an official car; a functionary of the security forces was taking him back to his office.

The victim and the executioner were riding together in the same vehicle.

"A ditch full of quicklime," he mumbled to himself.

The officer looked at him in surprise. "Here we are," he said, and stopped the car at the curb. The institute was close by.

He got out and for a moment didn't quite know what to do, whether to say thank you or goodbye. Instead, he just nodded and waited for the officer to drive away.

(March 1985)
Translated by Maya Latynski

Gustaw Herling-Grudzinski

SAN DRAGONE

*What is a dragon? An animal, one might say,
which looks or regards (Greek* drakon*): so
called, presumably, from its terrible eyes.*
—Norman Douglas, *Old Calabria*

I

I HAVE JUST RETURNED from Father Ilario Sterpone's funeral. Very few people attended, or so it seemed in the enormous nave of Santa Clara's—a bunch of students to the left side of the altar, fidgety after the long ceremony; to the right, Father Sterpone's sister and her husband, relatives from Calabria, colleagues from the university, and friends (such as myself). In the back, a handful of old women who can be seen in churches every day and at every hour, who love funerals and weddings, regardless of who died or is getting married.

The coffin, set up on the ground, was covered with wreaths with violet sashes. The golden letters on the wreaths bade farewell to "Our dearest brother and brother-in-law," "Wise teacher," "Dearest colleague," "Faithful friend." When the coffin was at last placed in the hearse, the sister of the deceased and her husband walked to the side of the church driveway. It was a signal for us to present our condolences. My turn came: "You spent so much time with him, sir. He talked to you about things."

The funeral procession wedged itself into the street crowd and the string of cars on Spaccanapoli just as the bell atop the campanile next to the church rang for noon. The Santa Clara's bell, which can be heard at this hour all over the city, had lately been the main thread connecting the deceased with Naples.

Yes, it is true, I did spend a lot of time with Father Sterpone—our last meeting took place a week before he died. Nothing then foreshadowed his death, even though he said to me on that occasion quite suddenly and sadly: "Everybody forgot a long time ago that I am still alive. I sometimes forget it myself."

There is an entry in my diary about how we first met, two years ago, soon after he was brought from the hospital (where he had been treated for nearly half a year for a cerebral hemorrhage) to his sister's apartment in upper Naples.

"He was sitting in an armchair," I wrote then, "slightly turned toward the window, from which one could see the whole bay: a sleepy sunny September day, hundreds and hundreds of colorful frozen sailboats, larger ships gliding slowly toward the islands. He seemed glad that I came, though I at once noticed a shadow of apprehension in his face. He spent the first half hour amusing himself with erudite memory exercises, which obviously were to serve as a kind of almost obsessively self-imposed brain test. Imprudently I asked him to repeat the title of a certain book. He reached out with his right—healthy—hand for the pad of paper with a pencil attached to it, placed it on his lap, scribbled a few letters with difficulty, glanced at his left arm, which hung inertly, and, resigned, covered the pad with his hand. He could not control his irritation for the rest of the visit, the conversation was lame, the silences long-drawn-out. When, suddenly overcome by embarrassment, I forgot myself and stared out at the bay, he turned his head and looked at me with eyes full of the emptiness of suffering. A moment of weakness redeemed as he whispered while saying goodbye: *Sto bene, sto sempre meglio.*"

II

Before his illness united us in friendship—perhaps even something larger than friendship: attempting to listen together to something riddle-like, mysterious, and very close to us both—we were for many years acquaintances.

For a long time, ever since 1955 when he came to Naples from Calabria as a teacher of philosophy in a monastery-run secondary school, he was in close and frequent contact with my wife's family. He was thirty-five then (almost exactly my age) and had been a priest for ten years. In 1970, he started lecturing at the university, but continued teaching in the lyceum and living in the monastery boarding school.

I would sometimes see him at friends' houses for tea, but our contacts were limited to casual conversations. Once, when he gave me his newly published translation of Plotinus with an intricate commentary, I decided to attend a presentation of the book at the Philosophical Society. I have no special memories of his lecture, other than a vague sense of having listened to a very personal confession concealed hermetically and very consciously in airtight language, a feeling unclear and obviously not lasting, for later we returned to the old casualness. It was only much later, when he talked to me during his illness, that he remarked in passing: "I don't think that anyone heard what I thought was really important in my lecture." He looked into my eyes with anticipation, as if for a moment he expected me to say, "I heard it." I said nothing, and he added: "Plotinus claimed that God, if one speaks about him without true virtue, is only a name. Is virtue sufficient for God to stop being merely a name for us?"

On that March morning in 1982, after the door had been forced open, he was found lying unconscious on the floor between the worktable and the bed. He had spent five and a half months in the hospital. He wanted no visitors except for his sister and brother-in-law. Eventually, the doctors sent him home (that is, to his sister's apartment), recommending physical therapy, though there was little hope for the future. He was expected to have a passive life, though still be clear of mind, sufficiently so for light reading and talking.

My wife visited him first. It struck her that he had moved into the distant past, into the years immediately following his ordination, when he served as a priest in a recently deserted parish in a small village between Catanzaro and Nicastro. Before his illness, he had never talked about those years; his life, one could have surmised, started later, in Catanzaro, where he began to study philosophy, while at the same time teaching religion at the local secondary school. Cantanzaro was also his hometown, it was there that his parents had died when he was young, his widowed and childless aunt lived there, there he had done his seminary studies. "What is the name of that village?"

"Rather strange—San Dragone. It's as if the name San Demonio should have been invented there."

It was because of that "strange" name that I later became a frequent visitor in Father Sterpone's house.

III

I had once read an article on San Dragone in an illustrated magazine, journalistically too jazzed up for me to get a clear idea of what had transpired and how, but interesting enough for the name of the little Calabrian village to lodge itself in my memory. I did not know then that there was a book about San Dragone, for the author of the article did not refer to it, as it appeared much later (in England, of all places; there is still no translation of the book in Italian, I have not seen any reference to it in the Italian press). It was that book that Father Sterpone mentioned in passing during my first visit, the title of which he was not able to write on the notepad. I went home intending to ask him about it later, in more opportune circumstances. But there was no need, as it turned out. The following morning, I found the book in my mailbox, with the sender's calling card attached to its cover. The book, entitled *The Hidden God*, numbered over two hundred pages and was richly illustrated and appended with "scholarly footnotes." The note on the dust jacket said that its young author, George Herbert Grudger, specialized in research "bordering on sociology and the study of religion," and that in 1952 he had spent two months in San Dragone.

I could of course refer my readers to Grudger's book and save myself the effort of writing this long exposition, but it is obvious that I should go on for reasons I need not even specify. And so I will provide here a concise summary of *The Hidden God* (published in London in 1957), and resume my story of what Father Sterpone told me during the years of our friendship.

The title page has a quote from Pascal that seems to justify the title: "If there were no darkness, man would not be aware of his sickness, and if there were no light, he would have no hope of healing himself. Hence, it is not only right but also useful that God is partly hidden and partly revealed, because it is just as dangerous to know God without knowing one's own misery as it is to know one's misery without knowing God."

In the introductory chapter, Grudger gives us a few historical facts about San Dragone which he sought out in archives, and in great detail describes the village, with references to particular photographs. The ruins of Torre Falconara, the remains of a tower from the castle of the Counts Falcone, date back to the late seventeenth century. The village was established on the hillside, next to the ruins, in the mid-eighteenth century, as a continuation of the former castle *borgo*, which had been destroyed or burned, together with the castle. At first it was called Falconetta; it was and still is mainly a village of shepherds. Surrounding the valley of the Chiariva River (or brook), the ring of hills is rich in shoals of grazing land easily accessible to flocks of sheep and goats. Its name was changed to San Dragone at the beginning of the nineteenth century for reasons that should perhaps be explained here more fully. There, in the ruins of Torre Falconara, in the wall of a large and dark cave (at one time dungeons), a huge crevice opened up and from time to time belched up wisps of smoke. Thus the legend of the Dragon was born. Renaming the village and placing it under the Dragon's protection must have been—according to Grudger—an act of appeasement to the Dragon. At that time the village had no church of its own and priests had to come to perform religious services from nearby Nicastro. Eventually, a church too grand for the small number of inhabitants was erected at the beginning of this century—under the patronage of St. Michael. "Semi-paganism," Grudger explains, "receded or abated, but the name San Dragone remained." Several stone quarries were opened up between the pastures after the First World War, and that made the village a much livelier place. After the Second World War it numbered over five thousand souls. In the photographs published in the book, one sees little houses piled up like swallows' nests, along narrow little streets that look like descending corridors cut in stone.

The central character of the story as told by Grudger is Gioacchino Scauro, also known in the village as Scuro (the dark one) because of his gloomy disposition and coarse, mean face. As a young boy, he tended his father's flock. He was often seen in the vicinity of the Torre Falconara ruins; motionless, he would stare for hours into the cave where the chasm had opened up, and would jump up and down excitedly every time a wisp of smoke slithered out and wound its way among the rocks. Scuro married a neighbor's daughter, Maria Minuzio, and started a carpentry shop. The couple were married in the newly built church by Don Pietro Vitale, San Dragone's first parish priest. Scuro became an ardent parishioner, prayed a lot, and often visited the parish house, doing, for free, small carpentry and masonry chores for the church. Conscripted into the army at the outbreak of the First World War, he left the village the father of three children— two daughters and a son. He returned from the war an invalid, with his right leg missing and with a bullet hole in his lung. He moved with difficulty, on crutches, and easily tired working in the shop. He spent much time reading—he had learned to read and write fluently during his convalescence in the military hospital.

IV

The longest chapter—nearly one-third of the book—is entitled "The Conversation" and contains such a multitude of documents, descriptions, digressions, and author's comments that only the barest outline can be attempted here. This impoverishes and "flattens" the story, of course, and lessens the credibility of the whole thing, but there is nothing I can do about it.

One night, in the year 1930, Scuro had a vision: a woman wearing a green dress appeared before him in his sleep, pointed to an oil lamp with three spouts, and ordered: "Light this lamp." And she added: "Your name is Levi, and you are to make light with this lamp." On the following morning, a man Scuro had never seen before knocked on his door and gave him a copy of the Bible: the man was a Protestant minister distributing religious literature from village to village in Calabria. Scuro began to read the Bible and, when he finished, became convinced that he had been living in a false faith. "He at last understood," as his daughter, quoted by Grudger, said later, "that the Old Testament is at the source of all religions, and therefore it alone is true, whereas the religions of the New Testament, Catholic as well as Protestant, were later additions and as such are false." He had no idea then that such people as the Jews existed; he thought that he was the one whom God entrusted with the mission of restoring the true faith to humanity. And so he started preaching the true faith—he reprimanded the "pagans" for worshipping icons and statues of the Virgin Mary, reminded them that Saturdays and not Sundays were the days of rest. Grudger quotes somewhere a peasant converted by Scuro: "There is only one God who gives us orders. He says: I am your Lord God, I saved you and led you out of Egypt. I am your jealous God all the way to the fifth generation. The Last Judgment will take place in the Valley of Jehoshaphat. Our

God does not forgive those who sin, as the Catholic God does. The Last Judgment will reward the righteous with eternal life and punish the ignoble with eternal death." Grudger's commentary: "What conquered his imagination was the unbending fairness of the Jewish God. The loving Christian God no longer appealed to the peasants of San Dragone: they preferred, like the ancient Jews, a just and implacable God."

Scuro, who asked everybody to call him Levi the Teacher and who saw himself as a descendant of the Levites and a priest of the community, had about fifty converts. Not one of them had any idea that there were believers in the Ancient Faith anywhere in the world. An itinerant peddler was the first person to tell them about their existence: he also wrote down the address of his Jewish friend in Naples in the Teacher's notebook. Scuro immediately wrote to the man in Naples and received in return the address of the chief rabbi in Rome. The next letter, this time addressed to Rome, went unanswered. The converts of San Dragone did not give up, though, and wrote again: again they announced that they had discovered the true religion and asked for help, because "they would like to become real Jews." This time an answer came. The rabbi of Rome wrote that at first he thought their letter was a joke, but now he knew better and was ready to send his representative to San Dragone. Indeed, a few days later an envoy from the rabbi appeared in San Dragone, spent a whole day in Scuro's house, and also visited the other converts. He listened to them carefully and in silence and, leaving them, said: "You are more Jewish than all the other Jews." Soon, religious brochures began to arrive in San Dragone, one entitled *The Straight Road*. But the printed word was not enough for the converts; they wanted to be accepted officially into the Jewish community. The Rome authorities hesitated. A delegate of the Jewish community visited San Dragone two more times and, following the passage of the Fascist racist laws, hid for a while in the village. "In 1938," reads one of the testimonies, "we learned that a new law had been passed forcing all Jews to declare themselves as Jewish. We wrote to Rome that we wished to register our race because we, too, were Jews like the others and wanted to suffer with the whole Jewish nation. But the answer from Rome was no."

And so the Jews of San Dragone patiently awaited recognition from Rome and practiced Mosaic law according to their own rules, which they interpreted on the basis of the books of the Old Testament.

The first great change in their lives came toward the end of 1943, after the Allies occupied southern Italy. One day they saw on the main road crossing the river in their valley eight army trucks with the Star of David; as they looked in amazement, they saw on the drivers' badges a word they had only known from books: Palestine. They gathered to greet the strangers. The soldiers of the Palestinian brigade could not quite understand what all this was about, but in the flood of foreign words the word *conversions* caught their attention and they later reported everything to the army rabbi in Cosenza. He paid a visit to San Dragone, where he was greeted with songs of the Lord of Hosts and of the Fortress of the Worlds. He was very much moved by the welcome and promised to intervene with the Rome rabbi as soon as the Italian capital was liberated. The patience of the converts was finally rewarded in the summer of 1946: the new chief rabbi of Rome himself came to San Dragone. The ceremony of accepting the converts as members of the synagogue took place just before sunset on the banks of the Chiariva.

But the new Jews felt in San Dragone the way their ancestors had felt in Egypt: they had to live in exile among "pagans." In 1948, Scuro learned that a Jewish state had been founded in Israel; he decided that all the converts were to go to the Promised Land, and so, early the following year, they sailed from Naples; in Israel, they were placed in a farming community where, in 1949, Grudger collected their depositions, the beginning of the book he had planned in London.

They all ended up in Israel, except Scuro himself. He had been widowed shortly before their departure; his wife's death worsened his condition; and the thought of parting from his native village suddenly seemed unbearable. He had a grandson, the son of his second daughter, an eight-year-old boy called Giosue, anemic, sickly, in danger of gradually losing his vision.

Grudger quotes a letter from Scuro to the rabbi of Rome, dated three months after the Jews' departure from San Dragone to Israel. It foreshadows a conflict, if not a complete break: "He who closes the heavens and says that there is no Vision, by rejecting the God of the Vision is also rejecting Moses and the Five Books of Laws. Thus I am telling You in the name of my Creator, who is also Your Creator, that if we are to overcome Evil, you must preach the Vision. There must also be founded a school of prophets, for in this way neither you nor we will grope around in the dark. You will certainly not be-what I have told you, yet without a Vision the shepherd is blind. Our God is not a dead God but a Lord of Hosts . . . If you scorn my words, you will be scorning not me but the God of the Vision who summons and changes the Wind as He likes. And there is no one who can ask Him: What are you doing?"

From 1946 on, one does not have to refer to Grudger's book. That was the year when the very old Father Vitale died and a young priest, Sterpone, took over, spending all together four years in San Dragone. Grudger visited him in Catanzaro in 1952: "He received me in his aunt's house—unfriendly, reluctant to talk, obviously full of tension, monosyllabic, almost rude. Those who introduced me to him had warned me that, following the tragedy of 1950, he had left San Dragone, with his superiors' permission, in a state of near nervous collapse."

V

There is no doubt that Father Sterpone's way of telling the story was affected by his illness. His narrative flowed like clotted blood. Some episodes, recollections, reflections, and emotions coagulated into clots, following one another, pause after pause, and what connected them seemed to break apart and then to heal itself: each part appeared to be a whole, loosely and vaguely attached to other parts; the story moved forward without too much regard for chronological or geographical accuracy, blurred and confused. This was tiring for the listener, who had a feeling that he was hearing a story created outside time and place and detached from reality. Ah, who knows, maybe the narrator's heart burst wide open one night, when all the separate clots, suddenly united, assaulted it during the sleepless and solitary hours of recollection.

And so we ought to ascribe the nature and form of Father Sterpone's narrative to illness. But not only to illness. For even as our friendship strengthened and deepened, I found myself resisting something that the author of *The Hidden God* had so clearly fought. Father Sterpone himself fought that something to the very end, I think, though at the same time he seemed, step by step, to be drawn irresistibly to confess.

Whatever the case may be, all I can do in the end is simply to try to make some sense and order of the whole thing, retrieving from the formless thicket a few clear and straight threads.

VI

It was said of old Father Vitale that he had died of remorse and despair, following the formation of the Jewish community in San Dragone. For his successor, the apostasy of fifty villagers was of course a shock, but certainly not a reason to despair. On the contrary, in his heart Father Sterpone saw the event as a sign of reaffirmation of God's presence in a country where religion had long become a tradition devoid of nearly all its content, as well as a kind of superstition and sorcery. He tried to get to know the members of the community, to knock on their doors, as he did on the doors of his faithful. They received him coolly. When he persisted, they would acknowledge his presence and bid him farewell, always with the same "We pray to the real God." They clearly imitated Scuro, because it was from Scuro that the priest had heard them for the first time on the doorstep of the carpentry shop, pinned down by the host's angry stare. He remembered that Scuro's wife had watched him silently, with what seemed like a smile, from the window of the house next to the workshop—hugging to her bosom her little grandson Giosue, a boy with a pale face and eyes squinting in the sun.

Scuro was in full control of "his people." They lived in different parts of the village, but every Friday evening and Saturday morning they would gather in the workshop converted into a house of prayer. A little cupboard containing a Torah sent from Rome stood in one corner. A wide ribbon of gray linen with Hebrew letters embroidered on it was nailed to the wall (similar hangings had been placed in the converts' homes over their beds, in the place of crucifixes and images of the Madonna). Scuro performed the services and he also had thought up a liturgy: a prayer composed by him was said by all in Italian; they listened to his sermons and then to his readings of selected fragments of the Old Testament. He also marked, and had a stone wall built around, a piece of barren land near the Torre Falconara, where the members of the community were to be buried. Scuro's wife, Maria, was the first to be laid to rest in the new cemetery, shortly before the mass departure from San Dragone for Israel.

At first, the villagers treated the apostates with indifference. Few bothered to condemn them. More often, people shook their heads in wonderment: "Who knows what the truth is, who can fathom it? We do what the priests tell us to do." The gradually deepening chasm was mainly the doing of the converts. They would spurn Father

Sterpone, saying: "We pray to the real God." To his parishioners they would say: "You are praying to a false God." A community of "strangers" emerged suddenly in San Dragone, which caused fear rather than hostility.

Fear—*timore*, at times even *timore religioso*—was clearly evident in Father Sterpone's narrative about his first two years in San Dragone. He sensed this fear in the sudden explosion of piety approaching ardor among his faithful: the church was full on Sundays; people prayed aloud, as if intending to outshout something unclear and disquieting inside themselves; they confessed and received Communion in great numbers, idled in good weather on the church steps, clung to the parish priest with excessive trust. He felt this fear even more keenly a year later in the equally sudden drop in fervor: the church was still filled on Sundays; people did not stop coming to confession and Communion, perched themselves on the church steps in the evenings; but they did all this in a kind of torpor, as though compelled; during Mass a hurried, soundless movement of lips replaced the supplications once chanted loudly to God. At that time, Father Sterpone experienced (as he put it) "a total solitude in the midst of people." I remember his exclamation: "Oh, how much God needs people so as to exist in more than name only!"

He of course deliberated with himself over what all this meant, what had really happened in San Dragone . . . He often mentioned Pascal's thought that Grudger used as the epigraph for his book; at times, in his incessant, stubborn references to a "revealed God" and a "hidden God," he completely forgot my presence. He was close to expressing a belief that God had revealed himself "in dual form," thanks to the conversion and apostasy of fifty inhabitants of the village, only to hide deeper than usual when He saw the growing split in the village. All the people of San Dragone were suddenly exposed to the knowledge of their own human misery and were being slowly enveloped by darkness. The apostates were being poisoned by the arrogance of possessing the only truth; the faithful were being consumed by the fear of living in a false faith.

He pored over his books late into the night, slept little and badly, was exhausted by passing bouts of fever, watched in terror as a soulless emptiness crept into his prayers. His solitude among the people was accompanied by a feeling of being lost to God. He was waiting for a kind of miraculous awakening, but with less and less hope that it would ever come.

One afternoon, when the church was empty, he dozed off on a pew in front of the altar. It was 1949, a sunny January afternoon that sprayed the stained-glass windows with a wintry gild. That morning the Jews of San Dragone had buried Scuro's wife in the new cemetery; a month later they were to leave their native village forever. A child's whimpering startled him out of his nap. He jumped up and ran in the direction of the crying, to a corner near the door immersed in semi-darkness. He saw little Giosue, crouched by the wall, helplessly batting his tiny hands in the air, like a fish caught in a net. He put his arm around the child, hugged him, and led him out of the church. Halfway down the steps, he saw Scuro standing, leaning on a crutch, and breathing heavily. When Father Sterpone gently pushed the boy toward him, Scuro put his left hand on his grandson's shoulder and with his right hand raised his crutch in a gesture of threat. This gesture was to haunt the parish priest of San Dragone for a long time.

VII

They walked down the steep, narrow streets to the two buses waiting on the road in the valley, weighed down with their still unsold possessions—men, women, children. The procession could be clearly seen from the window of the parish house. Scuro led the procession, holding little Giosue's hand in his own left hand. In front of their houses stood the "pagans." They watched the departing ones the way the villagers of southern Italy had for centuries viewed the course of life outside the walls of their homes: with a faded, empty look, in silence.

Father Sterpone slept in his chair next to the window; he was overcome by extreme tiredness, he could not even force himself to say a prayer for those departing. It was early morning of the last day of February, and a storm was gathering over San Dragone. Muffled shouts and calls came up from the valley road, and soon the human voices were drowned by the rumbling of engines. Then came silence.

Scuro returned home with little Giosue the next evening. He was later seen very rarely, no more than once a week. No one knew how he made a living, since he had abandoned carpentry—it is possible that he lived on what the community had left him. He refused to send Giosue to school, having decided to teach him himself, to bring him up in the only true faith. Whenever the boy came to the village store, people would ask him what his grandfather did all day. "He reads, writes, and prays to our God." People saw Scuro every Saturday as he ventured out with his grandson to visit his wife's lonely grave. He walked with difficulty, stopping every few steps, choked and clutched his throat in fits of coughing—an old sick man wearing the black hat of the Calabrian peasant, and a frail little boy walking cautiously, feeling the ground under his feet with the strained gaze of his sick eyes.

Grudger quotes Scuro's letter to the rabbi of Rome, full of bitterness (to say the least), dated three months after the Jews' departure from San Dragone for Israel. It was then—at the time when he sent the letter in which he appealed for the preaching of the glory of "the God of the Vision" and the founding of a "school of prophets"—that people began to see him more often, him and the inseparable Giosue. They would walk from the cemetery to the Torre Falconara, rest for a while on a large rock, perhaps the same rock on which Scuro as a child lay waiting for wisps of smoke to come out of the dark cave. The smoke would still emerge from the cave as before; nothing had changed over the years in that respect—nothing except perhaps that the memory of how the name San Dragone came to be had almost completely died. It was then perhaps (as Father Sterpone thought) that the image of a "shepherd without his herd" gazing into the opening of the cave, a leader of the "strange ones," stirred up in people dark and complex thoughts—associations—lit up in the ashes of memory a few still live sparks. For suddenly people began to see something sinister in Scuro's strange figure, to turn away and even to cross themselves in secret when they saw him.

I suspect that the phrase "lit up in the ashes of memory a few live sparks" was more than just a metaphor to Father Sterpone.

On a November night, Scuro's workshop, converted some time before into a synagogue, burned down. The circumstances will never be known. Was it arson, or did Scuro himself start a fire by throwing ashes on the glowing logs in the fireplace before going home? Father Sterpone was not clear, appeared to be agitated and distressed, as if it had happened the day before, and not many, many years earlier. The neighbors did not help to put out the fire—so much at least is clear. Scuro tried to run into the burning shack, but the blast of flames blinded him, hurling him back to the other side of the street. He was taken home; the women in his neighborhood washed his wounds and wrapped them in oil-soaked rags; he moaned and raved and at last fell into a convulsed sleep. Little Giosue could not be torn away from him; the child was obviously in shock. He was still in shock when Father Sterpone found him, having been awakened at dawn. He took the boy home with him. The injured man was taken to a hospital in Nicastro.

A week later a nun from the Nicastro hospital came to see them. The injured man was out of danger, but it would take several months for him to recover. Scuro was demanding to see his grandson; without him, he refused to accept food or medicine. What could anyone do? The nun came to take little Giosue away.

"In my four years in San Dragone," Father Sterpone said to me, "I was never so happy, so close to God, as during the week I took care of the little boy, trying to ease in him the memories of the shock he had lived through. I often thought about the time I found him in the church, about his crying in the corner by the door. Was that a sign of something? God revealed Himself at his fullest in the child's tear-stained face, in his half-blind eyes." And a moment later, his voice quavering: "Oh God, how I loved my little Giosue!"

VIII

Scuro was in the hospital until March 1950. Spring came early that year, the pastures greened quickly, herds of sheep and goats were soon grazing on the hills, early warmth brought life to the quarries.

One day Scuro came to the parish house with little Giosue to thank Father Sterpone for his having taken care of his grandson after the fire. He looked awful—a skeleton with burn-splotched skin stretched over it. Even more terrifying than his looks was a feeling that one was in the presence of someone who was not quite there. He wheezed out his thanks and refused to step over the threshold into the parish house; he leaned against the doorframe and stood staring at the crucifix on the wall. Listlessly, he stroked the child's head and babbled incomprehensibly, barely hearing what was being said to him and not answering questions. He left without saying goodbye. As they were descending the church steps, the boy turned back and called for both of them: *"Addio, Padre."*

A strange calm fell over San Dragone with the arrival of spring: a dead calm between a storm that had passed and the storm that was coming. Scuro locked himself up in his house, and little Giosue was rarely seen in the local shop. One day in early April, Father Sterpone knocked on the door of their house. There was no answer. He knocked harder, suddenly overcome with a certainty that he would never see them again.

The rest is legend. The tangible reality is Scuro's empty house and, found a few days later by the police, a black hat and a child's shoe abandoned on the path leading uphill from the rock near Torre Falconara to the mouth of the cave. And the legend . . . The legend is Scuro, who, following a wisp of smoke, is dragging little frightened Giosue into the subterranean abyss, as an offering, deep into the kingdom of Saint Dragon. Such is a legend born in the minds of the people of San Dragone, the truth hidden forever from our eyes.

IX

I began to compile this chronicle of events related to San Dragone on the day of Father Sterpone's funeral, October 29. I am finishing it today, on a wet November day, after my evening visit to his sister's house under the pretext of returning Grudger's book. I wanted very much, I do not know why, to take one more look at the room of the deceased.

The hostess left me there alone. The room had not been touched; on the night table by the bed, under the glowing lamp, I even found a little pad with a pencil attached to it and a thick folder containing a report of the proceedings of the Bologna symposium held in the seventies, *Studi sulla religiosita vecchia e nuova*, with the text of Father Sterpone's lecture. "We hear and read that God's image among people constantly changes, that our need to believe in Him weakens and gains strength, like a pendulum. I believe that Satan's face changes, takes on ever different expressions, while man, the eternal pilgrim ever in flight from Satan or perpetually yielding to his fascination, errs and circles, falls and rises."

I stood there for a while looking out onto the black bay through a windowpane lashed by rain. It was enough to switch off the lamp for the blackness over the bay to become light and cover itself with brightly burning flashes.

(January–February 1985)
Translated by Maya Latynski

ABOUT THE AUTHORS

MACIEJ BRONSKI is the pen name of Wojciech Skalmowski. Skalmowski was born in Poznan, Poland, in 1933, and studied Oriental languages and literatures at the Jagellonian University in Cracow, Humboldt University in East Berlin, and Teheran University. Since 1968 he has lived in Belgium, where he teaches linguistics, Oriental languages, and Polish literature at the University of Leuven. Since 1972 he has been a regular contributor to the Flemish journal *De Standaard*, where he publishes literary criticism of Russian and Slavic literatures. Skalmowski has been a regular contributor to *Kultura* since 1969. In 1981 the Institut Littéraire published *Texts and Pretexts*, a collection of his essays.

MIKHAIL HELLER was born in the Ukraine in 1922. He received his graduate and postgraduate degrees in "historical sciences" from Moscow University. He spent five years in Soviet prisons during the Stalinist era. Between 1957 and 1968 he lived in Poland, and since 1969 has lived in Paris, where he teaches Soviet history and literature at the Sorbonne. His works include *The World of Soviet Concentration Camps and Soviet Literature, Andrei Platonov in Search of Happiness,* and *Cogs in the Wheel: The Formation of Soviet Man,* as well as many articles and reviews. He is co-author (with Aleksandr N. Nekrich) of *Utopia in Power* (1986), described by *Le Monde* as "the most complete and without doubt the most satisfying history of the U.S.S.R. now available." Since 1969 Heller has been a regular contributor to *Kultura,* where—under the pen name Adam Kruczek—he publishes a monthly column "In the Soviet Press."

GUSTAW HERLING-GRUDZINSKI was born in Kielce, Poland, in 1919. He studied Polish literature at Warsaw University. At the start of World War II, he and his friends founded one of the first Polish underground anti-Nazi organizations in Warsaw. In 1940, after fleeing to the Soviet-occupied sector of Poland, he was captured by the NKVD, the Soviet secret police, and spent two years in a Soviet labor camp on the White Sea. After his release in 1942, he joined the Polish Army organized in the Soviet Union and went to the Middle East and then to Italy, where he took part in the battle of Monte Cassino. He was later awarded Virtuti Militari, the highest Polish military honor. After the war, he lived in Rome, London, and Munich, and finally, in 1954, settled in Naples, Italy. His experiences in Soviet camps are described in his book *A World Apart* (with a preface by Bertrand Russell), which went through many editions and was translated into several languages. His other works include *The Living and the Dead, Phantoms of the Revolution, The Second Coming, The Island: Three Tales, Journey to Burma, The Tower and Other Stories,* and *Night Journal.* He has been writing for *Kultura* since its inception. He is one of the magazine's principal contributors and divides his time between Naples and Paris, where he spends approximately four months each year at Maisons-Laffitte, *Kultura*'s headquarters.

KONSTANTY A. JELENSKI was born in Warsaw in 1922. He studied in Austria, Switzerland, and Great Britain (St. Andrew's University and Oxford). He left Poland in 1939 and in 1940 enlisted with the Polish Army in France. He was evacuated to England and later fought in Normandy in the Polish Armored Division. In 1952 he settled in France. Between 1952 and 1973 he was an active member of the Congress of Cultural Freedom and between 1952 and 1972 was one of the contributing editors of the French monthly *Preuves.* A noted publicist, art and literary critic, and translator, he frequently contributed to *Kultura* and many other publications. He wrote ten books, as well as many articles and reviews in Polish, French, English, German, and Italian, and translated works by Witold Gombrowicz and Czeslaw Milosz into French. He died in Paris in 1987.

LESZEK KOLAKOWSKI was born in Radom, Poland, in 1927. He studied philosophy at the University of Lodz and at Warsaw University. Before he left Poland in 1968, he was professor of the History of Philosophy at Warsaw University. In March 1968, during widespread student protests, he was considered one of the spiritual leaders of the rebellious students and was ousted from his university post, together with four other faculty members. Since 1970 he has lived in England, where he is a Fellow of All Souls College, Oxford; he also teaches at the University of Chicago, where he is a member of the Committee on Social Thought. He is the author of numerous works in Polish, including a book on Spinoza, *The Individual and Infinity.* His books published in the West include *Mensche Ohne Alternative, Les Chrétiens sans*

Eglise, The Positivist Philosophy, Marxism and Beyond, The Main Currents of Marxism, and *Religion.*

BOHDAN KORZENIEWSKI was born in Siedlce, Poland, in 1905. He graduated from the Faculty of Humanities of Warsaw University. Before the war, he also studied eighteenth-century theater in Paris, lectured on the history of theater, and published essays in theater criticism. During World War II he was active in the anti-Nazi resistance movement. He chaired a clandestine Council on Theater and worked for the Bureau of Information and Propaganda of the underground Home Army. In 1940 he was sent to Auschwitz and was released the same year. After the war, he worked as literary and artistic director at several Polish theaters, lectured at state theater and acting schools, edited theater journals, produced plays by Shakespeare, Molière, Mayakovsky, Sukhovo-Kobylin, Mickiewicz, Krasinski, and Fredro for theaters in Poland, East Germany, France, England, Czechoslovakia, and the Soviet Union, and wrote theater reviews and criticism. His works include *Discussions About Theater, I Want Freedom for Thunder . . . in the Theater,* as well as numerous translations into Polish of English, French, and Russian plays. He also published *Books and People,* a collection of short stories, some of which originally appeared in *Kultura.* He lives in Warsaw.

RYSZARD KUKLINSKI was born in Warsaw in 1930. He joined the Polish People's Army in 1947. In 1950 he graduated from military college, and in 1963 from the Military Academy of the General Staff. Between 1963 and 1976 he worked for the General Staff of the Polish Army, where his duties included planning military operations and training, and designing large military exercises to be conducted by the Minister of National Defense or the Chief of the General Staff. He witnessed the Soviet invasion of Czechoslovakia in 1968. In 1976 he attended (with General Czeslaw Kiszczak, the current Polish Minister of Internal Affairs) a special course on operations and strategy at the Soviet Military Academy in Moscow. He resumed his duties at the Polish General Staff as Chief of Department I for Strategic and Defensive Planning, a position which was later combined with that of Deputy Chief of Military Operations. In this capacity he participated in all meetings of the Warsaw Pact's Defense Ministers. It is not clear when Colonel Kuklinski established contact with the CIA. What is certain, however, is that in 1981 he supplied the U.S. government with the top-secret plans of the Soviet and Polish authorities, including details about the proposed imposition of martial law in Poland. He fled Poland in November 1981 and has since lived in the West.

JAN JOZEF LIPSKI was born in Warsaw in 1926. In 1944, as a soldier in the Home Army, he took part in the Warsaw Uprising and was seriously wounded. After the war, he studied Polish literature at Warsaw University. In the 1950s, he was a leading member of the intellectual Crooked Circle Club and was on the editorial board of the liberal journal *Po Prostu.* Later, in 1976, he was a founding member of KOR and then one of the leaders of Solidarity's

Mazowsze chapter. He was arrested in December 1981 with other Solidarity activists. In June 1989 he was elected senator to the newly created upper house of the Polish parliament. He is a senator from the electoral district of Radom, where, back in 1976, he—with other members and associates of KOR—organized legal protection and financial support for imprisoned workers. He is a literary critic, essayist, and the author of a critical biography of Polish poet Jan Kasprowicz. He lives in Warsaw.

JULIUSZ MIEROSZEWSKI was born in Cracow, Poland, in 1906. He studied law at the Jagellonian University in Cracow and graduated from the Higher School of Trade and Commerce. Until 1939, he was a contributing editor of a daily newspaper, *Ilustrowany Kurier Codzienny*, where he specialized in German affairs. In September 1939, he was in Bucharest, where, for the following year, he worked in the office of the Polish military attaché. Later he joined the Polish Carpathian Brigade, fighting in Africa, and subsequently the 2nd Polish Corps, with which he served until the end of the Italian campaign. After the war, he settled in London and from 1950 until his death in 1976 was *Kultura*'s London correspondent and the magazine's chief political commentator. In *Kultura*'s "inner circle," he was Jerzy Giedroyc's closest collaborator. He published several books in Polish, German, and English. His works include *What Europe Thinks of America*, *Political Neuroses*, and *Theory and Practice*, as well as numerous articles on political issues. He also translated into Polish the works of Arnold Toynbee, George Orwell, Bertrand Russell, and Lionel Trilling.

CZESLAW MILOSZ was born in Szetejnie, Lithuania, in 1911. He studied law at the University of Wilno. He helped form the literary group Zagary and quickly established himself as Poland's leading avant-garde poet in the 1930s. After his studies he went to Paris, and then worked for the Polish National Radio in Wilno and Warsaw. During World War II, he worked clandestinely in Warsaw as a writer and editor of underground publications. After the war he joined the Polish diplomatic service, and in the years 1946–51 held posts abroad in New York, Washington, and Paris. His disenchantment with communism led to his flight from Poland in 1951. He went to Paris and asked the French for political asylum. He stayed at *Kultura*'s headquarters in Maisons-Laffitte. Since 1951 he has been a regular contributor to *Kultura*, and most of his books were originally published by the Institut Littéraire. He first received international attention with *The Captive Mind* (1953), an examination of the power of communist ideology over Polish intellectuals. Since 1961 he has been professor of Slavic Languages and Literatures at the University of California at Berkeley, while continuing to translate and to write and publish poems and essays. He wrote several volumes of poetry, fiction, essays, and literary criticism, which were translated into many languages. He also wrote *The History of Polish Literature* (1969) and worked for years on a new Polish translation of the Bible. In 1978, Milosz received the Neustadt International Prize for Literature; in 1980, he received the Nobel Prize for Literature; and in 1981 and 1982 he delivered the Charles Eliot Norton lectures at Harvard University. He lives in Berkeley, California.

Slawomir Mrozek was born in Borzecin, Poland, in 1930. He studied art history and architecture and in the early 1950s worked as a journalist and a cartoonist and also published short satirical stories. Later he established himself as Poland's leading playwright. He left Poland in 1963 and first went to Italy and then to France, where he has lived since 1968. Both his plays and stories have been translated into many languages. His plays, which are produced all over the world, include *The Police*, *Tango*, *Striptease*, *Vatzlav*, *Emigrants*, *Humpback*, *On Foot*, *Ambassador*, *Alfa*, and *Portrait*. He is the author of several collections of short stories, including *The Elephant*, *Wedding in Atomice*, *The Rain*, *Two Letters*, and *Moniza Clavier*. He lives in Paris.

Marek Nowakowski was born in Warsaw in 1935. He studied law at Warsaw University. In 1957 he started writing and has since published several collections of short stories. In 1969 he began publishing his stories in *Kultura* under the pseudonym Seweryn Kwarc; since 1982 he has signed them with his real name. His book *The Canary and Other Tales of Martial Law* was translated into many languages. His more recent works include *Two Days with Angel*, *I Will Tell You, Grisha . . .*, and *The Feast and the Fast*. He lives in Warsaw.

Wlodzimierz Odojewski was born in Poznan, Poland, in 1930. He studied sociology at the University of Poznan. Between 1956 and 1960 he was on the editorial board of *Tygodnik Zachodni*, and between 1960 and 1971 he was a literary editor at Warsaw Radio. He left Poland in 1971 and went to Berlin and Paris. Since 1972 he has lived in Germany, where he works as a literary editor for the Polish Service of Radio Free Europe in Munich. He is a playwright, a literary critic, and the author of many collections of short stories and several novels, including *Island of Salvation* and *The Dying Day*. His prose has been translated into eighteen languages.

Jozef Szrett is the pseudonym of a writer who lives in Poland.

Leopold Tyrmand was born in Poland in 1920. He was educated in Warsaw and studied architecture at L'Académie des Beaux-Arts in Paris. During World War II, he was jailed by the Soviets in Poland and by the Germans in Norway. After the war, he returned to Warsaw, where he began a career as a journalist. In the early 1950s, he was a staff contributor to the Catholic-liberal weekly *Tygodnik Powszechny*, the only independent paper at that time in Eastern Europe. In 1965 he left Poland and in 1966 settled in the United States. He contributed to various publications, including *The New Yorker*, *The Reporter*, *The New Leader*, *Policy Review*, *Commentary*, *The Wall Street Journal*, *Kontinent*, and *Kultura*. From 1976 until his death in 1985, he was a director of the Rockford Institute and the editor of *Chronicles of Culture* and the *Rockford Papers*. He was the author of many books, including *The Man with the White Eyes*, *Journal 1954*, and *Seven Long Voyages*. In 1970 he edited two companion anthologies: *Explorations in Freedom: Prose, Narrative, and Poetry from Kultura* and *Kultura Essays*.